DATE DUE

Demco, Inc. 38-293

Brain-Compatible
CLASSROOMS

THIRD EDITION

In loving memory
of my dad,
who knew just
how to grow dendrites.

Brain-Compatible CLASSROOMS

THIRD EDITION

ROBIN FOGARTY

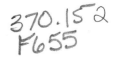

CORWIN
A SAGE Company

For information:

Corwin
A SAGE Company
2455 Teller Road
Thousand Oaks, California 91320
(800) 233-9936
Fax: (800) 417-2466
www.corwinpress.com

SAGE India Pvt. Ltd.
B 1/I 1 Mohan Cooperative
    Industrial Area
Mathura Road, New Delhi 110 044
India

SAGE Ltd.
1 Oliver's Yard
55 City Road
London EC1Y 1SP
United Kingdom

SAGE Asia-Pacific Pte. Ltd.
33 Pekin Street #02-01
Far East Square
Singapore 048763

Printed in the United States of America.

Library of Congress Cataloging-in-Publication Data

Fogarty, Robin.
Brain-compatible classrooms / Robin Fogarty.—3rd ed.
    p. cm.
Includes bibliographical references and index.
ISBN 978-1-4129-3886-0 (cloth : alk. paper)
ISBN 978-1-4129-3887-7 (pbk. : alk. paper)
    1. Thought and thinking—Study and teaching. 2. Brain. 3. Multiple intelligences.
4. Classroom environment. 5. Educational innovations. I. Title.

LB1590.3.F62 2009
370.15′2—dc22   2008056032

This book is printed on acid-free paper.

09   10   11   12   13   10 9 8 7 6 5 4 3 2 1

Acquisitions Editor:	Hudson Perigo
Editorial Assistant:	Lesley K. Blake
Production Editor:	Cassandra Margaret Seibel
Copy Editor:	Sarah J. Duffy
Typesetter:	C&M Digitals (P) Ltd.
Proofreader:	Susan Schon
Indexer:	Jean Casalegno
Cover Designer:	Scott Van Atta

Contents

Preface

The exploration of our "universe within" is in full swing. From designer drugs such as Prozac and Zoloft to catchy terms such as EQ and MRIs, the media is abuzz with the almost daily discoveries of how the brain functions and how that functioning can be monitored, improved, and even re-created. Popular magazines publish weekly articles on brain-related stories and feature editions that devote whole issues to the mysteries of the human brain.

In fact, the nation and the world are fascinated by the findings in brain research, including discoveries about sleep cycles, gender differences in physiology and processing, windows of opportunity and critical periods, and how the brain remembers, reads, and regenerates. Brain references pop up everywhere. People are aware of the dendrites in their brains, the myelination of the axons, the effects of nutrition and exercise on brain functioning, and the balance of the nature/nurture puzzle. The medical world taps into the research and discovers groundbreaking revelations connecting brain chemistry and disease. Many educators are tuning in to brain-friendly strategies for learning.

With all this interest in the brain and the vast amount of information about the brain inundating the media, the need for an informative and practical book for teachers seems imminent. Thus, it is the purpose of *Brain-Compatible Classrooms* (3rd edition) to bring the message of brain research and its implications for the classroom to educators in a user-friendly format.

Yet a word of caution is needed. The landscape of brain research changes almost daily. Be aware that information presented in this book is open to debate and alteration as new insights emerge. Take responsibility to read more on your own, concentrating on the resources cited within the past three years. Be a brain-wise consumer.

Robin Fogarty
Chicago, IL

Acknowledgments

In my search for understanding about how the brain works and how classrooms can become more brain-friendly, I want to acknowledge some leaders in the field: the pioneering work of Bob Sylwester and the caring advice he gave me, the generous sharing of Pat Wolfe, the wealth of ideas provided by Eric Jensen's books, the richness and freshness of David Sousa's compendium of "brain books," and the bridge to learning provided by Geoffrey and Renate Caine's principles of brain research.

In my quest for quality, I want to thank my editing and design staff for this third edition: Jean Ward for our early conversations on this new edition, Hudson Perigo for her direction and resources, and Desiree Enayati for her editorial guidance.

In my journey of lifelong learning, I want to mention three others: Brian for enduring endless hours of "brain tapes" as we traveled in the car, and Tim and Jeff for their unknowing contributions to my awareness of the brain and its inner workings.

I am indebted to all of the above.

Robin Fogarty
Chicago, IL

About the Author

 **Robin Fogarty** received her doctorate in curriculum and human resource development from Loyola University of Chicago. A leading proponent of the thoughtful classroom, Fogarty has trained educators throughout the world in curriculum, instruction, and assessment strategies. She has taught at all levels, from kindergarten to college; served as an administrator; and consulted with state departments and ministries of education in the United States, Puerto Rico, Russia, Canada, Australia, New Zealand, Germany, Great Britain, Singapore, Korea, and the Netherlands. She has published articles in *Educational Leadership, Phi Delta Kappan,* and the *Journal of Staff Development.* She is the author or coauthor of numerous publications, including *Brain-Compatible Classrooms* (2001), *Literacy Matters* (2001), *How to Integrate the Curricula* (2002), *The Adult Learner* (2007), *A Look at Transfer* (2007), *Close the Achievement Gap* (2007), *Twelve Brain Principles That Make the Difference* (2007), *Nine Best Practices That Make the Difference* (2007), and *From Staff Room to Classroom: A Guide for Planning and Coaching Professional Development* (2006).

Introduction

IN BRIEF

To briefly introduce this third edition—and what has been retained and reframed, what is new and renewed—the following summation is offered. It gives a glimpse of what the reader will find in exploring the new edition, whereas the longer, more detailed introduction shows how the material has evolved over time.

Retained material:

- The four-corner framework for quality teaching
- Visuals, quotes, stories, and graphics

Reframed material:

- Organization of the book—physiology, principles, strategies
- Applications—elaborated
- Research—updated

New material:

- Brain foods—a listing
- Gender research—updated
- Memory pathways—revised and elaborated
- Habits of mind—Costa and Kallick

Renewed material:

- Brain principles—Caine and Caine
- Rationale for differentiation—Tomlinson
- Role of data—Schmoker
- Research on teacher quality—Strong
- Four-corner framework—Fogarty/Pete
- Teachers Make the Difference

IN MORE DETAIL

This third edition of *Brain-Compatible Classrooms* (BCC) is a book with a bit of a history. The first edition was a reconceptualization of an earlier work titled

Patterns for Thinking, Patterns for Transfer (Fogarty & Bellanca, 1993). Based on a framework of four elements, *Patterns* presented a classroom model that advocates teaching for, of, with, and about thinking.

In essence, that same model was restructured in the second edition of *BCC*. Officially called the *four-corner framework for quality teaching*, this model addresses the same four elements: setting the climate for thinking, teaching the skills of thinking, structuring the interaction with thinking, and thinking in a metacognitive or reflective way. However, the second edition of *BCC* grounded the framework in the emergent brain research as well as in the sound pedagogical theory present in *Patterns*. Now, in the third edition of the *BCC*, the bridge between brain science and learning is elaborated and emphasized with a robust look at the principles of the brain and learning. In addition, separate chapters are included on brain science and cognitive science to further accentuate the linkages between what is known about the brain itself and what is known about how the brain learns. Thus, in this third edition the organization of the book has changed and the chapter headings have shifted.

The book is organized into three parts: Physiology and Brain Science, Principles for Teaching and Learning, and Brain-Friendly Strategies. These three parts create a balance of understanding about how brain science informs educational practices. With some foundational knowledge about the physiology of the human brain, supported by neurocognitive principles of how the brain learns and cognitive translations of what those brain-friendly strategies look like in the K–12 classroom, teachers are armed with an astonishing arsenal of tools for reaching and teaching all children. After all, brain science is the rationale for differentiating learning.

Part I: Physiology and Brain Science

Chapter 1 presents the basics of brain science in a brief discussion that is intended to provide an introductory awareness of the human brain and how it works. It begins with a thumbnail sketch of the exterior and interior physiology of the brain and ends with a description and explanation of the brain cell itself. While this opening section begins the conversation about the human brain, hopefully it also serves as a catalyst to further readings in the field of brain research.

Part II: Principles for Teaching and Learning

Chapter 2 opens Part II and builds on this research base by applying the findings to the four-corner framework. Using a brilliant synthesis of brain research, Caine and Caine (1991) and Caine, Caine, and Crowell (1994) have developed 12 principles that have compelling implications for the classroom. These principles guide the creation of the framework.

In sum, the climate for thinking is governed by a safe classroom setting and an enriched environment; skills of thinking encompass not only the types of skills but the developmental path of those skills; interaction with thinking targets active and experiential learning; and thinking about thinking highlights the reflection and assessment aspects of the high-standards classroom.

Chapter 3 explores the brain–mind connection and the role of cognitive science as it complements brain science. Discussions presented focus on the nature/nurture conundrum, the brain–mind connection, enriched environments, and the role of experience in building brain connections. In addition, windows of opportunity are explored as are the nutrition–cognition connection and the effects of abuse and addiction on the human brain. This chapter also presents information on the emotional brain, theories of the intellect and memory, and learning and the human brain.

Part III: Brain-Friendly Strategies

Chapter 4 describes the four-corner framework for a high-standards classroom and sets the stage for quality teaching. Chapters 5–8 extrapolate the principles assigned to each of the four areas. Chapter 5 discusses extensive strategies and options for setting a peak learning climate, and Chapter 6 exposes the essential macro and micro life skills and the natural developmental path from novice to expert to peak performance. Chapter 7 explores explicit strategies for active learners and the curricular models of authentic learning, and Chapter 8 discusses the roles of reflective thinking and balanced assessments needed for learners to demonstrate deep understanding and relevant transfer.

Within each of these four chapters, certain brain-compatible elements appear:

Brainwave: Theme
Big idea that relates to brain research and/or learning theory

Brainwise: Statements
Quips, statements, or memorable sayings about the brain and learning

Braindrops: Strategies
Strategies, tools, and techniques that help implement instructional methods based on brain research and learning theory

Brainworks: Activities
Activities or learning experiences for the reader or workshop participant to do and to actively think about in terms of the presented information

Brainstorms: Application
Personally relevant transfer by reader or workshop participant to tailor for immediate use

Braindrain: Reflection
Reflection and thought about the ideas and processes

While the first two chapters provide the soul of the book, these four middle chapters form the heart. They offer a wealth of practical strategies and usable techniques for teachers in today's classrooms. They give life to the theory and are intended to guide immediate application.

BCC also has two appendices and a glossary.

The book is designed as a comprehensive treatment of today's high-challenge classroom and the intricate complexities that make up that classroom. It is meant to provide a useful holistic model for teachers to use in designing their own classrooms. Thus, the reader may choose to devour the whole picture—page by page, chapter by chapter, as designed—or to sample bite-sized pieces at a more leisurely pace. In either case, there are certain advantages and disadvantages.

In approaching *BCC* as a complete framework for teaching and learning, the reader sees the big picture and the interrelationships among the four areas. The four-corner framework literally affords the reader a look at how it all fits together. On the other hand, by attacking the entire text as one piece, the reader may not have the luxury of immersion in content of specific interest. For example, there may be compelling ideas in the first chapter on the human brain that one wants to pursue before moving on to the practical implications of that information.

If, from the other perspective, the reader delves into separate sections that have personal relevance, the content may invite further investigation and in-depth exploration. Yet with the deep-dive approach, the framework may never emerge as a unifying thread. It is so easy to get lost within one section and miss the moment to bridge the various elements of *BCC* into a meaningful whole.

Still, it seems in keeping with the spirit of the book to trust the inquiring mind of the reader and advocate both approaches—whole to part and part to whole—as equally rewarding. After all, learning is personal, and each reader will do what he or she does naturally, regardless of the wishes or intent of the author. Ultimately, of course, the purpose of *BCC* is to inspire teachers in the architecture of their own uniquely designed brain-compatible classrooms. So off you go . . . read on.

Part I

Physiology and Brain Science

1 Brain Science

THE BRAIN IS THE UNIVERSE WITHIN

She's a brain! You're a numbskull! That's a harebrained idea! Have you lost your mind? Are you out of your mind? Put on your thinking cap. Use your noodle. I'm having a brain drain. Use your gray matter. I think I'm brain dead today. It's an idea that is swirling around in my mind.

These are just some of the remarks one hears in everyday references to the brain and the mind. In fact, these sayings offer concrete evidence for the common understandings people have, and have had for some time, about the human brain. Yet with the avalanche of information available through brain imaging technologies, interest in the brain is on the increase. As brain research explodes following what was known as the Decade of the Brain (Klein, 1997), parents, teachers, educators, and students themselves are now genuinely intrigued with the emergent knowledge of how their brains remember and learn.

HOW TO BE A CRITICAL CONSUMER OF RESEARCH ON THE BRAIN AND LEARNING

There is reason to be cautious and considered when reading and pondering ideas that are emerging about the human brain. *Brain science, brain fiction* is how Bruer (2002) refers to this fascination with research on the brain and learning. He has been the dissenting voice in the field, cautioning educators that it is far too early to make direct connections between research findings on how the brain learns and implications for teaching and learning. He specifically discusses and offers insightful comments about three big ideas: (1) in the early years of life, neural connections form rapidly, but we don't know if neural branching offsets neural pruning; (2) critical periods occur in development, but this may be a "myth of the first three years," as he calls it in the title of his book, because people seem able to acquire culturally and socially transmitted skills such as reading, mathematics, and music at any age; and (3) enriched environments have a pronounced effect on brain development, but our appeals to this research are often naïve and superficial, as neuroscience says nothing, really, about which environments are more or less enriched than others.

To be fair, in response, Wolfe (1996, 2001) argues with Bruer (2002) that brain/mind research supports sound pedagogy, as Brandt (1988) argues that educators need to know about the human brain and that it is not too early to search for the implications for education. While both Wolfe and Brandt rebut Bruer's view, it seems prudent, as consumers of current and ongoing information about brain physiology and brain functioning, that readers consider both sides of the issues whenever possible. Bruer provides a needed service by playing the devil's advocate, and readers need to seek out his writings as well as other dissenting voices. By reading opposing viewpoints, educators are forced to become more discerning consumers of cognitive and neuroscience research findings.

JUST THE FACTS! WHAT ARE THE FACTS ABOUT THE BRAIN?

Scientists have discovered numerous facts about the 100 billion nerve cells, called *neurons,* that make up the organ that is the human brain. This unique organ is protected by the cranium, or skull. The average brain weighs approximately three pounds (one and a half kilograms), is about the size of a small grapefruit or a cabbage cut in half, appears wrinkled like a walnut, and feels somewhat like a ripened avocado.

While the brain accounts for only 2 percent of a person's body weight, it uses 20 percent of the energy in the body and generates 25 watts of power (enough energy to illuminate a light bulb) when a person is awake. Messages travel within the brain through 30,000 miles of neural connections in the cerebral cortex at speeds of up to 250 miles per hour, and several billion bits of information pass through your brain each and every second of your life.

The study of the brain is considered science—biology, neurology, biochemistry, or neurochemistry—while the study of the mind is considered psychology or cognitive psychology. Both the neurobiological evidence and the cognitive-psychological findings offer scientists and researchers a better understanding of the brain and the mind and of their inner workings. While most educators are interested in how the mind works and what they can do to enhance learning, knowing how the brain itself works is an important prerequisite in shaping what is referred to here as *brain-compatible classrooms*: classrooms in which the teaching-learning process is structured to parallel the ways the brain obtains and retains information (Sousa, 2000; Wolfe, 2001).

To begin, let's focus on the brain and what is known about this amazing organ. Read the statements in Figure 1.1 and either agree or disagree with them in terms of your first thought or intuition. Then review the discussion comments immediately following the list of statements in Figure 1.1. Be aware that there are often differing opinions on these issues. They are presented here to stir up your prior knowledge about the brain and how it functions. This interactive reading is intended to precipitate a robust discussion about the human brain.

1. The brain is more like a sieve than it is like a sponge.

2. Critical periods (windows of opportunity) are not that critical.

3. Enriched environments grow dendrites.

4. Humans use only 10 percent of their brains.

5. The brain and the mind are one.

6. Memory is stored throughout the brain and must be reconstructed.

7. Brains are as individual as fingerprints.

8. Nurture rules over nature in brain development.

9. Experience affects how the brain is organized.

10. Our brains are plastic.

11. Alcohol kills brain cells.

12. Reasoning rules over emotions.

13. The brain "rewires" itself.

14. Male and female brains are different.

15. Music enhances general cognitive abilities.

16. The brain is not that much like a computer.

17. The brain is like a jungle ecosystem.

18. Pruning is a process that occurs in teenage brains.

19. "That added a wrinkle to my brain" means you just aged.

20. The brains of identical twins are not identical.

Discussion of the Statements

1. The brain is more like a sieve than it is like a sponge.

The brain is more like a sieve because it is designed to let go of information that is not important. It chunks information as it searches for connections that help keep the information in the sieve. The brain pays attention when the input is novel, relevant, or meaningful. Think of the implications for teaching . . . and the need for getting the attention of the learner.

2. Critical periods (windows of opportunity) are not that critical.

While there are sensitive periods when the brain seems more ready to learn some things, such as language and vision, the brain is able to learn those things beyond what is considered the sensitive period (Bruer, 2002).

3. Enriched environments grow dendrites.

Diamond and Hobson's (1998) *Magic Trees of the Mind* demonstrates the changes in the growth of dendrites when exposed to enriched environments. A key to this enriched environment with children is time to engage in that environment (Wolfe, 2001). It's not just about having a lot of stimuli.

4. Humans use only 10 percent of their brains.

Neuroscientists consider this idea a myth. If this were the case, the brain would compensate easily when damaged. However, some cognitive psychologists suggest that humans do not use the full power of their brains/minds, which might be where this 10 percent idea comes from (Gardner, 1999b).

5. The brain and the mind are one.

Scientists often say, "Yes, the brain is the brain is the brain is the brain." Psychologists often say, "The brain is physiological, the mind is psychological; the brain is the hardware, the mind is the software. They are different." Be aware when reading about the brain/mind and the language used. Think critically about authors' perspectives. Are they talking science or psychology? Do they use the term *brain* or *mind?*

6. **Memory is stored throughout the brain and must be reconstructed.**

Yes, it is now believed that memory is stored throughout the brain and is reconstructed in the mind. Different types of memory lanes are available to sort memory and to spark memory reconstruction. Memory is the only evidence we have of learning, according to Sprenger (1999).

7. **Brains are as individual as fingerprints.**

Yes, this is generally accepted. Each brain has its own unique wiring based on genetic codes and life experiences; each has a jagged profile of intelligences, according to Gardner's *Frames of Mind* (1983) and *Intelligence Reframed* (1999b).

8. **Nurture rules over nature in brain development.**

This points to the nature-versus-nurture question about brain and intellectual development. It is generally accepted that both are responsible, not one or the other (Sousa, 2000; Wolfe, 2001).

9. **Experience affects how the brain is organized.**

Yes, the organization of the brain is impacted by the environment. Read *Inside the Brain,* by Kotulak (1996).

10. **Our brains are plastic.**

The concept that the brain is dynamic and ever changing, continually forming new neural networks and pruning dendrites that are not being used, is called *plasticity* (Diamond & Hobson, 1998; Kotulak, 1996).

11. **Alcohol kills brain cells.**

Alcohol can cause extensive damage to the fetal brain, causing fetal brain syndrome. It is unclear whether alcohol kills brain cells in developed brains (Wolfe, 2001).

12. **Reasoning rules over emotions.**

Emotions seem to hijack other systems in the brain and take over momentarily. But cognitive functions may be alerted through signals from the emotions. There seem to be visceral reactions that cue the cognitive functions (LeDoux, 1998).

13. **The brain "rewires" itself.**

There is much evidence that the brain does rewire itself based on the experiences it has through sensory input of all kinds. Again, Kotulak's (1996) book *Inside the Brain* is one resource. Another is Diamond and Hobson's (1998) *Magic Trees of the Mind.*

14. **Male and female brains are different.**

Emerging evidence seems to show that male and female brains are physically different and that there are additional differences in how they process information. For example, the corpus callosum appears larger in female brains. In terms of processing information, the female brain seems to process language earlier and more easily, while male brains seem to process spatial information more readily (Sousa, 2000).

15. **Music enhances general cognitive abilities.**

While there is little real proof of what is termed the Mozart Effect (the idea that playing the music of Mozart will increase cognitive functioning), there seems to be some truth to the idea that music in general enhances cognitive abilities with more focus and concentration (Jensen, 1999).

16. **The brain is not that much like a computer.**

According to Sylwester (1995) and others, the brain is not as neat and tidy as the computer analogy suggests. In fact, in studies of artificial intelligence, scientists are not able to simulate the complexity of connections and problem solving that occurs in the human brain.

17. **The brain is like a jungle ecosystem.**

Edelman (cited in Sylwester, 1995) uses the analogy of a jungle ecosystem as a more apt description of the human brain in appearance and growth of dendrites.

Figure 1.1   *(Continued)*

(Continued)

18. **Pruning is a process that occurs in teenage brains.**

The brain does experience pruning at various times throughout life. Early adolescence seems to be a time of great pruning as the brain matures (Wolfe, 2001).

19. **"That added a wrinkle to my brain" means you just aged.**

There is a saying that when someone learns something or realizes an insight, the learning experience adds a wrinkle to the brain, meaning the brain grew bigger and had to wrinkle up more to fit under the skull.

20. **The brains of identical twins are not identical.**

The brains of identical twins are not identical because the twins have different sets of experiences that cause the brain to rewire accordingly. This is an example of the nature-versus-nurture argument. Both affect the brain: on the nature side, genetic makeup affects the brain; on the nurture side, learning is a function of experience (Wolfe, 2001).

Figure 1.1   The Human Brain: Agree/Disagree Discussion

MACROVIEW: A LOOK AT THE EXTERIOR OF THE HUMAN BRAIN

In an attempt to clarify and simplify the physiology of the brain, this discussion is divided into two parts: a look at the exterior of the human brain and a look at the interior of the brain. While this serves as an organizing principle for the discussion, it also presents some ambiguities. It is not an exact division of the exterior and interior of the human brain. Yet it does provide a way to read and understand complex information about the physiology of the brain.

Geography of the Human Brain (Topography)

Sometimes a visual helps anchor abstract ideas. To provide a big-picture look at the brain, Figure 1.2 depicts a general geography of the human brain. This is a grossly simplified version, but it does represent major areas and the accompanying functions of those areas.

To continue this discussion about the exterior brain, it is important to know that the neocortex is much larger than any other part of the brain. It has six complete layers of tissue and 30,000 miles (48,280 kilometers) of neural fibers. In fact, to more accurately represent the brain in terms of proportions, a simple model can be created using your right index finger, your left hand, and six sheets of newsprint. Simply hold up your right index finger to represent the brain stem (see Figure 1.3). Next, place your left hand over the right finger, forming a crescent (about the size of a bagel) to represent the interior limbic area. Finally, take the sheets of newsprint and crumple them up to fit as the neocortex over the brain stem and the interior limbic area. This physical model helps novices envision a mental model and gives a more accurate image of how big the neocortex is compared to other parts of the human brain.

The brain stem governs automatic functions of the body such as digestion, heartbeat, breathing, sneezing, and coughing. In addition, research favors the

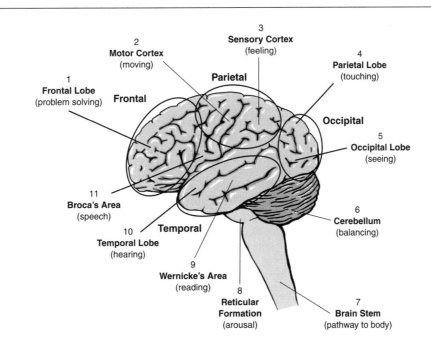

Geography of the Brain

1. This frontal lobe is future oriented and thinks creatively and analytically in a problem-solving mode. It also takes part in the complex behaviors called personality.

2. The motor cortex governs movement and overall motor control. It is seen as one of two distinctive channels in the neocortex.

3. The sensory cortex involves sensory input and appears as the second channel in the neocortex, near the motor cortex region.

4. The parietal lobe, located at the top of the brain, is often associated with touch and the sense of feeling received from all over the skin. It senses hot and cold, hard and soft, and degrees of pain. It also senses taste and smell and helps to integrate the senses.

5. The occipital lobe, located in the hind brain, at the base of the skull, rules over vision and the ability to see and observe. It works out shapes, colors, and movements and is the site center of the mind's eye.

6. The cerebellum, also part of the hind brain, is the center of balance for the human body. It coordinates movement as it monitors impulses from nerve endings in the muscles. The cerebellum is part of the memory system and retains muscle memory. It is believed to hold procedural memories that are part of step-by-step methodologies such as problem solving.

7. The brain stem, located at the back of the brain and extending to the spinal column, is the brain path to the body. It is the center for sensory reception and monitors vital bodily functions such as heartbeat, breathing, and digestion.

8. The reticular formation, located on the brain stem, is the trigger for arousal. It integrates the sensory information into a general level of attention. It acts as a chemical net that opens and closes to the incoming information flow.

9. Wernicke's area, located in the left temporal lobe, is considered the center of reading in the language region of the neocortex.

10. The temporal lobe in the neocortex, located above and behind the ears, is the center for hearing and auditory impact. It receives auditory signals and identifies sounds by comparing them with sound patterns in the memory banks.

11. Broca's area is the center for speech in the neocortex and relates to other language areas of writing and reading.

Figure 1.2

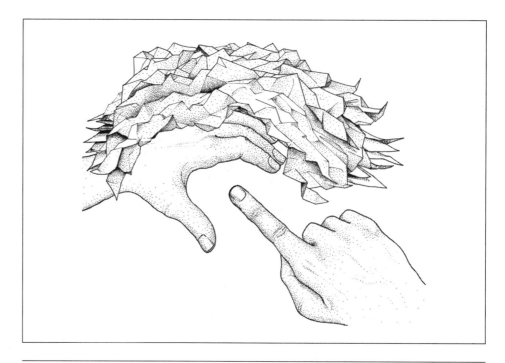

Figure 1.3   Brain Simulation

idea that the emotional functioning of the brain probably occurs throughout the entire brain, not simply in the limbic area. While the amygdala seems to govern some part of the emotions, LeDoux (1998), a widely respected expert in the area of emotion research, prefers to cross-categorize emotional functioning as processes that occur collaboratively with other brain areas.

The six sheets of newsprint in our physical model of the brain represent the massive amount of brain area designated to higher cognitive functions in the neocortex. This is where humans solve problems, make decisions, and do all kinds of critical and creative thinking.

Three Views of the Brain

To further illuminate a big-picture understanding of the human brain, three distinct views are offered for review: top to bottom, front to back, and left to right. Each view presents a slightly different perspective for consideration within the big-picture view.

Top-to-Bottom View

This view somewhat parallels MacLean's (1969) early image of the triune brain theory. Figure 1.4 depicts the top-to-bottom view of the brain. The top, or neocortex, is the outermost layer of the brain (the cortex, which means bark, constitutes four-fifths of the entire brain; Sylwester, 1995). This top layer is often referred to as the *thinking brain* because all higher-level cognitive functions happen in this folded section of the brain.

Moving from the top layer down, the middle section of the brain, or the limbic area, is key in the control of the emotions. It is part of the *feeling brain,* and it signals the body to receive or express emotions, to accept or reject

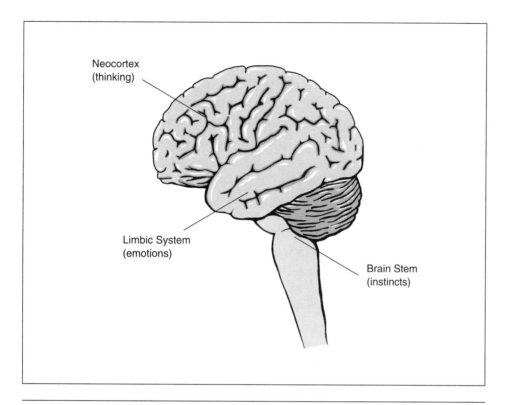

Figure 1.4   Top to Bottom

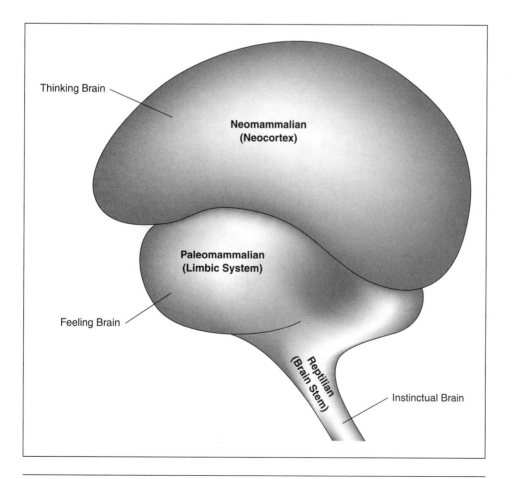

Figure 1.5   Triune Brain Model

possibilities. It is in constant conversation with the thinking brain above it and the brain stem beneath it.

Finally, at the bottom layer, or the brain stem, is the *instinctual brain,* which governs survival mechanisms. This is the part of the brain that alerts the body to the fight-or-flight syndrome and to territorial concerns and needs for survival. It is probably the oldest part of the brain, evolving from the reptilian era as the brain adapted to its environmental needs in a Darwinian way.

Front-to-Back View

According to Luria (cited in Rico, 1991), the frontal and hind lobes of the brain appear to sense temporal dimensions as well as spatial conceptual organization. This view of the brain from front to back is shown in Figure 1.6. The frontal lobe relates to the future. It is involved in planning, in making decisions, and in identifying one's sense of self. It is also the area where rehearsal takes place and where the brain allows risk taking (Sylwester, 1995, 2000a). It gives foresight (Rico, 1991) into situations. It is also the part concerned with problem solving and critical thinking. It helps make judgments, classify general categories, and estimate.

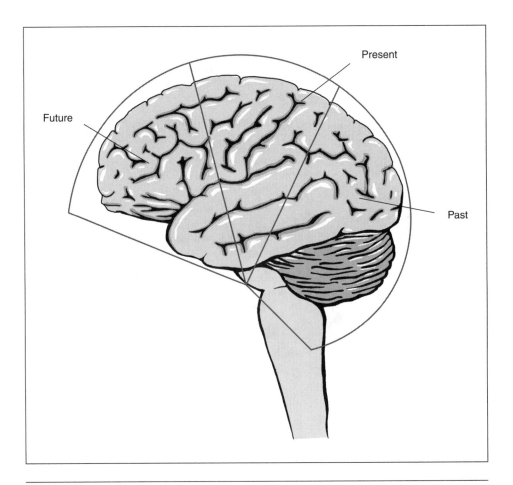

Figure 1.6 Front to Back

The middle section is most sensitive to stimuli in the present. Because it is the center of sensory and motor input, it makes sense that it "feels" the present situations.

The hind brain, situated farthest back, focuses on the past and is where memory is processed. In this area, the temporal lobes process hearing, and the occipital lobes process vision. This part of the brain collects and retrieves information. It contains the parietal lobe, which processes touch and the integration of the senses as memories are reconstructed.

Left-to-Right View

Viewed from above, the brain is divided into right and left hemispheres along a line running from the nose directly back (see Figure 1.7). The two sides are connected by the corpus callosum, which comprises a dense band of more than 200 million axons and acts as a bridge or pathway that interconnects the intricate hemispheric system.

Although lateralization (differentiation of tasks) does occur, the hemispheres are in constant communication with each other through the synchronization of the corpus callosum. Yet a closer look at the hemispheres reveals just how complex the tailoring of tasks for each side really is. Numerous researchers have documented this lateralization in terms of different ways of

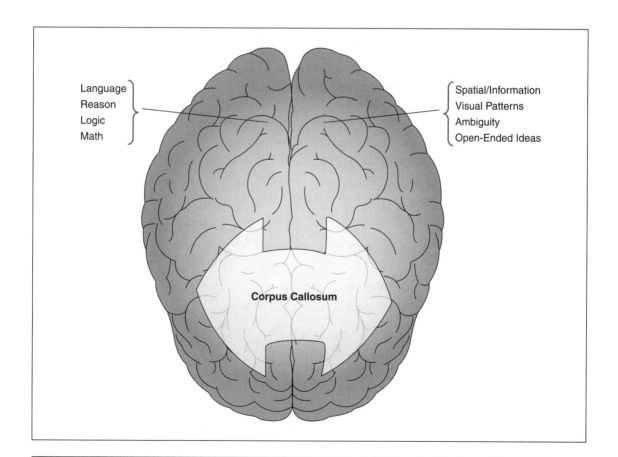

Figure 1.7 Left and Right Hemispheres

processing related information, helping the brain combine all the information to produce a more complete mental experience. For example, the left side of the brain is thought to process language-related ideas, reasoned judgments, and logical sequencing (Hart, 2002); provide literal interpretations (Barrett, 1992); give structure and order to thoughts (Jensen, 1996a); bring critical analysis to an idea (Sylwester, 1995); split and classify ideas (Rico, 1991); and deal with numbers and the calculations of arithmetic (Sousa, 1995). While this is generally true in most right-handed people, it is true for fewer left-handed people. In fact, some people have mirror brains, where everything is reversed, and some have quite mixed-up brains.

In contrast, the right side of the brain seems to process spatial information and visual patterns (Hart, 2002), scan images, utilize intuition, and take in data simultaneously (Barrett, 1992). In addition, the right hemisphere deals with spontaneous, random, and open-ended ideas (Jensen, 1996a) as well as novel situations, paradox, and ambiguity (Rico, 1991). It relates information; reads maps, graphs, and cartoons (Sylwester, 1995); and is able to go with the flow (Jensen, 1996c).

While hemisphericity in brain research made an early debut (Sperry, 1968), current thinking is cautious to apply the left/right processing concept too rigorously or too exclusively. Tempered with the overall understanding of synchronization of the two hemispheres, a more reasoned and generally accepted view of the bilateralization of brain processing is preferred. In addition, it is more acceptable to refer to left/right hemispheres than to left/right brains.

Continuing with the exterior brain, the stem is really an extension of the spinal cord, and it is about as thick as the middle finger on a person's hand (Wolfe, 2001). The swelling on the stem is called the medulla oblongata; it governs survival, sustenance, safety, and sex. It is the main controller of heartbeat, breathing, and other instinctual reflexes such as snoring, coughing, sneezing, and even digesting. It regulates instincts, including the reflexive activities of fight or flight. As one well-known writer on brain research says, this is the brain that automatically decides and responds to the questions: Do I eat it? Fight it? Run away from it? Or mate with it? (Sylwester, 1996, 2000b).

HOW HAS THE BRAIN EVOLVED?

Microview: A Look at the Interior of the Human Brain

The interior brain responds through its emotional system to all sensory input. It is located in the middle brain and includes the cerebellum. This midbrain surrounds the brain stem like a half-shell or half-donut and controls the sensory input of taste and smell, memory storage, motor muscles, and movement. It controls the ability to automate the skills of riding a bike, knitting, or keyboarding. The limbic system is believed to contain the thalamus (senses), hypothalamus (emotions, body temperature, hunger, thirst, and sex drive), pituitary gland (hormones for energy), pinal gland (rate of body growth), amygdala (trigger for anger), and hippocampus (new and short-term memories). In addition, the reticular activating system (RAS; Stevens & Goldberg, 2001) acts as a master switch that alerts the brain to incoming information and to the urgency or lack of urgency in the message.

The limbic area is often referred to as the sentry at the gate—the sentry of emotions at the gate of the intellect. Emotions are seen as the gateway to the thinking mind. If the emotional guard is up, little cognitive reasoning is likely to occur. Emotions rule over reason. In fact, emotions can highjack cognitive functioning, and thinking is often blurred when emotions are high. This is illustrated in a situation in which a person is so angry and emotionally upset that he or she cannot remember a well-known phone number.

This part of the brain regulates feelings of happiness, joy, sorrow, sadness, grief, jealousy, greed, and hate. It responds emotionally to stimuli and, in states of great threat, is the default system that activates first. MacLean's (1969) early theory suggests that the limbic system is the center of emotions, and Hart (2002) presents a concept of downshifting to this emotional brain in the face of threat. Yet more current theory suggests that the emotional brain alerts the body and threat is realized subconsciously in the emotional state before it is understood in the conscious rational state. In essence, the visceral reaction puts the entire body on alert.

The neocortex covering the mid brain is considered the thinking brain. It is located in the cerebrum and considered the center of academic thought and cognitive learning. It forms the top layer of the brain and is referred to as the forebrain, upper brain, or new brain. The neocortex actually comprises 85 percent of the total brain. The cerebrum, which is as thick as a tongue depressor, is full of convolutions. Known as the thinking cap, this part of the brain handles the cognitive functions of the brain and the mind. It predicts, classifies, judges, infers, reasons, puzzles, wonders, creates, reflects, and makes sense of things. This is the part of the brain that sets humans apart from other species of animals.

Brain Imaging: How We Know What We Know

Before getting into an in-depth discussion about the interior brain and describing how the brain actually functions, it seems appropriate to talk a bit about how researchers know what they know about the workings of the brain and what has caused this avalanche of ideas.

The major breakthrough in neurobiological research is attributed to advanced brain imaging techniques. A quick reference to these various methods reveals a concentration on three elements of brain function and neural organization: the chemical composition of cells and neurotransmitters (CAT, MRI), the electrical transmission of information along neural pathways (EEG, SQUID, BEAM), and the distribution of blood during brain activity (PET). This array of acronyms constitutes the brain imaging techniques (see Figure 1.8). Together, these techniques confirm earlier theories and revelations about how the brain functions and where particular functions occur. The explosion of information about the brain is unprecedented.

CAT: Computerized Axial Tomography

The CAT scan produces anatomical views of the brain that show three-dimensional graphical images of the density of tissue, such as bone and tumors. Multiple X-ray images can show depth of field and cross-sectional views on a computer monitor (Parker, 1995; Sylwester, 1995; Wolfe, 2001).

MRI: Magnetic Resonance Imaging

Unlike the CAT scan, the MRI focuses on soft tissue and provides a reverse image by responding to chemical differences in composition. New MRI techniques work so fast that researchers can monitor brain activity while a cognitive activity is happening (Barrett, 1992; Sylwester, 1995; Wolfe, 2001).

EEG: Electroencephalogram

Used for over 50 years, the EEG process reports patterns in electrical transmissions within an active brain. These patterns are recorded as a squiggly line graph on a roll of paper. Obtaining accurate readings and interpretations and translating a score is often difficult (Davis, 1997; Herrmann, 1995; Parker, 1995; Solso, 1997; Sylwester, 1995; Wolfe, 2001).

SQUID: Superconductivity Quantum Interference Device

The SQUID technique picks up small magnetic fields caused by the electrical current of firing neurons to pinpoint the exact source of brain activity. This identifies a more exact source of electrical activity (Barrett, 1992; Sylwester, 1995; Wolfe, 2001).

BEAM: Brain Electrical Activity Mapping

The BEAM machine records electrical activity in more precisely defined areas and uses color to represent positive and negative locations in the cerebral cortex (Sylwester, 1995; Wolfe, 2001).

PET: Positron Emission Tomography

The PET uses radioactive glucose to monitor blood flow through the brain as various areas are activated. This reveals information about how and where an experience is processed in the brain (Barrett, 1992; Sylwester, 1995; Wolfe, 2001).

Figure 1.8   Brain Imaging Techniques: A Glossary of Terms

HOW THE BRAIN WORKS

To fully understand how the brain works, it seems best to begin by identifying the parts of the brain cell: neuron, axon, dendrite, synapse, neurotransmitter, electrical impulse, chemical signal, glial cell, myelin, and neural network or pathway (see Figure 1.9). The brain is mostly composed of microscopic nerve cells called neurons, sometimes referred to as gray matter (Wolfe, 2001). Sylwester (1995, 2000a) describes the human brain as being composed of neurons and glial cells. *Glia* means glue, and glial cells are indeed an important part of the brain's architecture. They form part of a blood barrier to protect the brain from dangerous molecules that travel in the bloodstream. Glial cells also form a layer of insulation (myelin) around nerve fibers, which strengthens and increases the neural messages.

The neuron can be compared to a drawing of a human arm, hand, and fingers, as shown in Figure 1.10. The cell body is like the hand, the axon like the arm (acting as a conductor that sends the impulse to the next cell), and the

NEURON: nerve cell that comprises gray and white matter in the brain

GLIAL CELL: cell that splits and duplicates to act as glue to strengthen brain cells

MYELIN: coating on the axon that serves as an insulator and speeds up transmission for outgoing messages

AXON: long fiber that sends electrical impulses and releases neurotransmitters

DENDRITE: short branching that receives the chemical transmitters

SYNAPSE: small gap between neurons through which neurotransmitters move

NEUROTRANSMITTER: chemical molecule that travels within and between brain cells

ELECTRICAL IMPULSE: the nerve message received and sent out by the neurons

CHEMICAL SIGNAL: a message carried from neuron to neuron; chemical molecules called neurotransmitters travel across synapses

NEURAL NETWORK: a set of connected neurons that form a strengthened path that speeds the passage of the neurotransmitters

Figure 1.9   The Brain Cell: A Glossary of Terms

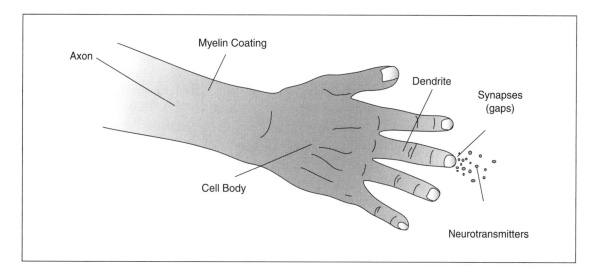

Figure 1.10   Physical Model of a Neuron

fingers form the equivalent of the dendrites, the receptors of the impulse (Sylwester 1995, 2000b).

When the neuron receives a message from the senses, muscles, or other neurons, it is received as an electrical impulse. This impulse is processed inside the cell and then sent out to other neurons by way of the axons (Wolfe, 1996). Traveling at speeds of 100 miles per hour, the impulse travels on the outside of the axon. When the electrical impulse reaches the end of the axon, near the dendrite branches, chemical neurotransmitters are released into the synapse

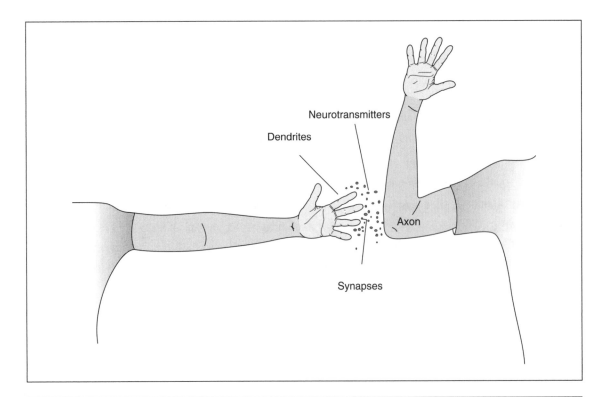

Figure 1.11   Synaptic Connection

and are received by the dendrite (Sylwester 1995, 2000b). These synapses allow neurons to communicate with each other (see Figure 1.11). Thus, the reaction along the axon is electrical, while the reaction between the cells is chemical (Parker 1995). This process results in electrochemical interactions.

The axon sends the electrical impulse to the dendrites through chemical messengers called neurotransmitters. The dendrites receive the messengers in little coves, or gaps, called synapses. The chemical message enters the neighboring brain cell and is translated into another electrical impulse within the cell. Brain cells talk to each other through the chemical messengers at the synaptic connections (Sylwester, 2000a; Wolfe, 2001).

A more scientific look at the synaptic connection highlights the strength of the dendrites (see Figure 1.12).

A still closer look at the synaptic connection reveals the intricate path of the neurotransmitters (see Figure 1.13).

Neurotransmitters

Neurotransmitters are the chemical messengers that communicate between neurons at the synapse, or the narrow gap between the axon and the dendrite. They are released as the electrical neural impulse is passed from one neuron to another (Sylwester, 2000b; Wolfe, 2001). Scientists have identified more than 50 neurotransmitters, but for the sake of this introductory chapter on the brain, only a few are defined in this text. They are grouped into three categories: amino acids, monoamines, and peptides (see Figure 1.14).

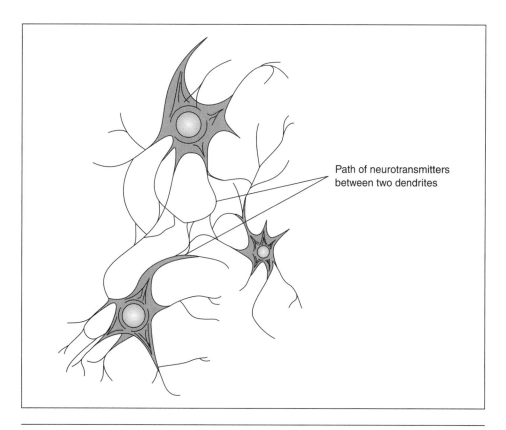

Figure 1.12   Neuron Communication

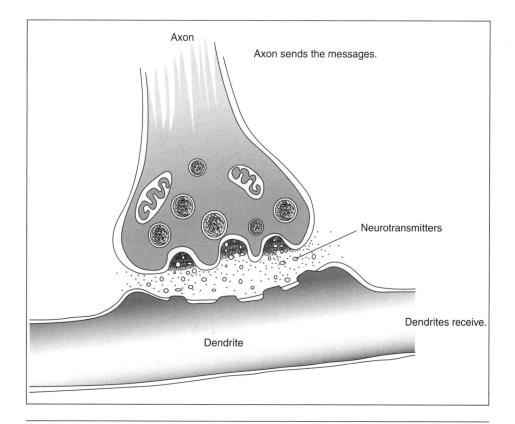

Figure 1.13   Synapse

Amino Acids (Principal)

SIMPLE GLUTAMATE: excitatory neurotransmitter (vision, learning, and memory)

GABA OR GLYCINE: inhibitory neurotransmitter (reduces anxiety and relaxes muscles)

Monoamines (Modified)

DOPAMINE: regulates complex emotional behaviors and conscious movements

SEROTONIN: regulates body temperature, sensory perception, and the onset of sleep

NOREPINEPHRINE: regulates arousal, activation, fight-or-flight response

Peptides (Complex)

ENDORPHIN: reduces pain, enhances euphoria

VASOPRESSIN: water retention, blood pressure, memory

Figure 1.14   Neurotransmitters: A Sample Glossary of Terms

Amino acids are the principal neurotransmitters. They carry excitatory or inhibitory messages. Monoamines determine whether the message sent is excitatory or inhibitory. Peptides, or classical neurotransmitters, affect complex behavior patterns such as pain and pleasure.

In this way, billions of nerve cells connect to each other in billions of combinations, forming trillions of pathways for nerve signals to follow. What results is referred to as dendritic growth, and the dendrites continue to grow and interconnect throughout a lifetime. These brain connections, or neural pathways, are wired and rewired constantly, continually, and incessantly as stimuli are processed by the brain (see Figure 1.15). The possible combinations are mind-boggling as the permutations expand (Sylwester, 2000a; Wolfe, 2001).

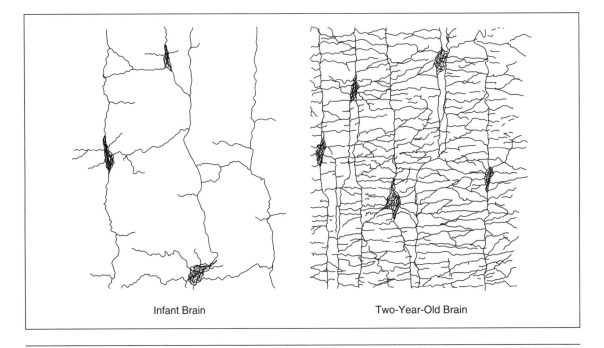

Infant Brain   Two-Year-Old Brain

Figure 1.15   Diagram of Growing Dendrites

Documented by Potter and Orfali (1993), an additional commentary on dendritic growth is the age-old axiom: Use it or lose it! (Wolfe, 2001). Just as stimulation fosters the growth of dendrites, the lack of stimuli causes the existing connection to weaken and even to disappear. While pruning (the natural weeding of old, unused dendritic connections, or neural pathways) is a natural process in growing dendrites, the concept of losing brain capacity refers to dramatic situations in which there is almost a total lack of stimulation for brain growth (Wolfe, 1996).

DIFFERENCES BETWEEN MALES AND FEMALES

Gender difference in brain physiology and functioning is an important concept to understand. It appears in literature about the brain, and it helps explain how the sexes process information differently. Gender differences occur in the area of emotions and in spatial navigation. Certain gender differences in brain functioning have been documented in terms of the location in which the processing occurs (Howard, 2006); for example, "the male's separation of language specialization in the left hemisphere and emotional specialization in the right helps to explain his traditional ineptness at talking about feelings" (p. 268). These and other differences, such as better visual perception and differentiation in males and greater verbal acuity in females, seem to appear most often after puberty.

There are differences in brain chemistry, length of nerve cells, density of nerve strands, and how information is processed in males and females. In fact, hormonal levels are the greatest indicators of gender-related differences in thinking and problem solving. In males, testosterone levels correlate with aggression, competition, self-assertion, self-confidence, and self-reliance. In females, when progesterone and estrogen levels are high, math and spatial abilities tend to be lower.

In terms of physiology and processing of information, Figure 1.16 depicts the most noticeable differences between males and females.

Males	Females
More cortical areas devoted to spatial-mechanical	More cortical areas devoted to verbal-emotive—use more words than males
Prefrontal lobe less active at earlier age—decision making more impulsive	Prefrontal lobe more active—can make less impulsive decisions, better literacy
Natural rest state many times a day—not as well suited to school day	Brain functioning stays active—more likely to retain information
Natural aggression—lateralize and compartmentalize in hemisphere	More cross talk between hemispheres—better multitasking
Visual system, type M ganglion cells—detect movement	Visual system, P ganglion cells—sensitive to color

Figure 1.16   More Than 100 Structural Differences Between Male and Female Brains

SOURCE: King & Gurian, 2006.

In brief, males and females process sensory input differently, using different parts of the brain. Although the brain is wired in the womb, the differences seem to be more noticeable after puberty. Gender differences are innately interesting, and the more that is known, the more educators are able to tailor learning to the preferences of both genders.

Part II

Principles for Teaching and Learning

2 Principles of the Brain and Learning

I think, therefore I am.

—Descartes

THE BRIDGE BETWEEN BRAIN SCIENCE AND COGNITIVE SCIENCE

Steeped in the knowledge of the brain and the workings of the brain, Caine and Caine (1991, 1993) have synthesized research-based information on the brain and learning into a set of 12 principles about how the brain learns. An overarching four-corner framework (Fogarty & Bellanca, 1993) and Caine and Caine's principles provide a basic schema that guide educators' work with students of all ages in the brain-compatible classroom (see Figure 2.1).

Principles	Making the Case for Best Practices
1. Learning is enhanced by challenge and inhibited by threat.	Case for high-level, complex performance tasks
2. Emotions are critical to patterning.	Case for emotional intelligence
3. Learning involves both focused attention and peripheral perception.	Case for enriched environments and time to engage in those environments
4. The brain has a spatial memory system and a set of systems for rote learning.	Case for both experiential and rote kinds of learning
5. The brain processes parts and wholes simultaneously.	Case for skill/drill and relevant application
6. Learning engages the entire physiology.	Case for nutrition, exercise, and relaxation
7. The brain is a parallel processor.	Case for multimodal instruction

Principles	Making the Case for Best Practices
8. Learning is embedded in natural, social settings.	Case for constructivist approach in hands-on learning environment
9. Each brain is unique.	Case for multiple-intelligences approach
10. The search for meaning is innate.	Case for activating prior knowledge
11. The search for meaning occurs through patterning.	Case for themes and threads to create patterns in an integrated curriculum
12. Learning always involves conscious and unconscious processing.	Case for more reflective processing and time to think things over

Figure 2.1   Using Principles About the Brain and Learning to Inform K–College Best Practices

THE BRAIN PRINCIPLES AND THE FOUR-CORNER FRAMEWORK

The origin of the four-corner framework is found in *Patterns for Thinking, Patterns for Transfer* (Fogarty & Bellanca, 1993). Based on an editorial by Brandt (1988) that appeared in an issue of *Educational Leadership,* the idea of teaching for, of, and about thinking emerged. Fogarty and Bellanca thought a fourth element was essential and added the idea of teaching with thinking. Thus, the four-corner framework of teaching evolved (see Figure 2.2). These four elements are held to be essential to the thoughtful classroom, to the classroom that requires rigor and vigor in thinking, to the classroom that values cognitive and cooperative structures for increasing student achievement and fostering high self-esteem, and to the standards-based classroom that honors the teaching-learning process.

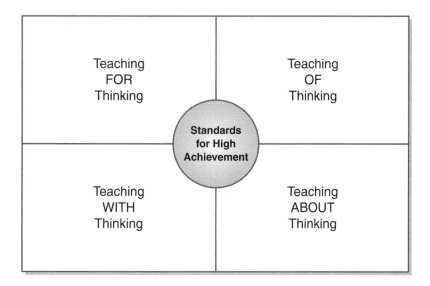

Figure 2.2   Four-Corner Framework

TWELVE BRAIN PRINCIPLES OF CAINE AND CAINE

Caine and Caine's (1993) principles (see Figure 2.1), within the four-corner framework, provide an understanding of how numerous educational innovations fit with brain research and sound pedagogy.

1. Learning Is Enhanced by Challenge and Inhibited by Threat

The brain loves a challenge and by nature is compelled to engage when a challenging puzzle, riddle, problem, or conundrum is presented. The brain naturally begins to figure things out. When the teacher has a "problem of the day" posted on the board, students automatically get hooked on solving the problem.

In turn, when teachers create a climate of threat, with dire consequences constantly the fare of the day, the brains of the students in those learning environments may not function as optimally as they could if they were learning in a more supportive environment. "This is going to be on the test." "If you don't know these things, you will most likely fail this course." These are not the words that challenge students to do their best thinking.

2. Emotions Are Critical to Patterning

Teachers have known for a long time that the affective and cognitive domains are inextricably linked. They are interconnected in ways that make it absolutely necessary to consider the impact of emotions on learning. This emotional impact works in two ways. One, as mentioned earlier, is the negative impact, evoking fear of threatening situations. This emotional link impedes learning or cognitive patterning. The other is the positive impact of getting students emotionally hooked and subsequently intensely involved in the learning so that cognitive patterning is internalized and anchored for long-term memory. Emotions engender focused attention. Attention engenders short-term memory. Short-term memory engenders long-term memory. And according to Sprenger (1999), memory is the only evidence we have of learning!

3. Learning Involves Both Focused Attention and Peripheral Perception

The human brain can readily focus on the task at hand or on the central idea presented. Yet at the same time, the human brain can pick up all kinds of other sensory stimuli that are occurring on the fringes of that central focus. Focused attention means just that: the brain is focused and alert and ready to connect to the incoming information.

Peripheral perception means that the brain is also taking in all kinds of surrounding stimuli, almost by osmosis. The brain is subconsciously aware of lots of peripheral input—visual, auditory, olfactory, kinesthetic, and taste. These peripheral sensory inputs can be as powerful and as long-lasting as the focused learning, especially once they become more explicit in the mind.

4. The Brain Has a Spatial Memory System and a Set of Systems for Rote Learning

The human brain has two kinds of memory systems. One is an explicit memory system, which requires practice, repetition, and rehearsal; the other is an implicit memory system that relies on experiences that invoke a more natural, spatial memory. The two memory systems work distinctly and in sync to form short-term memories that in turn become stored as long-term memories. The explicit memory systems include rote memorization of facts, repeated practices, and focused attention to procedures and routines. The implicit memory involves episodic memory, emotional memory, and spatial-experiential memory that occur almost automatically.

5. The Brain Processes Parts and Wholes Simultaneously

The human brain analyzes the discrete parts of information and at the same time discerns the big-picture look at the information. It is the dichotomy of the brain that involves the left and right hemispheres of the cerebral cortex. While the left hemisphere processes more analytically than the right hemisphere, which tends to synthesize the more holistic picture, the two are in constant communication with each other through a band of fibers, the corpus callosum, which connects the two sides of the brain.

6. Learning Engages the Entire Physiology

Learning involves heart, mind, and body. This principle epitomizes the mind-body connection of such regimes as yoga and Pilates. In fact, this principle involves emotional hooks, good nutrition, regular exercise, and time for relaxation. Learning that engages the entire physiology needs emotional connections to get students' attention. It needs healthy foods and nutrients to nourish the body and regular vigorous activity that sends the needed oxygen and nutrients to the brain. And finally, learning needs relaxation and meditation to create a mental focus for concentration and retention of information.

7. The Brain Is a Parallel Processor

According to this principle, when your mom said, "You can't do two things at once," she was wrong. The brain can and does do more than one thing at a time. The brain has four types of lobes in the cerebrum that process sensory input: the occipital lobes are the vision center of the brain, and the temporal lobes process auditory input. In turn, the parietal lobes integrate the various senses, particularly taste and touch, and the frontal lobes are the thinking and problem-solving centers of the brain, processing complex thought and emotion. These four lobes are able to process sensory input simultaneously. So, yes, a person can actually do more than one thing at a time.

8. Learning Is Embedded in Natural and Social Settings

Learning is most powerful when it is embedded in an experience that affords dialogue and discussion. We learn best when we have the actual experience and when we can talk about the learning. The experience taps into spatial memory (the time and space in which something occurred), and the dialogue taps into cognitive memory through verbal retelling of events and ideas. One can read about the zoo, or one can go to the zoo. Reading is not nearly as visceral as actually being there with the smells and sounds and images of the zoo.

9. Each Brain Is Unique

The fact that each brain is as unique as a fingerprint is astonishing. Every student sitting in a classroom has read different books, been different places, learned different words, and understood ideas and concepts in different ways and to different degrees. No two brains have exactly the same schema of prior knowledge because each brain has been exposed to background experiences. Thus, each brain connects the new learning in a different way. The fact that each brain is quite different in its cognitive schemes presents a daunting task to teachers as they try to connect with each student in meaningful ways.

10. The Search for Meaning Is Innate

The brain is a meaning-making machine, designed to make sense of all the sensory input it receives and create meaning of the world around it. The brain engages automatically when it is presented with a challenge or a conundrum, and it goes to work trying to sort things out. Yet while the brain is inherently designed to think and problem solve and make decisions, it also learns to be more skillful at these tasks with training in explicit thinking skills and problem-solving techniques. The search for meaning is as natural to the brain as breathing is to the lungs or pumping is to the heart. Thinking is what the brain does.

11. The Search for Meaning Occurs Through Patterning

The brain searches for recognizable patterns as it tries to fit the new information into its existing schema. It tries to slot the incoming stimuli into a proper place as it makes sense of it. One example of this is a toddler who is learning words as fast as he can. A bird flies by and the mom says, "Bird." The child repeats, "Bird." Over time he knows the object flying by is a bird. Yet when an airplane or butterfly flies by, the toddler often shows evidence of cognitive dissonance, slots these into his pattern of "birds," and inappropriately calls out "Bird" for these objects also. It is a great example of the brain slotting to a known pattern.

12. Learning Always Involves
Conscious and Unconscious Processes

The brain never really sleeps. In fact, when you are asleep, the brain is actually doing some of its most important work. It is doing the deep processing required to make meaning of ideas and put them into long-term memory and storage for later recall.

IT'S ALL ABOUT LEARNING

The principles of the brain and learning assembled by Caine and Caine (1993) provide the perfect backdrop to the teaching-learning scenario; they complement known best practices of instruction. They offer teachers a succinct resource of facts that explain how the brain learns best. By understanding, embracing, and applying these principles religiously in their instructional planning, teachers are better able to make relevant decisions about their teaching practices. The principles connect what is known about learning to what is known about teaching. This compendium is truly the bridge between brain science and cognitive science.

3 Cognitive Science

The Brain Is on My Mind

BRAIN SCIENCE AND COGNITIVE SCIENCE

The complement to brain science for educators is cognitive science. When the two come together, they provide a comprehensive frame for the teaching and learning process. This chapter unpacks the cognitive science component of the teaching and learning equation and discusses a number of elements that help explain and elaborate on the brain/mind connection.

NATURE VERSUS NURTURE (HEREDITY VERSUS ENVIRONMENT)

Perhaps the most obvious bridge between brain science and cognitive science is epitomized in the ongoing controversy about the role of heredity versus the role of environment—the nature-versus-nurture dilemma—that is always on the horizon. Evidence abounds (Diamond, 1988) that the role of environment is probably much more critical to the development of the brain function than was previously believed. Although most researchers agree that heredity plays a major role in determining the potential for brain growth and cognitive development, there is overwhelming evidence to suggest that an enriched environment stimulates brain activity and subsequent development of higher-functioning intellects (Diamond, 1988; Diamond & Hobson, 1998).

The ability of the brain to adapt to its environment by laying down essential neural connections is referred to as *neural plasticity*. Plasticity is seen as a result of experience. When researchers state that intelligence is a function of experience, they mean that experiences literally cause continual rewiring of the neural pathways within the brain (Sylwester, 1995, 2000a).

Although the previously held belief that the brain is a blank slate (*tabula rasa*) to be filled by experience is probably too radical an idea, the concept that it's all in the genes in terms of a person's "smartness factor" is also too drastic. Most likely, a reasoned voice would argue that a person's potential is governed by both natural genetic makeup and relevant environmental factors (Healy, 1990). In fact, the consensus seems to be that the ratio is about 50 percent nature and 50 percent nurture. The nature part of this equation is in the DNA; it literally is in the genes and is predetermined by the genetic code. Yet the nurture part is in the environment and is not predetermined, but rather available to influences from the environment. To unpack the concept of the influence that nurturing can have on the development of the human brain, the idea of enriching those environments is front and center.

ENRICHED ENVIRONMENTS

An enriched environment has a variety of rich sensory inputs and language experiences that literally stimulate a profusion of dendritic growth (Diamond & Hobson, 1998). The more dendrites one grows, the more pathways or connections one makes, the more capacity one has for establishing patterns and seeing the interrelatedness between ideas. This leads to the chunking of information so that information is remembered as a single item (Wolfe, 1996, 2001; patterning and chunking are discussed in detail later in this chapter).

More specifically, Healy (1990) speaks of enriched environments that involve basic considerations such as safety and regular contact with others. Enriched environments also include appropriate play materials such as blocks, clay, paints, and building sets; creative playthings that require intense, active learning; restricted television viewing time; and opportunities for daily outings. Wolfe (1994) makes a key point in her warning that no matter how well planned, how interesting, or how colorful or relevant the experience, if the child does not interact with that rich environment, little learning takes place and the dendrites are not stimulated to grow.

Jensen (1996c) includes a number of criteria in his discussion of enriched environments: room arrangement; formal and informal seating arrangements; appropriate lighting; ample water (8 to 15 glasses a day); clean air; real-world and multisensory experiences; multimodal experiences; challenging, novel, and rich activities; greater time flexibility (two-hour blocks); and opportunities for making choices.

Sylwester (1996) explains that because "neurons thrive only in an environment that stimulates them to receive, store, and transmit information, the challenge to educators is simple: define, create, and maintain an emotionally and intellectually stimulating environment and curriculum" (p. 140).

INTELLIGENCE AS A FUNCTION OF EXPERIENCE

In addition to and embedded in the idea of an enriched environment is the range of experiences students are exposed to both in school and outside of school. These experiences result from an extension of the enriched home or classroom environment and even reach out into the community and the world beyond.

These experiences imprint on the mind and stimulate brain growth and neural connections, just as the more formally planned experiences in the classroom do.

For example, a fishing trip with Grandpa, a walk along the wooded path, playing in the tree house, going to the museum, and even watching the clouds go by are the types of sensory experiences that children need. Having conversations with elders, laughing and teasing with siblings, and talking with friends are the kinds of language experiences that complement the parent-teacher dialogues and stimulate brain activity. Intelligence is truly a function of experience, so it is critical that whatever gifts nature endowed one with, these gifts are further enhanced and stimulated by rich and fertile experiences.

WINDOWS OF OPPORTUNITY

Closely connected to the concept of the role of nature versus the role of nurture and the accompanying concept of neural plasticity is the idea often referred to as *windows of opportunity.* Another way to think about these windows of opportunity is as sensitive periods (Bruer, 2002) in which the plasticity of the brain is at its peak for learning in a particular area. It's important to note that these periods are not critical but rather sensitive for certain kinds of learning. The windows do not close entirely except in a few isolated situations. In other words, there seem to be optimal times for the neural pathways to develop as larger and heavier cortical tissue, which means that future connections are made more frequently and more easily. These sturdy connections are sometimes referred to as *hardwiring* (Healy, 1990) in the brain. One example of this is binocular vision (the ability to coordinate the images from both eyes), which needs stimulation between birth and age three.

A partial listing of research results, while only a sampling of the concept, presents more on this idea of windows of opportunity:

- During the sensitive period from birth to three years old, the foundations are laid for vision, language, muscle control, intellectual development, and emotional development (Wolfe, 1996, 2001).
- At 24 months, babies who were consistently talked to by their mothers knew 295 more words than babies whose mothers did not engage them in conversation (Huttenlochner, cited in Wolfe, 1996).

The growing interest in and explosion of information about these windows of opportunity are evidenced by the number of popular magazines that are doing feature stories on the brain and its wiring. Among the popular literature, *Time* ran an article delineating wiring windows for vision, feelings, language, and movement and included suggestions for what parents can do to enhance this wiring (Nash, 1997b). And *Newsweek* published a special issue called "Your Child: From Birth to Three" (Gelber, 1997), which included a graph of the windows of opportunity for motor, emotions, vision, social, vocabulary, second language, math/logic, and music.

While there is still much to learn about these windows of opportunity, it makes sense to give children rich sensory input and robust language environments, especially in the early years when the plasticity of the brain is most pliable. Evidence indicates that if and when these critical periods are absent of any stimulation, children may develop the skill later but never with same ease or proficiency. In fact, when children learn certain skills later, they use different parts of the brain to accomplish the skill than if they had learned it earlier in the natural course of events (Healy, 1990). Further, Kotulak (1996) makes a convincing case for early childhood intervention for the economically, socially, and educationally disadvantaged to guide the massive "rewiring" that occurs in the brain in cognitively beneficial ways. In other words, the sense of threat that invades children's lives in those early years actually causes the brain to rewire itself in ways that tend to engage the instinctive brain and disengage the cognitive brain.

NUTRITION-COGNITION CONNECTION

Care and Feeding of the Brain

Lack of sufficient food has grave implications for the brain. The body uses what food there is in the following order: maintenance of vital organs, growth, social activities, and cognitive development (Wolfe, 1996, 2001). Interestingly, some studies suggest that if kids have a balance of food types available, they actually select a fairly balanced diet (Marcus, 2007; Shapiro, 1997). It is, of course, the adults' responsibility to ensure a proper diet, but there is also information about the workings of the brain that guides the options for nutritious, brain-compatible foods.

Marcus (2007) creatively describes three basic food groups: plant foods, animal foods, and junk foods (see Figure 3.1). The groupings provide a quick reference for students, teachers, and parents as they examine the three food options and this simple rule: In sum, the plate of food should have more plant foods than animal foods and more animal foods than junk foods. Marcus's description of nutritious meals and snacks continues with facts about junk foods as empty foods that offer no substantive nutrition.

Plant Foods
    Vegetables (e.g., lettuce, carrots, tomatoes, broccoli) and fruits (e.g., apples, grapes)

Animal Foods
    Meats (e.g., beef, chicken, pork)

Junk Foods
    Sugary and salty snacks (e.g., potato chips, candy)

Figure 3.1   The Three Food Groups

SOURCE: Marcus, 2007.

To continue the education about nutrition and the brain, it is important to explain how foods impact the workings of the brain. If what people eat affects the brain, it's important to know, for example, that neurotransmitters are made of amino acids and that amino acids are the building blocks of proteins. Therefore, protein in the diet before school facilitates brain activity. However, protein by itself tends to also make one sleepy. Protein with carbohydrates (high-energy foods) is the better choice for a hearty, brain-compatible breakfast.

Again, Marcus (2007) discusses the nutrients needed by the brain and the body in memorable terms that separate into four simple ideas: (1) proteins in beans, nuts, yogurt, and cheese as well as in fish and meats; (2) vitamins in fruits; (3) minerals in vegetables; and (4) fiber in cereals or fats.

Food sources, beyond the apple a day, include carbohydrates in cereals and grains for energy, chemicals in fruits and vegetables for fighting cancers, fiber in fruits and grains for warding off diseases, calcium in dairy products for teeth and bones, and fat (yes, fat) for energy and nerve growth. Since the brain gets the blood first, it almost always gets the nutrients it needs. The rest of the body will suffer from malnutrition before the brain will.

ABUSES AND ADDICTIONS

The alert about abuses and addictions is an important one. Without delving into great detail, there are a number of authors who devote their entire focus to the ideas of deprived, defective, damaged, abused, and injured brains. Kotulak (1996) looks at how nature builds the brain and then develops it during early life in response to its environment. He explores how the brain gets damaged from environmental threats, trauma, or alcohol and how aggression is triggered or controlled.

Wolfe (1996, 2001) graphically depicts the effects of fetal alcohol syndrome on the retardation of brain growth and goes on to explain that this inhibited dendritic growth is not recoverable—the damage is lifelong.

In yet another twist to this exploration of brains that are not properly nurtured or are damaged or abused in some way is the emerging evidence about addictions and the role of neurotransmitters. Researchers are linking the elevation of dopamine (a common substance in the brain that regulates complex emotions and conscious movements) to mood-altering drugs (Nash, 1997a); they increase or decrease levels of dopamine in the brain. Dopamine is associated with feelings of pleasure and elation and can be elevated by the potent pleasures that come from drugs (Nash, 1997a).

New Conclusions

While much of this information about the effects of environment on the brain is emerging literally on a daily basis, there is enough evidence to convince researchers that the nature-versus-nurture dilemma leans much more to the nurture side than previously believed.

Emotions and the Intellect

The sheer volume of information available about emotions (articles galore, audiotapes, whole books, thick chapters within books, and even terminology suggesting an emotional intelligence) provides the first clue to how important emotions are in the study of the brain. First brought to the forefront by studies of the limbic system, or the feeling brain, it is well documented that the emotions are the gatekeeper to the intellect (Goleman, 1995a; Hart, 2002; Isaacson, 1982; Kotulak, 1996). Sylwester (1995) says, "Recent research developments are unlocking the mysteries of how and where our body/brain determines what it likes, merely tolerates, and avoids. The emotional system emerging from this research is a complex, widely distributed, and error-prone system that defines our basic personality very early in life and is quite resistant to change" (p. 108). With that in mind, teachers should consider the following ideas about threat and challenge and the critical role of a safe, caring, and inviting climate for learning.

Safe Climate

Learners flourish in a safe and caring environment in which learning by trial and error, inquiring, and risk taking is the norm. In a classroom that is brain compatible, learners feel safe to take risks—including the risks of making mistakes and being wrong. In a safe climate, the brain is able to function at its highest cognitive level because learners do not sense threat and therefore continue in their cognitive mode. This is the climate most beneficial to enabling learning for all students.

Threat

The emotional brain, according to LeDoux (1998), is the default mechanism to stay alive. It senses threat subconsciously before the conscious mind is aware. In milliseconds, the heart rate increases, the palms get sweaty, and the body's state signals that something is wrong. What happens is a visceral response, and in fact the brain probably upshifts into a readied state of conscious alert.

This view of the brain sensing threat emotionally before it is cognitively aware, then signaling the mind to be on the alert through visceral responses, is in opposition to the previously held theory, which suggested that the brain perceives a threat and downshifts to a more primitive emotional state (Hart, 2002). However, in view of the theory of evolution and the concept of the human brain adapting to its environment for survival, the theory of the emotional brain as a default mechanism makes perfect sense—the brain's senses have allowed humans to survive as a species.

In brief, emotions drive attention and attention drives logic and reaction. When people are emotionally on alert, they are attentive and therefore at a higher state of readiness for whatever follows.

Challenge

Emotions have a positive side that can move life from the mundane to the joyful, from the boring to the immersed, from the interesting to the engaging.

In fact, Csikszentmihalyi (2008) describes a mental state of *flow* as an experience of creative oasis, relishing in the complexities and intricacies of a task. This transformational experience is achieved through the challenge of an engaging task or performance. And while this is the ultimate or peak learning experience, the concept of challenge is an enormously important one in designing classrooms that stimulate brain functions.

Simply put, when the brain faces challenging, intricate, and complex problems, all of its parts are engaged. Brain activity is evident throughout the cognitive and emotional realms. In fact, Goleman (1995a, 1995b) argues that reason without emotional input is impossible and suggests that gut feelings lend great credence to the decisions one makes. Along a similar line of thinking, Wolfe (1996, 2001) discusses the need for attention, meaning, and relevance for learning to take place. To pay attention, one must be emotionally secure and comfortably engaged—both are functions of the emotional brain.

In one sense, the emotional component can deter learning to the point of actually rewiring the brain to accommodate continual and unending threat (Kotulak, 1996). But positive feelings are necessary to give meaning to the experience (Goleman, 1995b) and to know deep joy in the learning experience (Csikszentmihalyi, 2008).

THE BRAIN AND THE MIND

To distinguish between the brain and the mind is not as simple a task as it appears. Some do not distinguish between the two at all (Hart, 2002; Jensen, 1996a; Kotulak, 1996; Rico, 1991; Sylwester, 1995, 2000a), while others are vigorous in their interpretations of each. F. E. Bloom and Lazerson (1988) make the unequivocal statement, "The mind is the product of the brain's activity" (p. 221). They see the mind as a function of the brain. Others distinguish between the brain and the mind in similar ways. Barrett (1992) suggests that the brain is part of the nervous system and is made of cells and fiber, while the mind is the part of a person that thinks, feels, perceives, and reasons. Sousa (1995) says that the brain is the physical organ in the head protected by the skull, and the mind transcends the head and operates throughout the body. The mind is aware, understands, makes meaning, and is the function of learning.

Brain Versus Mind

In its most simplistic sense, the brain is a concrete object that can be touched, but the mind is an abstraction that perhaps resides in the brain. The brain is physical; the mind is metaphysical. One can explore the biology of the brain but must explore the psychology of the mind. This is how Eisner (1997) explains it: "Brains, in contrast to minds, are biological—they are given by nature. . . . Minds are cultural—they are the result of experience. . . . Minds, then, in a curious and profound way, are made" (p. 350).

In a metaphorical reference to computers (that some researchers vehemently disagree with), some say that the brain is the hardware, while the mind is the software. (Maybe the dendrites are the Internet of the mind!) Speaking of metaphors for the brain, references range from a jungle ecosystem (Edelman, cited in Sylwester, 1995; Jensen, 1996a), to a symphony orchestra (Sylwester, 1995, 2000a), to a library (Sylwester, 1995), to a power plant or a highway system (Tierno, 1996). The possible number of metaphors to describe the relationship between the brain and the mind is endless, but each has its own limitations.

Although this discussion of the brain and the mind is somewhat unresolved, for the purposes of this book, the differences are of utmost concern. While information about brain physiology and about how the brain functions from a neurobiological perspective is paramount in educators' work with students, the workings of the intellectual mind seem just as important. Educators must be concerned not only with the development of the brain as an organ but also with the development of the intellectual mind. By understanding the intricacies of both, teachers can design learning in brain-compatible, mind-challenging ways.

It seems prudent to note that the use of the words *brain* and *mind* may signal an author's perspective or bias. For example, Sylwester (1995), a former biology teacher, prefers the word *brain* and does not use the word *mind;* in fact, it does not even appear in the index of his book *A Celebration of Neurons: An Educator's Guide to the Human Brain.* On the other hand, Pinker (1997), in *How the Mind Works,* refers to the human mind as he discusses the evolutionary functions of the human brain. He seems to prefer the concept of mind.

Just as in any emerging field of study, terminology is linked to one's understanding of a concept. Perhaps the best lesson here is to note, as one reads the volumes of information being produced about the human brain/mind, each author's terminology and to be aware of his or her perspective or point of view. Is the author a biologist or a psychologist? What bias may be represented by the language preference of brain/mind? In other words, read critically about the human brain/mind, and draw your own conclusions about basic assumptions.

Theories of the Intellect

The preceding discussion on the idea of a brain and a mind leads naturally to an exploration of the theories of the intellect. While the idea of intelligence has been around for some time (Barrett, 1992), emergent views of intelligence have abounded in the past several years. The theories described here include Spearman's theory of general intelligence (cited in Perkins, 1995), Feuerstein's (1980) theory of cognitive modifiability, Gardner's (1993) theory of multiple intelligences, Sternberg's (1997) theory of successful intelligence, Perkins's (1995) theory of learnable intelligence, Costa and Kallick's (2000) theory of intelligent behaviors or habits of mind, Goleman's (1995a) theory of emotional intelligence, and Coles's (1998) theory of moral intelligence.

General Intelligence Theory: Spearman

This theory is based on the idea that intelligence is inherited and unchanging and is measured by one's ability to score sufficiently on the Stanford-Binet intelligence test. On the Stanford-Binet test, an intelligence quotient (IQ score) is obtained by dividing a person's mental age by his or her chronological age, then multiplying by 100. A child with a mental age of 10 (based on the test) divided by a real age of 8, multiplied by 100 would yield an IQ score of 125. Traditionally, a score of 100 is considered average for any age (Barrett, 1992).

Theory of Cognitive Modifiability: Feuerstein

Working with disadvantaged children, Israeli psychologist Reuven Feuerstein (1980) challenges the traditional idea of a fixed intelligence and poses a theory that basically says intelligence is not a fixed entity but rather a function of experience, and it can be changed through guided mediation. This theory undergirds most modern theories of intelligence with the concept that human intervention and life experience impact intelligence. Feuerstein sees the human being as a guide or the mediator of learning, intervening to establish concepts that are approximately represented.

Theory of Multiple Intelligences: Gardner

Believing in a factored model of intelligence, rather than the general intelligence theory, Gardner (1983) posits the theory that there are many ways of knowing, learning, and expressing what one knows. Identifying several distinct intelligences, Gardner's theory embraces nine distinct intelligences: verbal-linguistic, mathematical-logical, bodily-kinesthetic, musical-rhythmic, visual-spatial, interpersonal-social, intrapersonal-introspective, naturalist, and existential. He sets strict criteria for identifying and classifying an intelligence, including biological evidence of brain tissue that processes an intelligence, and suggests that an intelligence functions in problem solving and in the creation of products.

Successful Intelligence: Sternberg

Also preferring a factored model of intelligence, Sternberg (1997) in his triarchic theory argues for three types of intelligence: analytical (compare, evaluate, judge, and assess), creative (invent, imagine, suppose, and design), and practical (practice, implement, show, and use). Based on his emergent theory, the analytical intelligence involves verbal abilities, the creative intelligence requires quantitative thinking, and the practical intelligence calls on spatial thinking. He refers to this combination of three intelligences as the *successful intelligence.*

Learnable Intelligence: Perkins

Perhaps the most palpable view of intelligence is presented by Perkins (1995) when he argues for a conception of learnable intelligence. He addresses these questions: Which mechanism underlies intelligence? Can people learn to be more intelligent? What aspects of intelligence need more attention? Perkins basically argues that a neural intelligence contributes to neural efficiency; an experiential intelligence stores personal experience in diverse situations; and a reflective intelligence contributes knowledge, understanding, and attitudes about how to use the mind in intelligent behavior. In brief, he makes a case for "knowing your way around" the good use of your mind, just as you know your way around a supermarket, an airport, or an opera. In turn, he believes in the metacognitive or reflective intelligence that is embodied in the idea of learning how to learn.

Intelligent Behaviors or Habits of Mind: Costa and Kallick

Looking at intelligence in terms of acquired habits of mind, or states of mind, Costa and Kallick (2000) outline a set of dispositions as evidence of intelligence. Included in the list of behaviors are persistence, reflectiveness, flexibility, metacognition, problem posing, accuracy, prior knowledge, precise language, enjoyment of thinking, and transference. These habits of mind are presented as teachable and, in turn, learnable.

Emotional Intelligence: Goleman

Among the emerging theories of intelligence is Goleman's (1995a) idea of an emotional intelligence. As conceived by Mayer and Salovey (cited in Gibbs, 1995), emotional intelligence refers to qualities such as understanding one's own feelings, exhibiting empathy for others, and regulating emotion to enhance living. In turn, Goleman delineates five elements of emotional intelligence: self-awareness (self-confidence and self-decisiveness), self-regulation (controlling impulsivity and handling emotions), motivation (hope, initiative in goal setting, zeal), empathy (reading others' feelings, caring), and social skill (influence, leadership, team building). Goleman argues that this emotional intelligence may be more important than IQ. He hypothesizes that emotional intelligence (a measure of the qualities of the mind) is a better predictor of people's success than the brainpower measured by standardized achievement tests. An illustrative story about this intelligence is presented in Figure 3.2.

Moral Intelligence: Coles

Using character development as the basis, Coles (1998) takes the position that a moral intelligence is a valid theory of intelligence. Coles shows how children can become smarter in their inner characters and can learn empathy, respect, and how to live by the golden rule through the living example of others

A favorite story that Goleman (1995b) tells is about the study of four-year-olds. A researcher invited the children, one by one, into a room and told each child that he or she could have one marshmallow right then or two marshmallows if he or she waited until the researcher came back. Then the researcher left each child alone in the room. Of course, some children grabbed for the marshmallow the moment the researcher disappeared through the door. Some waited a moment or two, then gave in and ate the marshmallow. Others were determined to wait it out. These children occupied their time with all kinds of diversions. They walked away, covered their eyes so they couldn't see the marshmallow, sang songs, tried to play games, licked the whole marshmallow, or even fell asleep. When the researcher returned, he gave the children who waited their hard-earned two marshmallows. Then, science waited for them to grow up.

The findings offer astonishingly predictive qualities. Those who had chosen to wait, to delay gratification, were reported to have generally grown up better adjusted and more popular, adventurous, confident, and dependable teenagers than their peers who had impulsively eaten the one marshmallow. Those who had eaten the one marshmallow were more likely to be lonely, easily frustrated, and stubborn as teenagers. They became stressed more easily and shied away from challenging tasks. In addition, when some teenagers from both groups took the Scholastic Aptitude Test, those who had held out and waited for the two marshmallows scored an average 210 points higher.

According to Goleman (1995a), it seems that this ability to delay gratification is a master skill in which reason triumphs over natural impulse, and he sees it as a sign of emotional intelligence that does not show up on an IQ test. However, be aware that emotional intelligence is not the opposite of IQ, but rather a complementary intelligence.

Figure 3.2   The Marshmallow Story

and through explicit dialogue about moral issues. The theory is based on how values are born and shaped through the *moral archeology of childhood.*

Memory, Learning, and the Human Brain

In this chapter on the cognitive science of the brain, it seems necessary to discuss, if only briefly, the relationship between memory and learning. Researchers often refer to memory when talking about learning because the two seem inextricably linked. Some say, "Memory is the thing I forget with," referring to the concept that the brain lets go of unneeded information. Others suggest that memory is the only evidence we have of learning (Sprenger, 1999).

According to Wolfe (1996, 2001), the learning process involves four interrelated processes: sensory memory, limbic system, short-term memory, and long-term memory. The senses focus on information (sensory memory), the brain determines whether the information is emotionally important (limbic system), the stimulation of brain cells produces more neurotransmitters as synapses are strengthened (short-term memory), and repeated activation causes changes in the neural networks so messages are sent more effectively and more permanently (long-term memory). In effect, the more these networks of neurons are used, the stronger they become and the more easily they are accessed and remembered.

Wolfe (1996, 2001) further describes this process by suggesting that memory is linked to three things: attention, meaning, and relevance. First, the brain must be aroused and then attend to the sensory input to capture it. Wolfe states that in terms of attention and focus, the input must hook in within 18 seconds or the brain loses the experience—the efficient normal brain acts as a sieve to sift out all extraneous information. Then, after the brain has paid attention to the idea, the learner tries to make sense or meaning of the input and attach personal relevance to it. In this way, the learner finds a pattern or another way of chunking the input so it can be connected through neural pathways to other ideas in the brain. That is how the new input becomes part of the long-term memory system. In Figure 3.3, the sequence of emotions to memory is delineated.

Emotions—Brain is aroused

Attention—Brain attends to sensory input

Meaning—Learner tries to make sense of input

Relevance—Learner attaches personal relevance to input

Figure 3.3   Memory Process

MEMORY METAPHOR

Is memory "the thing I forget with" or "the thing I remember with"? Pursuing that conundrum, consider the following: Using the computer screen as the memory metaphor allows one to look at the various phases of the memory/learning process (see Figure 3.4). This metaphor permits one to examine how the brain decides whether one can say, "It's on my screen," "It's on my desktop," "It's on my menu," or "It's on my hard drive." Let's unravel the function of remembering.

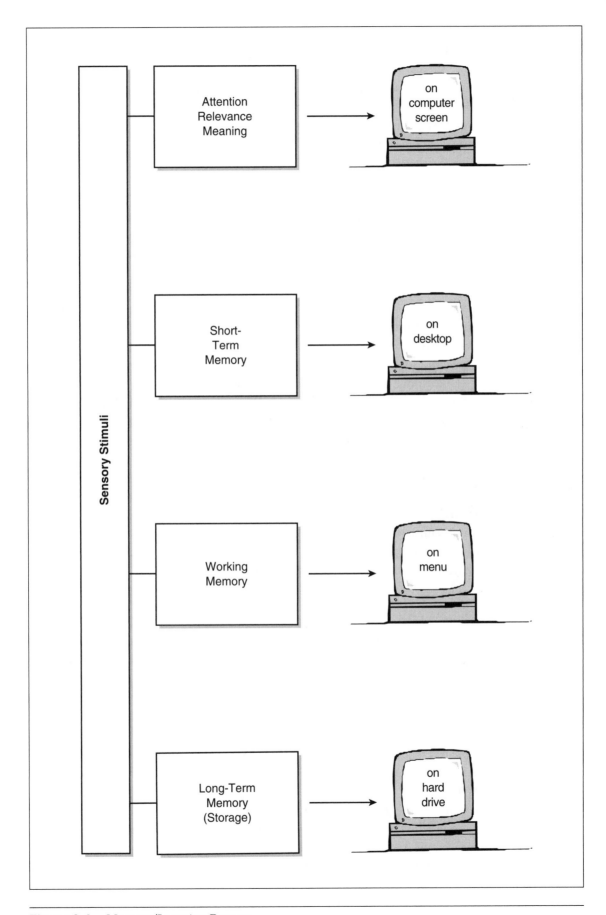

Figure 3.4 Memory/Learning Process

As alluded to previously, according to Wolfe (1994, 2001), there are a number of phenomena that influence memory: sensory input, attention, meaning, and relevance. Sensory memory results when sights, sounds, tastes, smells, and touch are noticed by the brain. If there is no notice taken or no attention paid to the incoming data, the information never gets into the brain in the first place. Therefore, sometimes it's not a matter of forgetting something, but rather a matter of never having noticed it at all.

It's on My Screen

Attention, then, comes into play. According to Sylwester (1995, 2000a), attention is the key to memory and learning. Attention can be an elusive thing. So how do we get the brain to attend to sensory input in ways that alert the memory system? The answer lies in the realm of the emotional intelligence system (Goleman, 1995a). It seems that without an emotional hook—some emotional connection to the incoming sensory input—the brain pays no attention to the information and, thus, no memory is made of it. In other words, sensory input must have an emotional tie-in to get the brain's attention. If it gets the brain's attention, "it's on my screen" and I can start to do something with it.

An example of this concept is when someone is introduced, and a moment later this thought occurs: "What was her name again?" The initial introduction, for some reason, does not alert the emotional brain to pay attention, so the brain simply decides that the information is not important enough to notice. If and when there is reason to know or to address the person, the brain is consciously on alert for the incoming input and will take notice of the name during the introduction. For example, when two sets of golf partners are paired together by the starter, the golfers pay attention to the subsequent introductions because the individuals will become a foursome for the day. The brain is attentive and awaiting the information for coding and placement in the memory system. That's when one can say, "It's on my screen."

It's on My Desktop

After the information is on the screen, one is able to start processing it to make sense of it. The brain searches for ways to connect this incoming information to something it already knows (Caine & Caine, 1991, 1993), that is, to tie it to some prior knowledge or past experience that has meaning. This is how the memory/learning system begins to put an idea into short-term memory. For example, as a person talks, suddenly he or she gets the attention of the listener with a reference to something meaningful. The mind immediately begins to create mental images of the scene based on previous pictures of similar scenes that are in the memory bank. Although the pictures may not actually be similar, they are in the mind because it's the only reference the mind has at that moment. It fits into the mind's schema. But, more important, the mind recognizes that at that moment, "it's on my desktop" because it is in working memory. The mind is doing something with the information. It's beginning to make sense of it and crystallize it. In the golfing example, the various people involved are consciously or subconsciously trying to find some way to recall the names.

It's on My Menu

The incoming information is beginning to have relevance because it's connecting personally in the mind and evoking emotional tie-ins. Relevance is another key to unlocking the mysterious marvel called memory. When the brain senses that something has relevance, it has reason to want to hold on to it. If the mind thinks it needs the data, it pays attention to, processes, rehearses, and stores the information. After storing it, of course, the expectation is that it can be readily retrieved.

To continue the computer screen metaphor, first, "it's on my screen" because there is an emotional hook to capture attention. Then, "it's on my desktop" because it becomes clearer and the mental connections take hold. The pragmatic learner looks for relevance and reason to continue to keep this information. After the brain knows that the information is useful, and that it's likely that it can be used in the future, "it's on my menu." Now it's in working memory for quick reference when needed. In the case of the names of the new golf partners, the names may hook into short-term memory with a reference to a place two of the golfers have in common, for example, Santa Fe. The mind has now connected these people to some experience, and the meeting has meaning.

It's on My Hard Drive

Later, at the mention of the new acquaintance in a letter to a friend in Santa Fe, the memory has transcended into a personally relevant episode. At this point, "it's on my hard drive" because the information has been placed into long-term memory for storage. It is now believed that memory is stored in multiple modes and the same memory chunk can be cued in a number of different ways. For example, this memory may be retrieved through the idea of Santa Fe, golfing at the same course again, or even by later writing the friend. In addition, it may be revisited through a visually similar face, a similarly sounding name, or even the sense of smell as the brain notices the fragrance of the cologne the person had been wearing.

With this recursive memory/learning process more fully exposed, the initial dilemma of memory as "the thing I forget with" or "the thing I remember and learn with" seems even more genuine. If a brain is to retain information, it seems that it must be emotionally linked to the incoming sensory input. Otherwise, the data never actually gets on a person's screen. It's not as much about forgetting as it is about whether the brain decides to hit the save key. After that miraculous memory cycle is ignited, through sensory input, attention, meaning, and relevance, you can be sure something's going to be on the screen!

TYPES OF MEMORY SYSTEMS

Short-Term Memory

LeDoux (1998) and Sprenger (1999) refer to two kinds of temporary memory: working memory and short-term memory buffers (see Figure 3.5). Working memory is located in the neocortex and holds thoughts for brief moments. It is understood that memory is able to handle seven items, plus or minus two, as the person continues to work with the information—social security numbers, zip codes, telephone numbers, seven habits of effective people, seven dwarfs, seven wonders of the world. Is this intentional or coincidental, based on some of the research called the *M factor* (Wolfe, 2001)? Short-term memory buffers are temporary storage areas in the occipital, parietal, and temporal lobes that are used to access and store information for long-term memory. And it is believed that the hippocampus plays a role in turning short-term memory into long-term memory and storage.

Working Memory	Short-Term Memory Buffers
Seven items, plus or minus two: social security numbers, zip codes, etc.	Stored for 15–30 seconds: phone numbers, names, etc.
Located in prefrontal cortex	Located in the temporal, occipital, and parietal lobes
Learning strategies: rote memory, configuration clues, patterns	Learning strategies: repetition, rehearsal, rote memory

Figure 3.5   Types of Temporary Memory

Several situations in which memory occurs are listed in Figure 3.6. Take a minute to review the instances that relate to your own experiences.

> . . . gone into one room for something, forgotten what you went into the room for, and returned to the original room where the thought occurred—and remembered what it was you were looking for? (declarative/episodic)
>
> . . . tried to find a piece of text on a page, knowing exactly where it is placed on that page (e.g., upper-right corner), but been unable to find it? (declarative/episodic)
>
> . . . read an entire page and then realized you had no idea what you had just read? (declarative/semantic)
>
> . . . driven home and had no memory of the actual drive? (procedural/emotional)
>
> . . . recalled a moment in time when a song unexpectedly played on the radio? (declarative/episodic)
>
> . . . had a sense of déjà vu—that something had happened before? (declarative/episodic)

Figure 3.6   Have You Ever . . .

Long-Term Memory

Different researchers use different terms to categorize the types of long-term memory (see Figure 3.7). Following is a discussion of these categories.

Episodic, Procedural, Conditional, and Emotional Memory

In one view of the relationship between memory and learning, Jensen (1997b) speaks of four kinds of memory. *Episodic memory* is location driven; it is the memory that is linked to a particular occurrence. People's ability to recall, in great detail, what they were doing when John F. Kennedy was killed, when the *Challenger* exploded on liftoff, and when the Twin Towers were attacked are examples of episodic memory.

Procedural memory is what is at work when people find themselves retracing their steps into the room they just left to try to capture the thought that has escaped them. Procedural memory is the muscle memory of keyboarding or snowboarding, and it is believed to be controlled, at least in part, by the cerebellum. On the other hand, *conditional memory* is the automatic memory that reminds people, for example, that the stove is hot and the edge of the cliff is dangerous.

Emotional memory is memory stimulated by feelings. For instance, the memories that rush back to people as they remember a lost love, a childhood sweetheart, or the absence of a beloved pet follow the emotional pathway of neural processing.

Memory Lanes: Semantic, Episodic, Emotional, Procedural, and Automatic

Sprenger (1999) delineates five specific kinds of memory or memory lanes that help the brain access memory or learning; these are similar to those discussed by Jensen (1997b), with one addition. *Semantic memory* is the memory of words and written language.

Declarative (Explicit) and Procedural (Implicit) Memory

The two most commonly recognized memory systems and perhaps the most clear and simple to remember are declarative or explicit and procedural or implicit. Wolfe (1996, 2001), Sylwester (1995, 2000a), Jensen (1996a), and Sousa (2000) discuss memory in these terms. *Declarative* memories are factual, label, and location memories. They define categories and are verbal and conscious. Some examples are names of things, classifications, and groupings. *Procedural* memories are automatic skill sequences. They are difficult to make but also difficult to forget! Some examples are riding a bike, typing, grooming, and skating.

Declarative memory is subdivided into semantic and episodic memory lanes (Sprenger, 1999). Semantic memory, as its name implies, governs semantics or words, learned language, facts, data, and other verbal information and general knowledge. Episodic memory, in turn, and as suggested by its label, is triggered by episodes or experiences in one's life, such as a family celebration, a week at basketball camp, or a spring dance. Both semantic and episodic memory lanes are explicit types of memory. They consist of abstract ideas. They are voluntary and often require practice, rehearsal, and repetition to put into long-term memory for storage and retrieval.

Declarative	Procedural
Explicit, voluntary, abstract, rehearsal	Implicit, involuntary, concrete, automatic
Semantic	*Automatic*
"The What"	"The How"
General knowledge, labels, names (facts, data, information, words)	Skill repetition, practice, rehearsal (driving a car, typing, riding a bike)
Located in the hippocampus	Located in the cerebellum
Learning strategies: graphic organizers, questioning, outlining, debating, paraphrasing, mnemonic devices	Learning strategies: performances, routines, procedures
Episodic	*Emotional*
"The When and Where"	"The Whatever"
Life experiences, location, spatial (songs, events, personal experiences, celebration, accident, death, divorce)	Deep, intense plus-or-minus emotional experience
Located in the hippocampus	Located in the amygdala
Learning strategies: novelty, bulletin boards, arrangement, role-plays, color handouts, position in room	Learning strategies: positive and negative emotional experiences, celebrations, debates, simulations, arguments, surprises

Figure 3.7   Types of Long-Term Memory

Procedural memory is subdivided into automatic and emotional memory lanes (Sprenger, 1999). Automatic memory lanes access motor or muscle memory skills and rote learning activities that have been practiced, rehearsed, and repeated many times. The learning is on autopilot, and the skills are grooved into place. One never forgets how to ride a bike, type, or play the violin. And with a mere whisper of a cue, the learner rattles off a poem, a prayer, or a song through rote memory recall. Emotional memory lanes are, in fact, linked to intense emotional experiences. These memory lanes are the most powerful, and they override every other kind of memory. There is often a visceral reaction as the memory is reconstructed. Extreme sadness or overwhelming joy may accompany the memory, or a smile may automatically appear as the memory manifests itself.

LEARNING THROUGH PATTERNS AND CHUNKING

The human memory is powerful and mysterious. Memory seems to be located everywhere and nowhere in the brain. Yet all learning depends on memory, including the simple recall of facts and data and the more complex memory system of remembering thinking patterns, conceptual frames, and complex ideas. The idea of "learning and the brain" suggests an intricate relationship between the two.

To assist the learning process, the brain does several other things beyond giving attention and focus to something. The brain creates *patterns,* or neural pathways, that are linked and connected in larger patterns (sets and subsets) of related information. These pattern-seeking devices in the brain are exemplified in the use of thematic teaching, in which a big idea provides an overall pattern for the brain to perceive. The brain is always seeking the big picture—the pattern of thought that is created by repeated use of familiar neural pathways.

Chunking (clusters or patterns of ideas that fit together; Sylwester, 1995) also aids the brain in memory and learning. It is a phenomenon that is achieved when a coherent group of informational items are rapidly combined and are remembered as a single item. One example of this is the chunk of letters that make up a word. In a more complex example, the difference between novices and experts in a given field appears to be that experts tend to organize information into much larger chunks, while novices work with isolated bits of information (F. E. Bloom & Lazerson, 1988). An example is the chess master who conceptualizes the whole process in a big-picture "first take" versus the novice who plots the game play by play.

Both patterning and chunking are responsible for enhancing memory and, thus, enhancing learning. For that reason, both are recursive themes in the text concerning the brain and the learner in brain-compatible classrooms.

IT'S ALL ABOUT TEACHING

The essence of this chapter on cognitive science is captured in the works of two great thinkers: Jean Piaget and Lev Vygotsky. Piaget (1954), often referenced as the father of constructivism, posits the idea that the brain "constructs meaning in the mind" and each learner must activate his or her own schema to connect the new and incoming input. Vygotsky (1978) discusses the idea of the zone of proximal development, in which he theorizes that the teacher must practice a gradual release of responsibility as the learner becomes more independent in the learning situation. Vygotsky believed that the learning is best internalized through this social interaction. These ideas are validated in the principles of the brain and learning delineated by Caine and Caine (1997), as described in Chapter 2 of this book.

With these parallel discussions of brain science and cognitive science, the educator has a comprehensive understanding of the human brain and how it functions, remembers, and learns. Now, the discussion turns to brain-friendly strategies that epitomize these findings. The next four chapters uncover these strategies for immediate K–college classroom use.

Part III

Brain-Friendly Strategies

4 Strategies for Brain-Compatible Classrooms

THE FOUR-CORNER FRAMEWORK

The origin of the four-corner framework is found in an earlier publication, *Patterns for Thinking, Patterns for Transfer* (Fogarty & Bellanca, 1993). Based on Brandt's (1988) editorial, the idea of teaching for, of, and about thinking emerged. Fogarty and Bellanca thought a fourth element was essential and added the idea of teaching with thinking. Thus, the four-corner framework of teaching for, of, with, and about thinking evolved (see Figure 4.1). These four elements are held to be essential to the thoughtful classroom, to the classroom that requires

Teaching for thinking	Teaching of thinking
Teaching with thinking	Teaching about thinking

Figure 4.1   The Four-Corner Framework

rigor and vigor in thinking, to the classroom that values cognitive and cooperative structures for increasing student achievement and fostering high self-esteem, and to the standards-based classroom that honors the teaching/learning process.

BRAIN-COMPATIBLE CLASSROOM

The four-corner framework of the brain-compatible classroom represents the many instructional innovations that comprise accepted understandings of pedagogy and best practice. In addition, the framework design is developed with a focus on teaching/learning behaviors. Teachers in brain-compatible classrooms set the climate for thinking, teach the skills and concepts of thinking, structure the interaction with thinking, and think about thinking (see Figure 4.2).

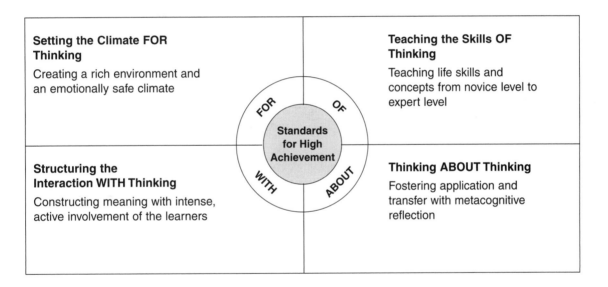

Figure 4.2   Brain-Compatible Classrooms: Description

To further understand how these four elements are critical to the learner-centered classroom and to clarify the implications for the teaching/learning process, a more thorough description of each element follows. In addition, the research base is stated (see Figure 4.3) as well as the names of the leading voices in the literature on brain research and learning theory (see Figure 4.4). The research is then bridged to the 12 brain-based principles (see Figure 4.5), enumerated by Caine and Caine (1991, 1993), in an attempt to "summarize the accumulated insights . . . [of the human brain] in a form that is of practical benefit to educators" (1993, p. 87). The principles also provide guidelines for programs and methodologies that are delineated as implications for learning (see Figure 4.6) and teaching (see Figure 4.7).

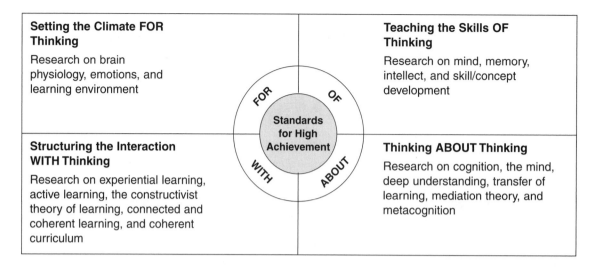

Setting the Climate FOR Thinking

Research on brain physiology, emotions, and learning environment

Teaching the Skills OF Thinking

Research on mind, memory, intellect, and skill/concept development

Structuring the Interaction WITH Thinking

Research on experiential learning, active learning, the constructivist theory of learning, connected and coherent learning, and coherent curriculum

Thinking ABOUT Thinking

Research on cognition, the mind, deep understanding, transfer of learning, mediation theory, and metacognition

Figure 4.3   Brain-Compatible Classrooms: Research Base

Setting the Climate FOR Thinking

- Sousa (biology)
- Wolfe (biology)
- MacLean (triune brain)
- Diamond (environment)
- Hart (emotions)
- Isaacson (limbic system)
- Ornstein & Sobel (healthy brain)
- Goleman (emotional intelligence)
- Mayer & Salovey (emotional intelligence)
- O'Keefe & Nadel (memory)
- Lozanov (limbic)
- Jensen (movement)

Teaching the Skills OF Thinking

- Epstein (education)
- Hart (learning)
- Luria (higher cortical functions)
- Sylwester (learning, acquisition)
- Sternberg (successful intelligence)
- Gardner (multiple intelligences)
- Goleman (emotional intelligence)
- Coles (moral intelligence)
- Perkins (intelligence)
- Costa & Kallick (intelligent behavior)
- Mayer & Salovey (emotional intelligence)
- Jensen (learning)
  - Sousa (learning)
  - Wolfe (learning)
  - Spearman (intelligence)
  - Sprenger (memory)

Structuring the Interaction WITH Thinking

- Ornstein & Sobel (parallel processing)
- Healy (active learning)
- Gardner (multiple intelligences)
- Caine & Caine (connections)
- Bruner (learning theory)
- Dewey (experience)
- Brooks & Brooks (constructivism)
- Beane (coherent curriculum)
- Harmin (active learning)
- Piaget (constructing meaning)
- Bloom (active learning)
- Goodlad (active learning)
- Johnson & Johnson (cooperative learning)
- Vygotsky (social interaction)

Thinking ABOUT Thinking

- Luria (cognition)
- Vygotsky (mind)
- Feuerstein (mediation)
- Perkins (transfer, deep understanding)
- Perkins & Salomon (transfer)
- Hart (transfer)
- Palinscar & Brown (metacognition)
- Costa (metacognition)
- Flavell (metacognition)
- Swartz & Perkins (metacognition)
- Gardner (deep understanding)
- Costa & Kallick (habits of mind)

Figure 4.4   Brain-Compatible Classrooms: Researchers

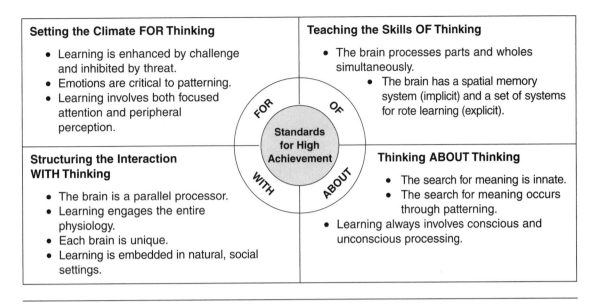

Setting the Climate FOR Thinking

- Learning is enhanced by challenge and inhibited by threat.
- Emotions are critical to patterning.
- Learning involves both focused attention and peripheral perception.

Teaching the Skills OF Thinking

- The brain processes parts and wholes simultaneously.
  - The brain has a spatial memory system (implicit) and a set of systems for rote learning (explicit).

Structuring the Interaction WITH Thinking

- The brain is a parallel processor.
- Learning engages the entire physiology.
- Each brain is unique.
- Learning is embedded in natural, social settings.

Thinking ABOUT Thinking

- The search for meaning is innate.
- The search for meaning occurs through patterning.
- Learning always involves conscious and unconscious processing.

FOR OF WITH ABOUT

Standards for High Achievement

Figure 4.5 Brain-Compatible Classrooms: Principles

Teaching FOR Thinking: Setting the Climate

Teaching for thinking is about setting the climate for thinking. It means creating a learning environment that offers a safe and caring place for all learners—regardless of race, color, creed, age, aptitude, or abilities—to go about the business of learning. In setting a safe climate for thinking, risk taking is the norm and learners understand that to learn is to make mistakes as well as experience successes. The ideal learning environment presents a rich and stimulating setting for learners to explore, investigate, and inquire.

Research Base—Physiology, Emotions, Environment

Research on brain physiology (MacLean, 1969, 1978; Ornstein & Sobel, 1987) and the development of neural networks provides empirical evidence related to setting the climate for thinking. More specifically, two distinct lines of research relate to this critical element. One group of studies (Goleman, 1995a; Hart, 2002; Isaacson, 1982; Mayer & Salovey, cited in Gibbs 1995) concerns the role that emotions play in the teaching/learning scenario, and another set of investigations (Diamond, 1988) targets the concept of enriched environments (see Figures 4.3 and 4.4).

To summarize the critical findings on emotions as succinctly as possible: emotions are the gatekeepers of the intellect. Emotional hooks are necessary for long-term learning; negative emotions can become blocks to learning. The findings on the benefits of an enriched environment, although convincing, invariably lead to the age-old controversy concerning nature versus nurture. Basically, the question is: Are people born, by nature, with an unchanging brain/mind/intellect, or does nurturing through a rich environment impact the brain and increase the neural pathways of intellectual activity? The jury is still out on the balance of natural endowments and the nurturing environment, but most researchers agree that the nurturing side of the equation is a critical component. In fact, there is some consensus that the balance is about 50 percent nature and 50 percent nurture.

Setting the Climate FOR Thinking

Verbal and nonverbal signals

DOVE guidelines

Emotional intelligence

Moral intelligence

Three-story intellect

Fat/skinny questions

People search

Wait time

Response strategies

Socratic dialogue

Student groupings

Blocks of time

Year-round schools

Room arrangement

Equipment and supplies

Sensory input

Language stimulation

Learning centers

Teaching the Skills OF Thinking

Microskills

- Collaborative skills
- Thinking skills
- Academic content skills and concepts
- Technological skills
- Performance skills

Macroskills

- Problem-solving skills
- Decision-making skills
- Communication skills
- Research skills
- Word-processing skills
- Innovation skills
- Production skills
- Performance skills

Skill Development

- Direct instruction
- Development of skill and content

  Training
  - Embedded application
  - Peak performance
  - Flow

FOR · OF · WITH · ABOUT

Standards for High Achievement

Structuring the Interaction WITH Thinking

Cooperative structures

Graphic organizers

Multiple intelligences (verbal-linguistic, logical-mathematical, bodily-kinesthetic, musical-rhythmic, visual-spatial, interpersonal-social, intrapersonal-introspective, naturalist-physical world)

Integrated curriculum

Performance tasks

Themes

Problem-based learning

Projects/service learning

Case studies

Thinking ABOUT Thinking

Personal relevance

Knowledge construction

Deep understanding

Generalizations

Engagement

Cognitive mediation

Metacognitive reflection

Direct application

Transfer levels and enhancing transfer

Traditional assessment

Dynamic assessment

Performance assessment

Learning logs

Mediated journals

Figure 4.6   Brain-Compatible Classrooms: Implications for Learning

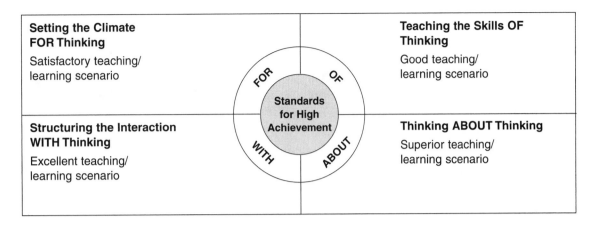

Figure 4.7   Brain-Compatible Classrooms: Implications for Teaching

Principles of Brain-Compatible Learning

The following are Caine and Caine's (1991, 1993) principles that seem to relate to setting the climate for thinking (see Figure 4.5):

1. *Learning is enhanced by challenge and inhibited by threat.* The brain learns optimally when appropriately challenged; thus, a safe, rich environment fosters a state of relaxed alertness for learning. The mind becomes engaged in problem solving and decision making, especially in open-ended problem scenarios. For example, in lab settings, rather than telling students what to do, teachers guide the process as students figure out what seems best.

2. *Emotions are critical to patterning.* Emotions and cognition cannot be separated; thus, positive emotional hooks, such as intriguing questions, puzzles, conundrums, and open-ended problem scenarios, tend to enhance learning. Other ways to tap into emotional intelligence include role-plays in which there is some emotional risk, surprise introductory sets that encourage students to be curious, public opinion polls that encourage safe risk taking, and relevant stories that pull at the heartstrings.

3. *Learning involves both focused attention and peripheral perception.* The brain responds to the entire sensory context; thus, in an enriched environment, peripheral information can be purposely organized to facilitate learning. For example, informative bulletin boards, instructional graphics on the board, appropriate background music, varied lighting, posters, charts, and maps are all part of the learning environment that influence learning.

Implications for Learning

Implications for learning (see Figure 4.6), based on brain research and pedagogy, are that certain methodologies are more brain-compatible or more in sync with how the brain takes in information, remembers it, and, in turn, triggers that information for relevant use. In essence, techniques that set a safe climate and challenge the brain in engaging ways are implied or hinted at by the findings about how the brain works.

Because brain functioning is enhanced by challenge and inhibited by threat and learning involves both focused and peripheral learning, certain instructional methods and climate-setting techniques are dictated for the brain-compatible classroom. For example, higher-order questions, time to think before answering, room arrangement, and enriched environmental stimuli seem more brain compatible or conducive to learning in ways that are easily adapted to how the brain works. The following are some ways to set the climate in a brain-compatible classroom:

- Be aware of verbal and nonverbal behaviors
- Establish classroom guidelines
- Use DOVE guidelines for brainstorming (**d**efer judgment, **o**pt for unusual, use a **v**ast number of ideas, **e**xpand by piggybacking)
- Recognize emotional and moral intelligence
- Ask high-level questions (fat/skinny, three-story intellect)
- Probe for depth in answers (people searches, wait time, response strategies, Socratic dialogue)
- Group students diversely (by age, ability, etc.)
- Schedule blocks of time
- Consider a year-round school schedule
- Arrange the classroom for learning
- Create a rich environment (equipment, supplies, sensory input, language stimulation)
- Set up learning centers
- Utilize learning stations within one class period for multiple ways to learn

Implications for Teaching: Satisfactory

Based on the four-corner framework for the brain-compatible classroom, if teachers set a warm, safe, and inviting climate for thinking and authentic student learning, they are doing a satisfactory job in terms of quality of teaching. Immersed in a rich, secure environment, students learn. In fact, they learn naturally, in the inductive way they learn outside of the formal school setting.

Teaching OF Thinking: Instructing Skills and Standards of Learning

Teaching the content and process standards of the various disciplines as well as the skills of thinking encompasses the life skills and concepts that thread through all subject matter content in a standards-based curriculum. These skills range from communication and social skills, to the microskills of thinking and reflecting, to the technological skills of the information age, to the skills needed for solving algebraic equations and for computer programming, to the skills training involved in a craft or athletics. Direct instruction of skill development moves through predictable stages from the novice, to advanced beginner, to competent, to proficient, and finally to expert.

Research Base—Brain, Mind, Intellect

Early research on the brain/mind/intellect focused on understanding the relationship between the brain and the learning process (Hart, 2002; Luria 1976). More current research on the brain and its implications for learning (Epstein, 1978; Jensen, 1996c; Sousa, 1995; Sylwester, 1995; Wolfe, 1996, 2001) is appearing at an incredible rate. In addition, emergent theories of the intellect, including the traditional general intelligence (Spearman, cited in Gould, 1981), multiple intelligences (Gardner, 1983), successful intelligences (Sternberg, 1986), emotional intelligence (Goleman, 1995a; Mayer & Salovey, cited in Gibbs, 1995), moral intelligence (Coles, 1998), and intelligent behaviors or habits of mind (Costa & Kallick, 2000) as well as ways of outsmarting IQ (Perkins, 1995), are inextricably related to this element of the skills and concepts that thread through our lives (see Figures 4.3 and 4.4).

Principles of Brain-Compatible Learning

Continuing with Caine and Caine's (1991, 1993) principles, the following are the ones that relate to teaching the skills of thinking (see Figure 4.5):

4. *The brain has a spatial memory system (implicit) and a set of systems for rote learning (explicit).* There is a natural, spatial memory that needs no rehearsal and affords instant memory, and there are facts and skills that are dealt with in isolation and require practice and rehearsal; thus, teaching must focus on both the personal world of the learners to make the learning relevant and rote memorization techniques to foster long-term learning for transfer. Rote memorization requires more conscious effort because the facts being memorized may have little meaning or relevance to learners. When the brain senses that there is no need to remember (i.e., lack of relevance), it tends to let go of the information. Thus, rote memorization of isolated facts often needs more explicit work to learn and recall information, whereas spatial memory has built-in cues that help in the retrieval of information. For example, spatial memory can be used to prepare students for a big test by having them study in the same room and at the same desk—essentially the same exact location—as they will be when they take the actual test. Students will mentally "see" notes that had appeared on the board during the initial learning. For rote learning, students need a lot of practice and repetition in various contexts: flash cards, musical lyrics, rhyming sounds, acronyms, and repeated rehearsals.

5. *The brain processes parts and wholes simultaneously.* Bilateralization of right and left hemisphere processing, though inextricably interactive, allows the brain to reduce information into parts and, at the same time, to perceive and work with it as a whole; thus, immediate application of direct instruction allows learners to perceive the information from both

perspectives. Examples include teaching adverbs through a skill/drill method and accompanying the drill with an exercise that requires students to explicitly use adverbial phrases in their writing; learning multiplication facts and then applying them to story problems; and working with punctuation and then using specific kinds of punctuation in journal writing, lab reports, and expository essays.

Implications for Learning

The knowledge that the brain processes parts and wholes simultaneously and that memory is both spatial and rote implies that learning in the classroom needs to happen in ways that are compatible to brain functioning. Included in these brain-friendly methods is direct instruction in skill and concept development, accompanied by application of the learned skills and concepts in authentic situations. The following are ways to teach skills in the brain-compatible classroom:

- Promote collaboration (leadership, communication, conflict resolution, team building)
- Foster critical and creative thinking
- Develop academic content skills and concepts (math, science, social studies, language arts)
- Incorporate technology (literacy, graphics)
- Require performance tasks (athletics, visual arts, performing arts, practical arts)
- Apply problem-solving and decision-making skills
- Support communication
- Build a knowledge base (research, word processing)
- Use innovation skills
- Develop production skills
- Incorporate embedded application
- Incorporate performance skills
- Use direct instruction
- Develop content and process skills/concepts
- Identify peak performance and flow (Csikszentmihalyi, 2008)

Implications for Teaching: Good

Teaching that develops skills, concepts, and attitudes through direct instruction techniques and teaching that creates a risk-free climate within rich classroom environments are considered good teaching. This kind of teaching moves beyond the first element of climate setting and combines two essential elements by teaching for thinking and by teaching the skills and concepts of thinking. This combination of elements is considered better or more skillful than merely setting a safe, enriched environment because the learning is guided explicitly by the teacher. In this way, learners are moved more directly to specific realms of learning—to areas of study that they may not have approached without intervention and guidance.

Teaching WITH Thinking: Structuring Interactions

Teaching with thinking is about structuring the interaction with thought-provoking activities that require intense involvement from learners. Learning is shaped by an internal process and by social interaction (Vygotsky, 1978). Active learning permits learners to construct meaning in the mind; thus, optimal teaching/learning situations invite learners to become an integral part of the learning process through hands-on learning and dialogue with others. This includes the use of cooperative learning, graphic organizers, multiple intelligences, and authentic curriculum models such as case studies and problem-based learning.

Research Base—Active Learning/Constructivist

The research basis for the element of structuring the interaction with thinking comes from literature on experiential learning (Bruner, 1973; Dewey, 1938), the constructivist theory (Brooks & Brooks, 1993; Piaget, 1970), the active learning theory (Harmin, 1994), Caine and Caine's (1991; Caine, Caine, & Crowell, 1994) synthesis of brain research and their subsequent call for more connected and interrelated ways of learning, as well as related work about developing a coherent curriculum (Beane, 1995; see Figures 4.3 and 4.4).

Principles of Brain-Compatible Learning

The following are Caine and Caine's (1991, 1993) principles that relate to structuring the interaction with thinking (see Figure 4.5):

6. *Learning engages the entire physiology.* Learning is as natural as breathing, yet neuron growth, nourishment, and emotional interactions are integrally related to the perception and interpretation of experiences; thus, stress management, nutrition, exercise, and relaxation become a focus of the teaching/learning process. For example, providing nutritious snacks of nuts, fruits, and cheeses for school celebrations; incorporating frequent movement into the classroom regime; and building in opportunities for down time to foster reflection and deeper understanding are strategies that honor this principle.

7. *The brain is a parallel processor.* Thoughts, emotions, imagination, and predispositions operate simultaneously; thus, optimal learning results from orchestrating the learning experience to address multiple operations in the brain. For example, complex performance tasks such as producing a dramatic play, authentic projects such as creating a brochure, and service learning that requires complex negotiations with community agencies are the types of orchestrated learning that engage the brain most fully.

8. *Learning is embedded in natural, social settings.* Specific items are given meaning when embedded in ordinary experiences, such as learning grammar and punctuation and applying the learning to writing; thus,

experiential learning, which affords opportunities for embedding learning, is necessary for optimal learning.

9. *Each brain is unique.* While most normal brains have a similar set of systems for sensing, feeling, and thinking, this set of systems is integrated differently in each brain; thus, teaching that is multifaceted with inherent choices and options for learners fosters optimal learning. For example, classrooms in which approaches honor students by creating freedom of choice within a given structure—choices in terms of multiple intelligences (verbal, visual, mathematical, musical, interpersonal, intrapersonal, bodily and existential; Gardner, 1993) or types of media to use, kinds of processes required, and end products accepted—are classrooms in which students embrace diversity and uniqueness.

Implications for Learning

With an understanding that each brain is unique, the brain is a parallel processor, learning engages the entire physiology, and learning is embedded in natural, social settings, the implications for learning are clear (see Figure 4.6). The multiple-intelligences approach taps into the uniqueness of each brain, while collaborative and experiential kinds of learning are useful tools for embedding the learning into natural memory pathways and engaging the learner holistically in sensory stimuli. The following are ways to structure interaction in a brain-compatible classroom:

- Use cooperative learning and collaborative models
- Use graphic organizers
- Target the nine multiple intelligences (Gardner, 1993)
- Design integrated curricula
- Create performance tasks
- Develop thematic units
- Do problem-based learning
- Design projects or service learning opportunities
- Use case studies

Implications for Teaching: Excellent

Teaching that focuses on creating a safe and caring climate within an enriched environment setting; targeting specific skills, concepts, and attitudes necessary for high achievement; and intensely involving learners in active and interactive experiences is considered excellent teaching. When attention is focused on climate, skills, and interaction, students are invited into learning in irresistible ways. Complex tasks, problems to encounter, and time to dig into learning are key.

Teaching ABOUT Thinking: Reflecting Metacognitively

Teaching about thinking is teaching about reflection, self-regulation, and self-assessment (see Figure 4.3). Teaching about one's own thinking is called metacognitive (beyond the cognitive) reflection. It is about self-awareness and subsequent self-regulatory processing, or self-evaluation. This is the element in the brain-compatible classroom that requires students to engage in self-regulated goal setting, self-monitoring, and reflective actions and teachers to give reactions and feedback to students about their learning. It is the cornerstone of the learner-centered concept that drives personal application and transfer of learning.

Research Base—Deep Understanding/Transfer

The research basis for this element of metacognitive reflection, or the idea of thinking about how you think and learn, is grounded in literature on cognition (Luria, 1976), the mind (Vygotsky, 1978), transfer of learning (Fogarty & Pete, 2007; Hart, 2002; Perkins, 1986; Perkins & Salomon, 1989), mediation theory (Feuerstein, 1980), deep understanding (Gardner, 1993; Perkins, 1986), and metacognition (Costa, 1991; Flavell, cited in Costa, 1991; Brown & Palinscar, cited in Costa, 1991; see Figures 4.3 and 4.4).

Principles of Brain-Compatible Learning

The following are Caine and Caine's (1991, 1993, 2008) principles that relate to thinking about thinking (see Figure 4.5):

10. *The search for meaning is innate.* The search for meaning cannot be stopped, only channeled and focused; thus, classrooms need stability and routine as well as novelty and challenge, and the learning can be shepherded explicitly through mediation and reflection. Teachers might foster the search for meaning in students by, for example, encouraging students to see patterns, themes, and big idea concepts; chunking or rearranging information in meaningful ways; and connecting the new learning to past learning or to future applications through skillful questioning.

11. *The search for meaning occurs through patterning.* The brain has a natural capacity to integrate vast amounts of seemingly unrelated information; thus, when teaching invokes integrated, thematically reflective approaches, learning is more brain compatible and learning is subsequently enhanced. For example, the use of integrated thematic instruction within or across several disciplines naturally produces patterns and themes. The structure of the cell, the sentence, the music, and the architecture all reinforce the concept of structure.

12. *Learning always involves conscious and unconscious processing.* Enormous amounts of unconscious processing go on beneath the surface of awareness; thus, teaching needs to be organized experientially and reflectively to benefit maximally from the deep processing. Although it is hard to do sometimes in the heat of the action in the classroom, providing for down time, when students can think, write reflectively in their journals, and enjoy moments of quiet and solitude fosters reflective, subconscious processing.

Implications for Learning

Based on the principles that the search for meaning is innate and occurs through patterning, and that both conscious and unconscious processes occur in learning, the call for the mediation of learning is clear (see Figure 4.6). Through reflection, metacognitive monitoring, and explicit transfer strategies, the processing becomes more brain compatible, or aligned to how the brain puts learning into long-term memory. The following are ways to promote and explicitly teach students to think about thinking in the brain-compatible classroom:

- Create personal relevance
- Construct knowledge
- Foster deep understanding
- Make generalizations
- Promote mindful engagement
- Use mediation strategies
- Embrace metacognition (planning, monitoring, evaluating)
- Move to application and use of ideas
- Shepherd the transfer of learning
- Check for understanding (traditional assessment, dynamic assessment)

Implications for Teaching: Superior

When one enters a classroom in which superior teaching is clearly the norm, it is immediately and visibly evident. When superior teaching is taking place, the climate is warm and accepting, the environment rich and inviting; appropriate skills and concepts are targeted for mastery; and students are actively engaged in experiential learning. But one other element surfaces beyond the others, and the difference in the learning atmosphere is astonishingly obvious. The critical element is a combination of self-reflection and self-monitoring. In this classroom, the teacher believes in students' innate ability to make meaning of their world. That is to say, there are clear and explicit expectations for high standards and high achievement for all students to not only learn but to be in charge of their own learning.

DEFINITION AND DESCRIPTION OF BRAIN-COMPATIBLE CLASSROOMS

Brain-compatible classrooms are brain-friendly places. They are classrooms in which the teaching/learning process is dictated by how the brain functions and how the mind learns. The distinguishing feature of brain-compatible classrooms (or brain-based classrooms) is that they link learning to what is known about the human brain.

These classrooms are set up with safe, stimuli-rich environments and a balance between direct instruction for skill development and authentic learning that immerses learners in challenging experiences. In addition, brain-compatible classrooms tap into the uniqueness of each learner and shepherd relevant transfer for future application of the learning.

To illustrate how brain-compatible classrooms differ from other classrooms, consider the following examples:

- Since brain research suggests that the brain learns by patterning ideas or chunking notions that seem to go together naturally, classrooms in which themes are used frequently to connect ideas are more brain friendly than classrooms in which information is doled out in discrete pieces.

- Since brain research suggests that an emotional and visceral reaction happens when the brain senses a threat, testing situations in brain-compatible classrooms are managed explicitly by the teacher to diminish anxiety and fear and thus enable learners to function at their highest cognitive levels.

- Since findings on brain functioning suggest that learning involves the entire physiology, real or simulated experiences that tap into the many ways of learning are more brain friendly. For example, problem-based learning scenarios in which students take on the roles of stakeholders address those findings.

In brief, not all classrooms are brain compatible, or brain friendly. While they may appear to be places of learning, they may not explicitly target the principles of brain research. The brain-compatible classroom is specifically designed to teach for, of, with, and about thinking based on emergent findings about how the brain works and how the mind remembers and learns.

Figure 4.8 depicts the essence of the material presented in *Brain-Compatible Classrooms* through a series of themes, or brainwaves. Each corner of the four-corner framework comprises two brainwaves that provide the focal point for the discussion and strategies, or braindrops, in that area. For example, in the climate corner the brainwaves are emotions and enriched environment.

RESEARCH ON TEACHER QUALITY

Superior teachers continually foster increased student achievement. They embrace specific and definable qualities (see Figure 4.9) that recur in their work with students of all ages, abilities, genders, races, and ethnicities. These teachers set high expectations for all students to achieve to their highest potential. They challenge kids to think, ponder, wonder, problem solve, and make sound decisions (Marzano, Pickering, & Pollock, 2001). They require rigor in their classrooms in every realm, from speaking and writing in the formal register, to student demeanor and deportment, to student pride in their work. These teachers leave nothing to chance, differentiating instruction to ensure that everyone has an entry point to learning. They make no excuses about the kids they have, the facilities they work in, or the materials afforded them. Teachers of quality insist on results by using data to inform their instructional planning and by examining student work with multiple measurement systems.

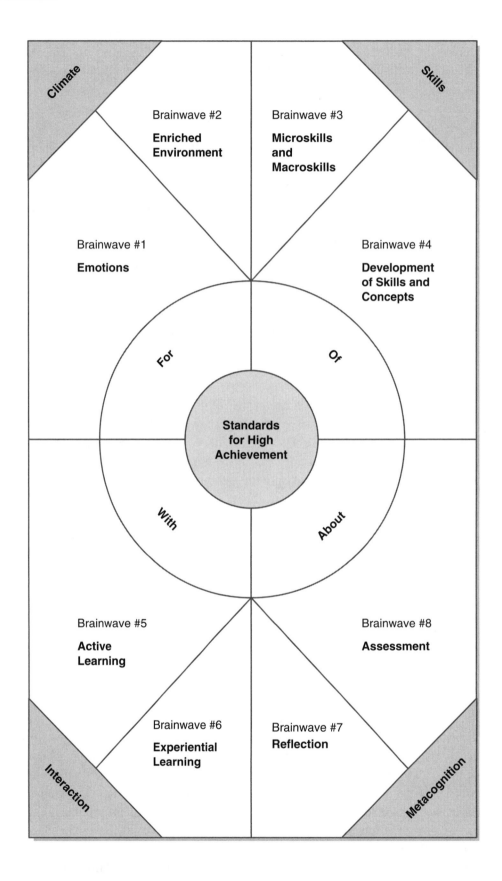

Figure 4.8 Brainwaves in the Four-Corner Framework

Set high expectations	Leave nothing to chance
Challenge students to think	Make no excuses
Require rigor	Insist on results

Figure 4.9 Teacher Quality: Characteristics

What Teachers Say

When teachers are asked to identify the best teacher they ever had—the one they remember by name, the one they feel had the most positive influence on them—they list a number of qualifiers. After they name a specific teacher, these teachers say that the best teachers they ever had . . .

- made school fun, interesting, and kid friendly
- were experts in their content and knew a lot
- were passionate about their subjects and made this passion contagious
- believed in them and communicated that belief to them
- encouraged them and kept them going when things were difficult
- empowered them by gradually releasing responsibility to them
- cared about them in genuine and authentic ways

What Experts Say

By contrast, yet sharing significant similarities in their delineation of the characteristics of quality teachers, experts discern the following list among the traits from their findings of a meta-analysis of the research (Strong, 1996):

1. High expectations that translate to **rigor** in their classrooms

2. "Eyes in the back of their heads," suggesting enforcement of **rules** for managing their classrooms

3. Robust teaching repertoires for **richness** and differentiating instruction

4. Positive attitudes that manifest as **rapture** and joy in their teaching

5. Clear communications so students see the **relevance** of the learning

6. Work with students and establish **rapport**

7. Show evidence of student learning that yields **results** in increased achievement

8. Practice lifelong learning with their own professional work and act as **role models** for young people

What Kids Say

And last but by far not least, what do students themselves say? They say that good teachers . . .

- are good listeners; they believe kids have ideas to share
- have a sense of humor; they think it's natural for kids to laugh
- make the class interesting; they understand that kids must be enticed to tune in to learning
- have knowledge of their subjects; they know that kids can and will think when they are provoked with thought-filled teaching
- explain things clearly; they know that it is vital that the kids get it
- spend time helping students; they put kids first and foremost before content or anything else
- develop good rapport and have credibility; they understand the importance of trusting relationships and that kids know whether or not teachers are genuine
- have respect; they honor kids as important and credible
- are available; they are visible, accessible, and available to students

A FRAMEWORK FOR QUALITY REVISITED

Figure 4.10 illustrates an agree/disagree anticipation guide on Quality Teaching. It is a prompt for thinking about this important topic. The four-corner framework pictured in Figure 4.11 shows the various dimensions as they are developed in this book. Moving from the bottom of the figure to the top, the six views begin with the basic overview: setting the climate for thinking, teaching the skills of thinking, structuring interaction with thinking, and thinking reflectively about thinking.

---

1. An enriched environment in the classroom is ever changing.

2. Emotions are the gatekeeper of the intellect.

3. Direct instruction is a viable teaching method in the constructivist classroom.

4. Experts think about their performances differently than novices do.

5. Active learning is the same thing as engaged learning.

6. Learning is a function of experience.

7. Learning is processed consciously and unconsciously.

8. Transfer of learning occurs naturally as part of the teaching/learning process.

9. Teachers make *the* difference, not teachers make *a* difference.

10. It's the art of teaching, not the science of teaching, that creates great teachers; teachers are born, not made.

Figure 4.10   Agree/Disagree: Quality Teaching

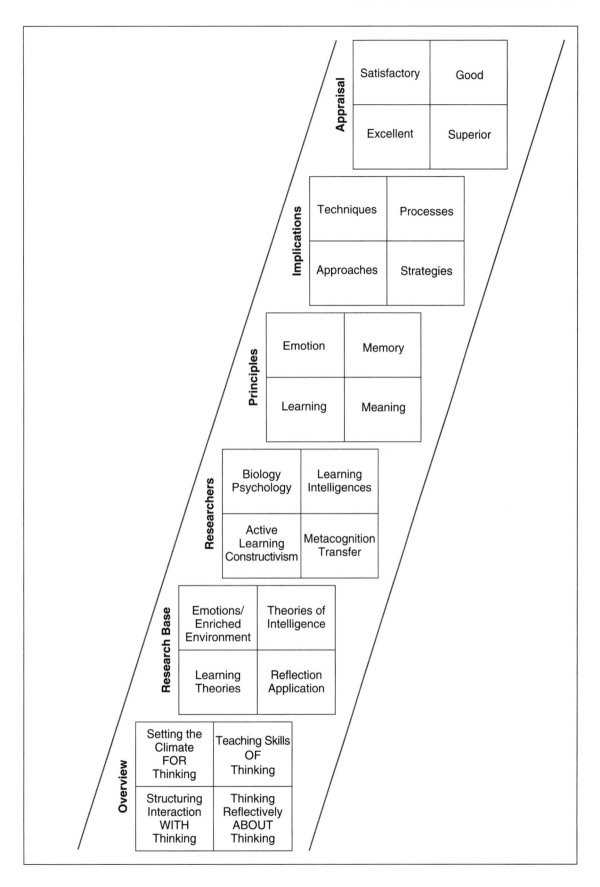

Figure 4.11   The Brain-Compatible Classroom in the Four-Corner Framework

In the second view, the dominant research base for each element is summarized: climate is grounded in the brain research on emotions and enriched environments; research on skills and concept development comes from the various theories of intelligence; structuring the interaction is rooted in learning theories, such as active learning and constructivism; and thinking about thinking takes its theory from writings on reflection and application.

The third view delineates the various areas into which the work of researchers is organized.

Climate: Sousa, Wolfe, MacLean, Diamond, Hart, Isaacson, Ornstein and Sobel, Goleman, Mayer and Salovey, O'Keefe and Nadel, Lozanov

Skills: Epstein, Hart, Luria, Sylwester, Sternberg, Gardner, Goleman, Coles, Perkins, Costa and Kallick, Mayer and Salovey, Jensen, Sousa, Wolfe, Spearman

Interaction: Ornstein and Sobel, Healy, Gardner, Caine and Caine, Bruner, Dewey, Brooks and Brooks, Beane, Harmin, Piaget, Bloom, Goodlad, Johnson and Johnson

Metacognition: Luria, Vygotsky, Feuerstein, Salomon, Perkins, Hart, Palinscar and Brown, Costa, Flavell, Gardner, Fogarty and Pete, Costa and Kallick

The fourth view highlights the areas into which Caine and Caine's (1991, 1993) principles fit.

The fifth view focuses on the instructional, curricular, and assessment implications of the elements and their predicating principles. This schema of the educational implications forms the heart and soul of this book, and here is a brief synthesis:

Climate: techniques that create a safe climate and an enriched environment

Skills: content and process standards that foster skill building, conceptual thinking, communicating, and technology skills and social skills

Interaction: approaches that engage learners actively and experientially

Metacognition: strategies for reflection, application, and transfer

In the sixth and final view, the framework acts as an overlay for teacher appraisal. In this view, teaching performance is depicted as satisfactory, good, excellent, and superior as the various elements are carefully integrated into the high-standards classroom.

Together, these six views of the four-corner framework depict the essence of this book and provide a road map to subsequent chapters.

Setting the Climate for Thinking 5

We must have . . . a place where children can have a whole group of adults they can trust.

—Margaret Mead

In the discussion that follows about setting the climate for thinking in the learner-centered classroom, the focus is on two interdependent themes: the emotional climate and the learning environment. Within the scope of these two overlapping ideas, this chapter discusses the roles of emotions and environment in the brain-compatible classroom and leads the reader into implementation ideas for immediate classroom use.

When setting a warm, safe, and caring emotional climate, two aspects of brain activity are relevant: threat and challenge. One phenomenon under the emotional umbrella concerns how the brain viscerally reacts to threatening situations. The other is about engaging the brain with intriguing and inviting intellectual challenges.

To provide an enriched environment for students to flourish, both organizational structures and sensory and language stimuli are involved. Organizational structures range from how students are grouped and how time is scheduled to how the classroom is arranged, while the sensory and language stimuli cover the scope of available media from paints, clay, and videotapes to books, magazines, and print-rich materials.

BRAINWAVE #1: EMOTIONS
Goleman/LeDeux/Coles

Diminishing the sense of threat and establishing a warm, caring climate are paramount concerns in the brain-compatible classroom. The existence of a safe learning environment is obvious the moment one enters a classroom that possesses these qualities; it is felt immediately and unmistakably. But what are the qualities that create this sense that it's safe to take risks in this classroom? That it's OK to make a mistake, and in fact it's expected? What is it in this classroom that says this is a place of learning, a place for explorations and investigations? What tells students that this is the classroom for trial-and-error learning; messy problem solving; constant, continual movement of student-directed activity; and lively, animated conversations in which "I wonder" is the norm? What is it that says that this classroom unequivocally belongs to the learners?

BRAINWISE STATEMENTS

- Emotions are the gatekeeper of the intellect.
- Challenge causes engagement.
- Threat alerts the body.

Braindrops: Strategies

A closer look reveals a set of strategies that eliminate threatening conditions that cause visceral reactions in the body and, instead, invite student curiosity and a sense of challenge (see Figure 5.1). The strategies at play in a nonthreatening climate include nonverbal signals the teacher consciously or subconsciously gives, guidelines that everyone adheres to, and understanding and implementation of the principles of emotional and moral intelligence theories. On the other hand, the strategies that set up a challenging classroom climate tend to focus on the verbal exchanges in the classroom, especially the question-and-response patterns set by the skillful teacher. In addition, the challenging classroom environment fosters problem solving and inquiry learning.

Threat Alerts the Body	**Challenge Engages the Intellect**
Verbal and nonverbal signals	Three-story intellect
DOVE guidelines	Fat/skinny questions
• Defer judgment	People search
• Opt for the outlandish	Wait time
• Vast number of ideas	Response strategies
• Expand by piggybacking on others' ideas	• What else?
Emotional Intelligence	• Tell me more!
• Self-awareness	• Give me an example.
• Self-regulation	Socratic dialogue
• Motivation	• Activity justifier
• Empathy	• Socratic questioner
• Social deftness	• Summary provider
Moral Intelligence	• Process coach
• Empathy	• Genuine participant
• Respect	
• Character shaping	
• Value shaping	

Figure 5.1   Strategies That Foster Emotion

Threat Alerts the Body

All of the strategies listed in Figure 5.1 target setting a safe emotional climate in which all students feel free to take risks, make mistakes, play around with ideas, and mess around with learning. The emotional climate is the key to opening the mind to explorations and investigations. When students feel safe, the cognitive brain is able to engage and process rather than allow the emotional brain to take over in the face of anxiety, fear, and threat. The following strategies are examples of some ways to foster a safe, warm, caring climate.

Verbal and Nonverbal Signals

Subtle verbal and nonverbal cues are crucial to setting a safe climate. These cues range from facial expression and body language to tone of voice and even to the mobility of the teacher around the classroom. The research on teacher expectation and student achievement provides invaluable data on verbal and nonverbal cues in the classroom that affect student-teacher interactions (Kerman, 1979). Facial expressions and body language can encourage and affirm thinking or discourage and inhibit further thought. Smiles, nods, and pats on the back say, "Keep thinking. You're on to something." Frowns, finger pointing, and lack of eye contact mean certain disapproval. Even the absence of an affirming comment is sometimes construed as a negative cue by the unsure student.

In addition, although the words may sound all right, the tone of voice may convey a different message. The comment "That's an original idea, Joey" might lead to positive feelings if the teacher says it enthusiastically, or it might lead to negative feelings if the student thinks the teacher is being sarcastic, cynical, or disapproving.

Another obvious signal to students is triggered by the mobility of the teacher. If the teacher remains somewhat stationary in one spot in the front of the room, the line of the teacher's eye contact inadvertently follows that of an inverted T. By continually changing positions in the room, the inverted T moves, allowing the teacher to focus on different students. This simple strategy encourages more students to be actively involved in teacher-directed discussions and activities because it allows the teacher to practice the strategy of proximity, prompting students to be alert and attentive to the instructional moment.

DOVE Guidelines

In some classrooms, guidelines are explicitly developed to create clear and accepted rules of order for everyone to adhere to. These can be general guidelines for the classroom as a whole, or they may target specific exercises or activities. The DOVE guidelines are one set of explicit guidelines that foster the generation of many ideas. When brainstorming . . .

D—Defer judgment

O—Opt for the outlandish

V—use a Vast number of ideas

E—Expand by piggybacking on others' ideas

Although these guidelines appear fairly simple and straightforward, they send a subtle message to students that all ideas are valued and that students are to listen to and value other people's opinions. These are powerful messages for students of all ages to learn as they become empowered in the brain-compatible classroom.

Emotional Intelligence

Goleman (1995a) has signaled a call to action regarding emotional intelligence and its impact on learning. His seminal work, *Emotional Intelligence: Why It Can Matter More Than IQ*, outlines five elements that constitute the emotional climate of the learner: self-awareness, self-regulation, motivation, empathy, and social deftness (see Figure 5.2). Teachers who create a climate free of fear and threat work at building students' self-confidence, helping them control their impulsive behavior and be aware and in control of their emotions. These teachers understand how to develop intrinsic motivation and create a climate for goal setting and feelings of joy in the accomplishment of those goals. These teachers also help kids care about others to the extent that they feel the feelings of another and foster the skills of team building and leadership.

Self-awareness	"I feel a little down in the dumps today."
Self-regulation	"I think I'll feel better if I go work out."
Motivation	"I am excited about starting my new job."
Empathy	"I feel your pain. It must hurt so much."
Social deftness	"I appreciate your apology. It feels good."

Figure 5.2   Five Domains of Emotional Intelligence

To look further at the concept of emotions, read Aristotle's Challenge (see Figure 5.3) about the emotion of anger and reflect on a situation in your own life that might apply. Then ask yourself if you responded in the "right" way according to Aristotle's criteria.

> Anyone can become angry; that is easy. But to be angry with the right person, to the right degree, at the right time, for the right purpose, and in the right way, that is not easy (Goleman, 1995a).

Figure 5.3   Aristotle's Challenge

To be in touch with one's feelings is not as easy as it might seem. In fact, because emotional intelligence training is often not part of the school curriculum, it's often hard to fully or precisely describe one's feelings to someone else. Use the list of feelings in Figure 5.4 to help students become more familiar with the language of emotions. Use the phrase: "I feel _____."

accepted	hopeful
adventurous	inferior
awkward	jealous
bewildered	lonely
bold	overjoyed
cautious	peaceful
compelled	refreshed
confident	rejected
daring	stunned
defiant	stupid
disappointed	surprised
eager	trapped
embarrassed	uncomfortable
empty	worried
free	worthy

Figure 5.4 Feeling Words to Describe Emotions

Moral Intelligence

In a similar vein, Coles (1998) builds on the idea of an emotional climate in his seminal work on the concept of moral intelligence. Coles touches on the idea of learning to empathize with others as a sign of moral intelligence and suggests that respect for oneself and others is embodied in the development of moral intelligence. His concept of a moral archeology of childhood suggests that morality and the shaping of character and values are the wellspring of the young years—the modeling and teachings children are exposed to in their developmental path toward adulthood. While these are not new ideas, the framing of character traits as moral intelligence creates a fresh window on morality and its place in the schooling of children. Is there moral intelligence, and if there is, what is its impact on the climate for learning in the brain-compatible classroom?

Challenge Engages the Intellect

According to the experts (Caine & Caine, 1991, 1993; Sylwester, 1995; Wolfe, 1996), when the brain is challenged, it becomes engaged in intense activity. Puzzlement, wonderment, and curiosity cause the brain to kick in and begin its intense search for patterns and connections. There seems to be nothing more engaging for the mind than to have a challenging problem to solve. In fact, the brain is a natural problem solver, continuing to process information even when the person is asleep.

To create models that challenge the brain and engage the intellect, complex thinking is involved. The three-story intellect, fat/skinny questions, the people-search strategy, wait time, response strategies, and Socratic dialogue are just some of the critical tools that challenge and engage the brain.

Three-Story Intellect

One compelling concept that exemplifies a safe-risk challenge for the brain-compatible classroom is captured in the metaphorical structure of the three-story intellect. It is Bloom's taxonomy (B. S. Bloom, Engelhart, Furst, Hill, & Kratwohl, 1956)—knowledge, comprehension, application, analysis, synthesis, and evaluation—synthesized in poetic form by Oliver Wendell Holmes (see Figure 5.5).

There are one-story intellects, two-story intellects, and three-story intellects with sky-lights. All fact collectors who have no aim beyond their facts are one-story [minds]. Two-story [minds] compare, reason, generalize, using the labors of the fact collectors as well as their own. Three-story [minds] idealize, imagine, predict—their best illumination comes from above, through the skylight.

—Oliver Wendell Holmes

Figure 5.5   Three-Story Intellect

For teachers, the three stories of the intellect serve as easy reminders of the types of thinking required in a challenging learning environment. Of course, students must be able to gather the needed information. But beyond the gathering of facts and data, they must also be ready to process the input—to analyze, classify, and compare and contrast the information in meaningful ways. It is through this processing that the information becomes meaningful for students. So, too, in the usual course of events, the final stage of application must play a role. After all, this is the point of learning—to find uses for the learning that are relevant and helpful.

Thus, in Holmes's version of the three-story intellect, teachers have a handy reference tool for the students to use in their work. When teachers supply students with a model of the three-story intellect (see Figures 5.6 and 5.7), students have a quick guide to reference as they investigate and explore ideas and execute projects.

Fat/Skinny Questions

Another critical element for creating challenge in the classroom is verbal dialogue. Thinking is embedded in the language of the classroom. If the teacher uses questions that call for one right answer or yes/no/maybe answers, the depth of the thinking stays at the surface. However, if the questions probe deeper for thoughtful answers, by asking for agreements and disagreements to an idea or by pushing for a clear example of what the student means, then the response becomes more elaborate and the thinking is extended and deepened. In fact, some prefer to label this idea of fat/skinny questions as *deep dive and surface* questions.

The strategy of fat/skinny questions guides the teacher to ask higher-level questions (see Figure 5.8). Fat questions require thought and time to answer.

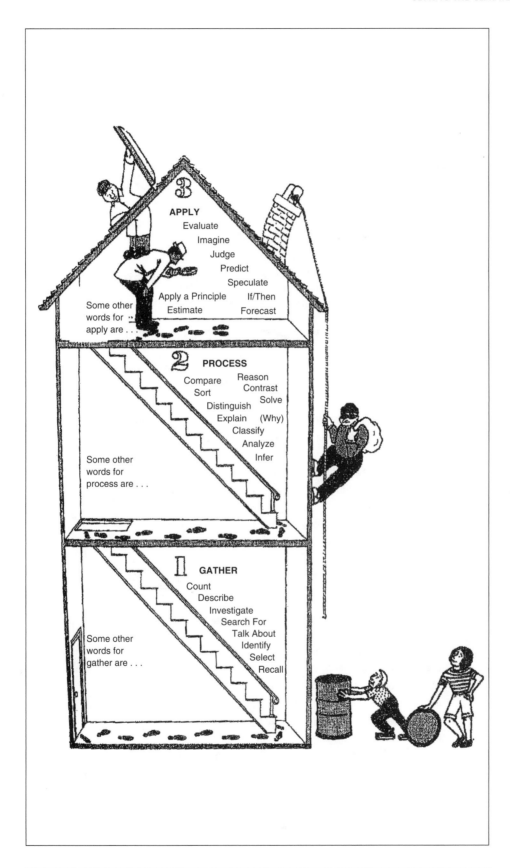

Figure 5.6   Three-Story Intellect Model

SOURCE: Bellanca & Fogarty, 1991.

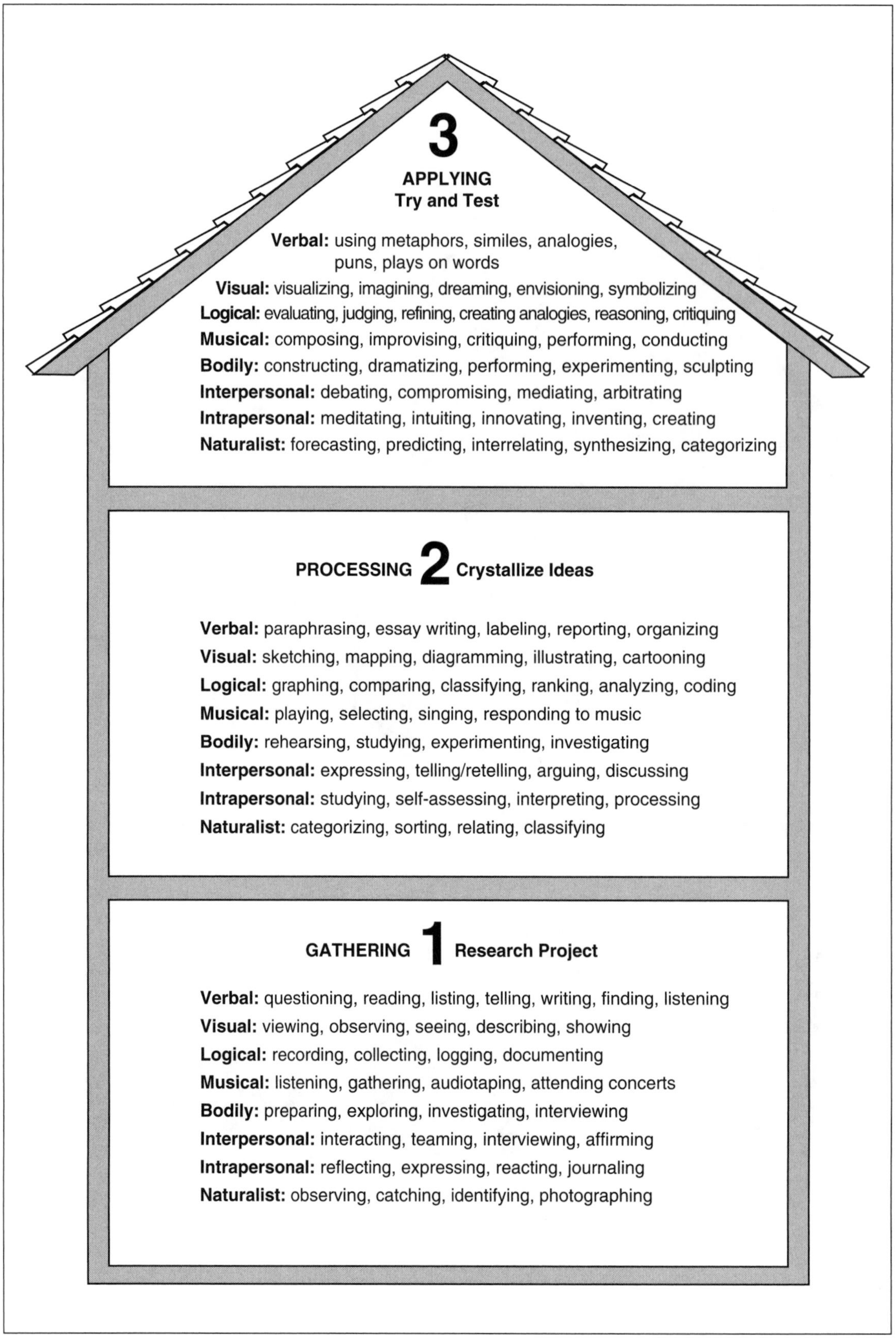

3
APPLYING
Try and Test

Verbal: using metaphors, similes, analogies,
puns, plays on words
Visual: visualizing, imagining, dreaming, envisioning, symbolizing
Logical: evaluating, judging, refining, creating analogies, reasoning, critiquing
Musical: composing, improvising, critiquing, performing, conducting
Bodily: constructing, dramatizing, performing, experimenting, sculpting
Interpersonal: debating, compromising, mediating, arbitrating
Intrapersonal: meditating, intuiting, innovating, inventing, creating
Naturalist: forecasting, predicting, interrelating, synthesizing, categorizing

PROCESSING 2 Crystallize Ideas

Verbal: paraphrasing, essay writing, labeling, reporting, organizing
Visual: sketching, mapping, diagramming, illustrating, cartooning
Logical: graphing, comparing, classifying, ranking, analyzing, coding
Musical: playing, selecting, singing, responding to music
Bodily: rehearsing, studying, experimenting, investigating
Interpersonal: expressing, telling/retelling, arguing, discussing
Intrapersonal: studying, self-assessing, interpreting, processing
Naturalist: categorizing, sorting, relating, classifying

GATHERING 1 Research Project

Verbal: questioning, reading, listing, telling, writing, finding, listening
Visual: viewing, observing, seeing, describing, showing
Logical: recording, collecting, logging, documenting
Musical: listening, gathering, audiotaping, attending concerts
Bodily: preparing, exploring, investigating, interviewing
Interpersonal: interacting, teaming, interviewing, affirming
Intrapersonal: reflecting, expressing, reacting, journaling
Naturalist: observing, catching, identifying, photographing

Figure 5.7 Three-Story Intellect With Multiple Intelligences

SOURCE: Bellanca & Fogarty, 1991.

They are not questions that have rote answers in the book; rather, they are questions whose implications go far beyond the facts and data found in text references. For example, fat questions ask a lot of *how* and *why* questions; they ask students to reason and figure things out, to take a stand and advocate a position, to support that position with facts, to justify and argue that position, and to persuade others to take that position. Fat questions get fat answers.

Skinny questions, often found in textbook material, can be fattened. For example, when a question requires students to list some information (skinny), changing the word *list* to the word *rank* fattens up the question, and the level of the thinking becomes more complex. Now, the student must place a value on the list of items. The fat question contains the information of the skinny question and more!

Skinny Questions

Skinny questions require simple yes/no/maybe or one-word answers, or a nod or shake of the head. They take up no space or time. Examples:

- Did you like the story?
- Who is your favorite character?
- What is the main idea?

Fat Questions

Fat questions require a lot of discussion and explanation with interesting examples. They take time to think through and answer in depth. Examples:

- How might you compare and contrast the two characters?
- Why do you agree with the author's perspective?
- If this is so, then what do you anticipate will happen next and why?

Figure 5.8   Fat/Skinny Questions

SOURCE: Bellanca & Fogarty, 1991.

If the words *fat* and *skinny*, though embraced and understood easily by students of all ages, are bothersome, teachers can label the two types of questions *convergent* and *divergent*, *closed* and *open*, or *telling* and *thinking*. The labels are synonymous—the concept remains constant. Whatever the choice, teachers need to make the students aware of the differences so they become empowered in the use of both types.

In addition, questions may fall in between fat and skinny. Students call these chubby questions. "What do you think?" could be a skinny question, and the student could answer, "Nothing!" Yet there is an implied "Tell me something about your thinking" that suggests a certain chubbiness in the intended response.

People Search

People searches are interactive strategies to get students moving about and talking to each other about a given topic. They are often used as prelearning pieces to stir up prior knowledge about a topic or concept. Figure 5.9 uses the FRIENDS acronym to explain why people searches are valued in the high-challenge

Focus on content. As students move through the various lessons of the day, it becomes critical for teachers to provide a timely focus for the content to be presented. Carefully designed search statements lead students toward the target lesson.

Reinforce learning through articulation. Much of the research in the area of reading suggests that recitation by students, rephrasing in one's own words, is a powerful way to help place material into long-term memory. By talking with each other, all students have an opportunity to articulate their conceptions.

Invite meaningful interaction. As teachers promote thinking for all students in the classroom, getting students to interact with each other about the material is vital. Seeking out friends with whom to discuss the lesson content does just this.

Exemplify a model of the safe-risk climate. By structuring statements on the people search as open ended and divergent in nature, students are safe to risk their interpretations of an answer because there are as many answers as there are student connections.

Note the value placed on people as resources. "Cooperation and communication are valued" is the message modeled in this strategy. Teachers demonstrate the resources available among the members of the group. Students sense that it's not only OK to talk with classmates, but expected as part of the learning process.

Diagnose prior knowledge for new learning. As teachers participate actively in the search, they sense the readiness of the group and note whether the preconditions to the proposed learning are in place. From the information learned in this activity, teachers adjust subsequent plans.

Signal priorities of the unit or semester. Teachers can flag the primary concepts, objectives, and goals of the unit (or semester) through the people search. The message to students is: "These are the important things. If you understand these, you have a solid grasp of the material."

Figure 5.9   FRIENDS: Why Do a People Search?

classroom. Figures 5.10, 5.11, and 5.12 are examples that illustrate people searches on various levels.

To form high-quality questions or statements for a people search, teachers can use the cue words from the three-story intellect (see Figure 5.6). These verbs force students into higher mental processes. For example, as mentioned earlier, instead of asking students to list items, the statement could require them to rank items. *Rank* means not only to recall the list but to process that list and place value on each item. Thus, the statement leads to more sophisticated mental processing.

Teachers should try to write the search in such a way that the key issues are "spirited through the back door." The search should not read like a pre- or posttest or quiz. It should be focused and fun. For example, instead of asking students studying a DNA unit to define *genes,* the teacher asks them to find someone wearing *jeans.* The teacher triggers an analysis level of thinking by subtly interjecting a homonym into the search. Students think of jeans and genes, which leads them to compare the two concepts. It requires complex thinking, beyond just recall.

Wait Time

Asking questions, even in the structured sequence of higher-order questions, does not accomplish the goal of involving all students in the discussion.

Level: Elementary School

Fish Stories

Find someone in our room who . . .

knows the difference between Flipper and Charlie Tuna.	has a parent who loves to cook fish.	can stay under water for 30 seconds.
owns a green scale.	knows someone named Gil.	has touched a fish.
has met a red snapper.	can tell a fish story.	can make a noise like a fish.

Figure 5.10   The People Search: A Sponge Strategy for Transition

Level: Middle School

"My Furthest-Back Person—'The African'"

Find someone who . . .

attended a family reunion last summer.	has a living great-grandparent.	knows what countries his or her ancestors came from.
can describe what a family tree contains.	has a relative who learned English as a second language.	can locate the Gambia River and Annapolis, Maryland, on the map.
uses a name different from that on his or her birth or baptismal certificate.	can list the circumstances in which oral tradition might be considered dependable.	can defend the African's need to keep his name Kinte and not be called Toby.

Figure 5.11 The People Search: A Poststrategy for Review

Level: High School

DNA Search

Find someone who . . .

has experienced a spiral staircase or slide.	is wearing clothes with a zipper.	knows someone named Watson.
knows what to do with a phosphate.	likes to eat sugar.	can make up three words with base in them.
would be a good pair with you.	can name a cell in his or her body that is reproducing right now.	knows an identical twin.
has jeans on.	knows the difference between a female and a male gene.	ate a protein today.
can name a commercial product that has an enzyme in it.	knows triplets.	knows several symbols in Morse code.
knows a president of a company.	knows someone who uses blueprints.	can take the 1st, 5th, and 20th letters of the alphabet and construct three different words.

Figure 5.12   The People Search: A Prestrategy for Focus

The strategic use of what science researcher Rowe (1996) calls *wait time* must go with the questions.

If there is a single strategy that yields immediate and dramatic increases in student involvement and interaction, that strategy is wait time. What is it? It is simply SILENCE! SILENCE! MAGICAL SILENCE! That's it—waiting three to ten seconds after asking a question. Teachers can count silently, grit their teeth, even pick at their fingernails! But they need to wait and watch what happens. Not only does the length of student response increase, but the probability of clarification, extension, justification, and on-task conversation increases, too. Students begin to listen to each other. Expecting immediate teacher verification and not getting it, classmates nervously support and defend their own or each other's points of view. They elaborate and give personal, relevant examples. They begin to bridge the new concept to past learning, and they demonstrate evidence of thinking. Student participation noticeably increases with silence.

Although wait time is not new, it is essential to the thinking classroom. Research documents the effect of rapid-fire questioning patterns: students soon learn that the teacher really isn't interested in thoughtful answers, only quick

---

Student Behavior

1. The length of the students' responses increased.

2. The number of freely offered and appropriate student responses, unsolicited by the teacher, increased.

3. Failure to respond—"I don't know" or no answer—decreased.

4. Inflected responses decreased, thus students appeared to be more confident in their answers.

5. The number of speculative responses increased, thus students appeared to be more willing to think about alternative explanations of the subject matter at hand.

6. Students worked together more at comparing data.

7. Students made more inferences from evidence.

8. The frequency of questions raised by students increased.

9. The frequency of responses by students who were rated as relatively slow by their teachers increased.

Teacher Behavior

1. Teachers became more flexible in their responses; for example, they were more willing to listen to diverse answers and to examine their plausibility.

2. Teachers' questioning patterns became more manageable; questions decreased in number but showed greater variety and quality.

3. Some evidence suggests that teachers raised their expectations of students who had been rated as relatively slow.

Figure 5.13   Wait Time Study Results

answers. The effective teacher communicates that effective thinking by all is a preeminent expectation. Thus, that teacher waits three to ten seconds after each question before calling on any responder; waits three to ten seconds after the last response before introducing a new question; seeks multiple responses to the same question, even when recall is used; moves close to a student who doesn't usually answer; asks the question to the class, waits, and then calls on the first student; and establishes eye contact and cues the students. Figure 5.14 outlines how to use Rowe's (1996) wait-time strategy, and Figure 5.15 defines the average teacher.

1. Wait at least three seconds after asking a question to let the student begin a response. Say to yourself, "One thousand one, one thousand two, one thousand three . . . ." It sounds simple, but the silence can be deafening the first few times.

2. Wait at least three seconds after any response before continuing the question or asking a new one. This second wait time recognizes the possibility that the student may wish to elaborate on the initial response.

3. Avoid verbal signals—positive or negative—in asking questions. Among the most common cues are "Isn't it true that . . .?" and "Think!"

4. Eliminate mimicry (i.e., repeating the response a student has just made).

5. Eliminate verbal rewards ("okay," "fine," "good," "right") and negative sanctions (the typical "Yes, but . . ." pattern, in which the teacher completes the answer or restates the question).

Figure 5.14   How to Use Wait Time

- Wait time #1 = 1 second
- Wait time #2 = .9 second
- Asks three to five questions in a minute, sometimes ten questions per minute.
- Asks 400 questions in a short class session.
- Repeats (mimics) every student response.
- Uses words such as *very good* and *wonderful* 25 percent of the time.
- Rewards indiscriminately.
- Looks for the answer.

Result: The focus is on the teacher, not on the content.

Figure 5.15   Average Teacher

Based on Rowe's (1996) seminal work on wait time, the poem in Figure 5.16 summarizes the findings that setting high expectations for all students is necessary if all students are to achieve to their fullest. As suggested in the poem, the average child is just as in need of attention and focus as are the children at the high or low end of the infamous bell curve. In Rowe's work, all students were given equal opportunity to respond in depth.

I don't cause teachers trouble

my grades have been OK.

I listen in my classes

and I am in school every day.

My teachers think I am average

my parents think so, too.

I wish I didn't know that

cause there's lots I'd like to do.

I would like to build a rocket.

I have a book that tells you how.

Or start a stamp collection

well no use in trying now.

'Cause since I found I am average

I am just smart enough you see

to know there is nothing special

that I should expect of me.

I am part of that majority

that hump part of the bell

who spends his life unnoticed

in an average kind of hell.

—Anonymous

Figure 5.16   The Average Child

Response Strategies

There are three simple response strategies that challenge students to keep thinking and to think deeply about an idea: What else? Tell me more. Give me an example. The first response that leads to multiple answers is "What else?" When sampling answers from students in a brain-compatible classroom, teachers use this question to elicit multiple answers from a variety of students. By saying "What else?" after one response, teachers signal students to keep on thinking and encourage them to generate more novel ideas more often.

Another response that pushes student thinking to more depth is "Tell me more." This truly probing phrase to encourage depth of thinking is a cue for elaboration, detail, and examples or illustrations of an idea. It is a statement that says the teacher wants to hear about the idea.

The third response strategy calls for specificity. "Give me an example" tends to move the response from a simple recall to a specific illustration that makes the point. This often leads to clarification and deeper understanding by all students as they visualize the example being discussed.

Socratic Dialogue

While the three-story intellect, fat/skinny questions, people searches, wait time, and response strategies are clear conceptual techniques to incorporate into the interactions of the brain-compatible classroom, Socratic dialogue techniques offer still another idea for study and consideration. Socratic dialogue, or Socratic practice, is based on the belief that it is not enough to encourage students to ask questions. Instead, teachers must develop a classroom culture in which the experience of asking questions is consistently rewarded by teachers and peers, a culture in which the goal is to learn, not just to know. In this ideal classroom, the habit of hiding one's ignorance or lack of understanding is overridden by the need to inquire, know, and understand.

From a practical perspective, according to Michael Strong's (1996) *The Habit of Thought*, there are five roles to the Socratic leader:

Activity justifier. The activity justifier provides a clear rationale for why a particular activity is occurring. The rationale can range from enlightenment (thinking for oneself) to brain growth (contextual, complex thinking results in greater brain development) to job skills (people with high social and intellectual skills are valued in the workplace).

Socratic questioner. The Socratic questioner tries to understand exactly why beliefs are held or why people interpret an idea as they do ("Does that mean . . . ?"). This role is like playing the devil's advocate, or in a more positive vein, always being open to another view.

Summary provider. The summary provider or synthesizer pulls together the threads of the conversation, provides succinct summaries and insightful syntheses, and clarifies the concepts and ideas that have come up ("It sounds to me as though . . .").

Process coach. The process coach develops a real awareness beyond the intellectual content to the processes being used. This person processes during the conversation (speaks to everyone), debriefs afterward ("One thing the group could do differently is . . ."), performs individual processing outside the conversation ("I was especially impressed with the comment you made about . . ."), and structures related activities (creates self-assessments and extensions of the topic).

Genuine participant. The genuine participant offers his or her own opinion in appropriate circumstances to build trust in the group and to be a part of the intellectual exploration ("My personal thoughts are based on . . .").

Although Socratic dialogue may require more elaboration before many teachers feel comfortable using the techniques, some of these roles are already part of the thoughtful classroom. Lipman, Sharp, and Oscanyan (1980) assembled a comprehensive listing of the types of questions that encourage Socratic dialogue. These questions tend to help students make their views more explicit; interpret meaning; become consistent and logical; and recognize assumptions, fallacies, and faulty reasoning in their thinking. Figure 5.17 shows the types of questions often asked in the midst of a Socratic dialogue.

What reasons do you have for saying that?

Why do you agree or disagree with that point?

How are you defining the term?

What do you mean by that expression?

Is what you're saying now consistent with what you said before?

Could you clarify that comment?

When you said that, what was implied by your remark?

What follows from what you just said?

Is it possible that you are contradicting each other?

Could you clarify that remark?

Are you sure that you are not contradicting yourself?

What alternatives are there?

Could you give an example of that?

Are you familiar with incidents of this sort?

Why did you find that interesting?

Are you saying . . . ?

I wonder if what you're saying is . . . ?

So, you see it as . . . ?

Is that the point you're making?

Can I sum up what you've said by . . . ?

Are you suggesting . . . ?

If you're correct, would it follow . . . ?

The implications of what you've said seem far-reaching if . . . , then . . . ?

Aren't you assuming . . . ?

Is what you've just said based on . . . ?

What is your reason for saying that . . . ?

Why do you believe . . . ?

What can you say in defense of that view?

How do you know?

Couldn't it also be . . . ?

What if someone . . . ?

Figure 5.17   Socratic Questioning

Brainworks: Activities

People Search

Create your own people search using Figure 5.18. To practice divergent strategies as you create your people search, scan the examples provided in the Fat/Skinny Questions section of this chapter. Then select your topic, select your verbs from the Three-Story Intellect, and write away!

Level: _____

Topic: _____

Find someone who . . .

Figure 5.18   The People Search: Write Your Own

Fat/Skinny Questions

Refer to the Brainteasers People Search (see Figure 5.19) and the people search you created in Figure 5.18. Now review the questions (or statements), and code them as fat questions or statements that require a full, elaborated response or as skinny questions or statements that get a simple yes/no/maybe response.

Code: F = Fat, elaborate response   S = Skinny, yes/no/maybe response

Once the coding is done, revisit your people search and fatten up any skinny questions you have.

The Human Graph

Using some of the comments from the Brainteasers People Search (see Figure 5.19), select your position on them using the human graph illustrated in Figure 5.20.

Select a spot along the continuum for each item, and think about the intensity of your agreement or disagreement as well as the rationale for your decision of where you are on the graph. For example, using the statement "About the brain, I know . . . ," decide how you feel about that idea and take that position in the human graph.

Finally, refer to the human graph, and take a stand on the idea that "neurons that fire together wire together" by choosing a spot along an invisible line that goes from strongly agree to strongly disagree (strongly agree, agree, neutral, disagree, strongly disagree); justify your position. Consider the need to think deeply about issues and why it is important to take a position. Think about how it feels to make opinions public and how to ease the fear of public ridicule by peers. Think about the feelings and emotional climate needed for risk taking and how you might facilitate that in your classroom.

Brainstorms: Application

Think of the issues, concerns, and strategies about the principles of brain-compatible classrooms that have unfolded in this chapter—that threat causes a visceral response and challenge engages the mind cognitively and fosters more thought-filled reactions. Then make a strategic plan to use one of the techniques discussed earlier. Be specific about the application for immediate use in your classroom or work setting. Map the strategy into a relevant use so that students have a sense of purpose about why they are using it.

For example, plan a discussion using the Socratic dialogue technique. Introduce the Socratic terminology to students, label the roles as you use them, and talk about how Socratic dialogue differs from ordinary classroom discussions.

Find someone who . . .

can tell a personal story about this statement: Emotions are true gatekeepers of the intellect.	can explain how neurons that fire together wire together.	can justify this saying: Your brain is smarter than you are.
can take a stand on the following: Practice makes perfect or practice makes permanent?	can create an apt analogy for the brain/mind: The brain is to _____ as the mind is to _____.	can apply the saying "Use it or lose it!" to an understanding of how the brain develops.
can brainstorm five ways to grow dendrites.	can agree or disagree with this statement: Reason rules over emotion.	can describe their theory on the controversy over nature versus nurture (heredity versus environment).

Figure 5.19   People Search: Brainteasers

Figure 5.20   Human Graph

Braindrain: REFLECTION

- Take some time to reflect on the following ideas. Relate one to a personal experience, and write about the experience as a journal entry.
- *Idea 1:* Emotions rule the mind—they can take over reasoned thinking. Yet there needs to be some emotional hook to one's thinking.
- *Idea 2:* The sense of challenge is difficult to achieve. There is a fine line between challenge and engagement versus struggle and frustration.
- *Idea 3:* Threatening situations are sensed by the entire body.

BRAINWAVE #2: ENRICHED ENVIRONMENT

Diamond/Conyers and Wilson

A second and complementary part of setting a safe emotional climate is to create an enriched environment that invites learning. In a safe and caring climate, learners naturally begin to explore and investigate. The discussion about an enriched classroom environment encompasses two realms: the organizational (or structural) environment and the sensory environment. Based on those two arenas, the focus of this section is to delineate the various structures that support the brain-compatible philosophy and the sensory inputs necessary to foster brain growth.

BRAINWISE STATEMENTS

- It's not nature versus nurture but rather nature and nurture.
- Enriched environments grow dendrites.
- A nurturing environment enhances the gifts of Mother Nature.

Braindrops: Strategies

The discussion about creating an enriched environment for learning can be titled "How to Grow Dendrites," as it outlines the key environmental factors needed for intellectual development (see Figure 5.21). The discussion of organizational enrichments includes descriptions of various student groupings that facilitate learning in natural ways and the actual structuring of the school year and the school day. In addition, things as obvious as room arrangements and the use of existing facilities are of concern here.

Sensory enrichment, on the other hand, involves both the stimuli for the senses as well as language stimuli. Included in this discussion are things such as equipment and supplies, learning centers, and other sensory input.

Organizational Enrichments

Based on the premise that organizational enrichments stimulate brain growth, one question begs for an answer: What are the organizational structures that ease the way for learning? Student groupings, daily schedules, length of the school year, and the learning facility all seem to be obvious concerns for the student-centered classroom, and, of course, the impacts of these elements have been studied and documented. Yet many schools, trapped in the traditions of the past, neglect to evaluate the effectiveness of current practices.

Organizational Enrichments

- Student grouping
- Blocks of time
- Year-round schools
- Room arrangement and facility utilization

Sensory Enrichments

- Equipment and supplies (availability, accessibility, flexibility)
- Sensory input (touch, smell, hear, see, taste)
- Language stimulation (print rich, language rich)
- Learning centers

Figure 5.21   Strategies for Creating an Enriched Environment

This discussion hopefully will serve as a wake-up call to carefully look at all of the components of brain-compatible learning, including things as mundane as the room arrangement, as well as the availability, accessibility, and flexibility of equipment and supplies for fostering brain-compatible classrooms.

Student Grouping

Two ideas jump out in the discussion of how to group students. One is the concept of small schools, and the other is the idea of Freshman Academies. Following the tragic student shootings at Columbine High School, in Colorado Springs, Colorado, Bill and Melinda Gates, of Microsoft fame, created a multi-million dollar fund to promote the small schools concept in an effort to eliminate the huge impersonal high school models that permeate our communities. As a result, the redesign of the high school is front and center in today's schools. In these designs, students are clustered into "houses," "families," or "academies" in an effort to develop smaller, more student-centered high school environments.

The houses or families are usually heterogeneous groupings of 400–500 students, assigned to a team of teachers and geographically located in a specific area of the building. Each house or family may have its own principal. While each grouping may have a specific academic focus (e.g., law and jurisprudence, business and industry, medical and health-related policies), those called academies always have the umbrella of a definite academic focus. In these models, students select an area of interest and apply to that house or academic family. In this way, their academic program has a career relevance built in, unlike that of the traditional large high school model.

As with any other radical change in the design of schools, moving into a small-schools model takes strategic, long-term planning with graduated implementation in phases that occur over the course of three to five years.

The second innovative student grouping idea that is fast finding its place in our nation's high schools is the formation of Freshman Academies. Although this is an easier shift to make, compared to the small-schools concept, the reasoning falls along the same lines. The overriding goal is to manage the transition into large high school settings with more care and attention paid to the students and their transitional adjustments. Specific teachers are assigned specific students, so students are monitored more closely and potential problems are averted before they manifest as student failures or dropouts.

Blocks of Time

Goodlad (1980) and Sizer (2004) call for blocks of time, clusters of students, and teams of teachers as sensible and learner-centered ways to organize a school. A close cousin to the student grouping ideas discussed previously, the case for block scheduling also advocates teaching teams, with students clustered in houses or families. Pioneered by the middle school movement, the concept of moving from a bell schedule to some version of the block schedule is taking high schools by storm. In fact, it is one of the most radical changes instituted at that level in decades, and it is the initiative that often leads to the small-schools concept.

The shift to a block schedule has been and is being made for solid philosophical reasons. It's not about time; it's about learning. Each school's administration and teaching staff seem to have a couple of driving questions that lead to the block concept: What can we do to build relationships in the school? How can we facilitate learning? The actual block schedule adopted varies from school to school based on a balance of needs and constraints: 4x4 (four classes a day that change four times each year), modified 4x4 (four classes a day, with one block using an AB schedule), AB (four classes a day on alternating days for a total of eight classes), modified AB (four classes a day, alternating every other day except Friday, when all eight classes meet for shorter periods), Copernican (two classes a day of 120 or 240 minutes, changing every 30 or 45 days).

Block scheduling often leads to or incorporates the concept of a core teaching team that provides instruction in essential academic disciplines either in traditional subject matter courses or interdisciplinary courses. The inclusion of teaching teams as part of the block idea greatly enhances the possibility that teachers do two things more skillfully: enhance the lesson (not merely extend the lesson to 90 minutes) and prioritize and focus on the curriculum (not just cover the content less, but spend more concentrated time on the content).

The purpose of the block of time is to enhance learning in dynamic, hands-on ways for deep understanding of key concepts. This requires knowledge, skill, coordination, and commitment on the part of the teachers and is facilitated by collegial support and professional dialogues.

Year-Round Schools

One other macro-organizational change in the educational community is the concept of year-round schooling, or year-round education (YRE). While this concept is always the subject of much skepticism, I predict that YRE will become more commonplace in the next decade. Why? It makes sense in terms of learner-centered schools and the current understandings of how the brain grows and develops. Many students lose academic ground over the summer months, and they may even be losing those critical dendrite connections. One thing is certain: neural pathways that are strengthened through concept attainment and concept formation exercises are probably more dormant when lacking the rigor of academic stimulation. The jury is still out on this innovation, but schools fostering brain-compatible classrooms are likely to look into the case for YRE.

Room Arrangement and Facility Utilization

Learner-centered classrooms and the relationship to how the classroom is arranged seem obvious enough. However, grounded in emergent brain research about the impact of an enriched environment on actual brain growth, the classroom environment issue takes on new dimensions. Is the classroom learner friendly? Does the environment invite learners to dig in, mess around, and play with objects and ideas as they explore, investigate, and inquire about their world? Is the room set up in a way that invites conversation and collaboration? It's hard to talk to the back of someone's head when seated in rows, all facing the front of the room.

Also, the noise level in a room full of inquiring minds dictates room arrangements that foster small-group work, separated areas designated for particular tasks, and some accommodation for large-group discussions and more direct instruction. Quiet zones can be built in for particular kinds of activities that require a library atmosphere.

This brings the discussion to how the whole facility is utilized. The learner-centered classroom often extends beyond the classroom walls into the halls, in the byways between doors, down the hall, and into other rooms, libraries, computer labs, art studios, and even outside into the courtyard, on the lawns, or on sidewalks that surround the building. In short, brain-compatible classrooms often are not, literally speaking, just the actual classrooms; the school and even the community may fall within the usable perimeters.

Sensory Enrichments

What are the sensory enrichments that facilitate learning? As silly or simple as it may seem, sensory enrichments range from the equipment and supplies available to the learner, to opportunities to use the senses, to language stimulations, to learning centers that invite learner involvement. What is sometimes overlooked in this idea of enriched environments and rich sensory inputs is the time needed to investigate, experiment, and become intensely involved in the learning environment. Without sufficient time to truly engage with sensory stimuli, learning is short-circuited and may be superficial and shallow.

And don't be mistaken, very young children are capable of long-term engagement in an investigation with the senses. Witness two toddlers at the seashore, engaging with the wave action, running in to meet the wave, and squealing as they try to outrun the rushing water as it covers the beach. These two little ones will repeat that activity with the environment for hours on end, all the while hypothesizing as they try out different methods of attack. This is just one example of real time for playful engagement. There are many others, but the point is made: enriched environments are most beneficial when learners are given the proper time to interact with sensory input. Learners need more than just glimpses and glances of sensory stimuli; they need opportunities to explore and to delve into the explorations.

Equipment and Supplies

Naturally, the most basic items that enrich the classroom fall under the category of equipment and supplies. Textbooks, paper, pencils, crayons, markers, chalk and chalkboard, staples, glue, paper clips, and tape are essential. In addition, ready access to recorders; CD players; film, slide, and transparency projectors; video monitors, computers, and handheld wireless devices; and the Internet are necessary in today's classroom.

In the enriched classroom, supplies and equipment include science and technological equipment such as hands-on science kits, lab setups, plants, animals in cages and aquariums, calculators, computers, hard drives, CD-ROMs, DVDs, and online services. Also important are materials and supplies for the practical and fine arts, including paints, easels, kilns, tools, wood, tile, coils, springs, screws, material, sewing machines, drafting paper, T squares, printing presses, and drawing tables.

If the school is unable to supply the items needed to create a rich and inviting sensory environment, then it falls to teachers and students to find a way to get them. In a number of classrooms, teachers solicit supplies from parents and students at the beginning of the year or as special projects arise in the course of classroom activities. Notes or letters home can bring a surprising flood of goodies to enrich the classroom.

For the classroom to be truly brain compatible, that is to say, a classroom that fosters brain growth and a flourish of dendrites, the equipment and supplies must not only be in or near the classroom activities, but also be available and accessible to students. In addition, students must have some level of freedom and flexibility to use the equipment and supplies in creative ways. While that is not to say that there are no rules or guidelines for use, there is nothing sadder to see than a room filled with inviting objects that are off limits to the students. Remember, if students are not using it and doing it, the learning is, at best, minimal.

Sensory Input

Based on the five senses that humans use to take in information, the sensory-enriched environment is filled with opportunities for students to see, hear, touch, taste, and smell. Much like a children's museum that is organized to be a sensory-rich experience, if the classroom is to be brain compatible, it should be steeped with irresistible, intriguing, and curious materials, tools, and objects relating to various topics. Although this sounds more like an elementary classroom, there are great examples of middle, high school, and college classrooms that exude rich stimuli for the curious learner. Figure 5.22 lists several examples of stimuli for each of the senses.

Sight: film, video, multimedia, posters, bulletin boards, books, pictures, paintings, drawings, sketches, games, statues, writings, blackboards, whiteboards, cartoons, caricatures, people, places, things, periodic table, beakers, electrical circuitry, bottles, containers, letters, plants, animals, rocks, stones, seashells

Hearing: rap, rhythm and blues, jazz, classical music, folk music, Christmas carols, bands, symphony orchestras, bells, choirs, choruses, radios, televisions, head sets, CDs, CD-ROMs, people, peers, teachers, other adults, children, voices, audiotapes, audiobooks, foreign languages

Taste: classroom cooking, snacks, ethnic foods, healthy foods, snack food, junk food, soft drinks, juices, fruits, vegetables, legumes, sweets, starches, dairy products, grains, breads, muffins, cookies, cakes, puddings

Touch: clay, sand, sandpaper, finger paints, textures, paper, cloth, blocks, puzzles, keyboards, musical instruments, paintbrushes, canvas, easel, papier-mâché, puppets, dolls, plants, flowers, toys, tools, pencils, pens, markers, crayons, chalk

Smell: paint, markers, ink, glue, chemicals, foods, paper, chalk, flowers, plants, animals, people, clay, books, aromas, pungent odors, fresh air, rain

---

Figure 5.22   Stimulating Classroom Environments

Language Stimulation

Language stimulation involves both a print-rich environment and a wealth of oral language in the form of dialogues, songs, conversations, and articulation among peers, adults, and others. In fact, the impact of language stimulation is so critical in the early years that curriculum needs to focus around the idea of what has been called language experience; whole language; or the current euphemism of choice, literacy. Regardless of its title, the meaning is clear—language is the doorway to learning.

Language is what sets humans apart from other species in the universe. Language is the result of connected and connecting neural pathways in the brain. Humans think in pictures, but thinking is also filled with language that is invisible and inaudible to others. Oral and written language gives voice to thinking through reading, writing, speaking, and listening.

Understanding the adage that "the person doing the talking is the person doing the learning" is at the heart of this drive for a language-rich environment. When students are required to speak in formal English, to use complete sentences in all of their communications in the classroom, they are given the gift of fluency and finesse in their oral and written usage of the language. This gift translates into an educated, well-spoken person who is skilled and ready to enter into the world of advanced educational study or the world of work.

In turn, the classroom that is print-rich is overflowing with books, magazines, newspapers, articles, written papers, poetry, letters, student work, first drafts, final publications, student-produced books, big books, stapled booklets, calligraphy, printed pages, handwritten notes, labeled drawings, sketches, cartoons, paperback books, picture books, textbooks, and reference materials, such as maps, globes, dictionaries, thesauri, and books of sayings and quotations. These materials should abound throughout the room so that students are inundated with printed information. If the classroom shelves are stuffed full and the walls are dripping with papers, students are bombarded with the printed language from every direction.

In addition to the printed word, as explained earlier, students in a stimulating language environment are exposed to and immersed in the spoken language in every form. Included in this concept are oral directions, teacher instructions, discussions, partner sharings, tellings, retellings, poetry readings, stories and short stories read aloud, plays, role-plays, monologues, dialogues, questions, responses, dialects, foreign languages, lyrics, raps, operas, and folk songs. Oral language permeates every sector of the classroom as students learn the lingo for each discipline: biology—microscope, DNA, genetic code, recessive gene, heredity; English literature—Victorian, genre, voice, novel, epic, classic, mystery; geography—plain, terrain, tributary, desert, fjord; computer science—bits and bytes, hard drive, CD-ROM, disk, floppy, bug, virus; art—palette, color wheel, blend, brighten, lighten, Cubism, abstract.

Learning Centers

A fairly common scene in today's elementary and middle school classrooms is the arrangement of learning centers: areas of the classroom designated for certain types of learning experiences. There might be a writing center filled with writing prompts that relate to a classroom topic or unit of study or a math center stocked with calculators, exercises, and problems of all sorts. Sometimes these centers are developed around a current academic theme, around Gardner's (1993) theory of multiple intelligences, or in more traditional ways such as subject matter content. Chapman (1993) calls these *flow centers* in reference to Csikszentmihalyi's (2008) theory of the state of flow that is reached when one is intently engaged in a task.

In upper-level classrooms, these centers may not be stationary but may develop as a unit unfolds. They may be called stations, rather than learning centers, as they are more temporary in nature. For example, a French class set up a series of four stations for students to rotate through as they applied various techniques to learn their vocabulary words for a particular unit. Also, in a math class, three stations or centers were used to give students three experiences with parabolas. In one center they used the textbook exercise, in another they used circular graph paper, and in the third they worked with a hands-on project involving wax paper models of the graphed lines. Figure 5.23 extends the learning center examples.

Brainworks: Activities

Four Corners

Do a four-corner activity using the four corners of a piece of paper, labeling them Multiage Groupings, Block Scheduling, Year-Round Schools, and Teaching Teams. Then choose a corner that interests you, and write about that idea. Feel free to write about more than one idea. In fact, you can use all four corners if you wish.

Imagine how these centers might be filled with sensory and language-rich experiences for the appropriate grade levels and subject areas.

Elementary School: A Multiple Intelligences Approach to Centers (Armstrong, 1999)

- Word smart
- Picture smart
- Music smart
- Number smart
- Game smart
- People smart
- Self smart
- Nature smart
- Spirit smart

Upper-Level School: A Biographical Approach

- Georgia O'Keeffe center for art
- Joyce Carol Oates center for writing
- Maria Callas center for music
- Madame Curie center for science
- Wilma Rudolph center for health and fitness
- Hillary Clinton center for leadership
- Emily Dickinson center for reflection
- Margaret Mead center for naturalist studies
- Mother Teresa center for spiritual awakenings

Figure 5.23   Learning Center Ideas

Brainstorms: Applications

Sketch on paper your current classroom layout, and label all sensory and language stimuli that are apparent and visible in the room. Revisit your room design, and apply the ideas about enriched environments by redesigning the room with additional enrichments; use graph paper, and prepare to discuss enhancements in terms of brain research. Consider including the learning centers in your redesign or as temporary stations that change periodically.

Braindrain: REFLECTION

Compare the before and after versions of your room arrangement using the Comparison Alley graphic in Figure 5.24.

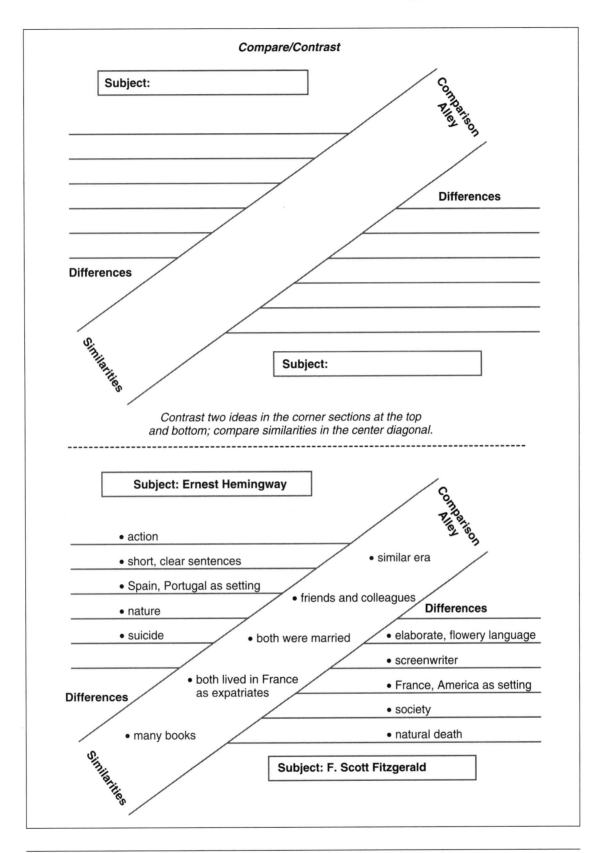

Figure 5.24   Comparison Alley

6 Teaching the Skills of Thinking

A school should not be a preparation for life. A school should be life.

—Elbert Hubbard

A major curriculum focus must be on the skills used to function in and make one's way around this world—life skills such as problem solving and decision making. Skill development is vital to the learning process. Skills are embedded in every discipline, content subject area, and field of study and are the keys to understanding and becoming proficient in any chosen pursuit. For example, in the area of writing, skills of organization, fluency, and structure are necessary to develop a coherent piece of written work. Another example of skill training that leads to proficiency and production is in the field of computer technology. The more adept one becomes at keyboarding, word processing, and graphic design, the more likely one is to use those skills purposefully in the creation of a useful product.

To illustrate process standards or life skills, think about the collaborative skills of leadership, teamwork, conflict resolution, and communication. Or consider thinking skills that are both creative and critical in nature. Other life skills include the skills of technology and the performance skills necessary for the visual and performing arts, athletics, and the practical arts.

On the other hand, content standards concern the various disciplines and their subject matter content. In math, there is content about number sense, computational skills, problem solving, and reasoning. In the sciences, content is organized around understanding motion, energy, and forces as well as biological data, chemical compounds and reactions, astronomy, earth science, and biochemistry. Social studies content embraces concepts about civilization, historical data, politics, economics, geography, and the humanities.

Note the content required in the area of literacy. In reading, content focuses on decoding and word analysis skills, fluency, comprehension, vocabulary development, critical analysis, and genre. In writing, the skills and concepts encompass organization, outlining, note taking, and structures and formats from letter writing to creative essays. In the area of speaking skills, content standards target language usage, public speaking, debates, dialogues, proper English, and conversational English. Figure 6.1 shows a chart of these skills and concepts. While not comprehensive, the list suggests the content and process standards required.

Microskills

Collaborative Skills
- Leadership
- Communication
- Conflict resolution
- Team building

Thinking Skills
- Creative
- Critical

Academic Content Skills and Concepts
- Math
- Science
- Social
- Language arts

Technological Skills
- Literacy
- Graphics

Macroskills

Problem-Solving Skills

Decision-Making Skills

Communication Skills

Research Skills

Performance Skills
- Athletics
- Visual arts
- Performing arts
- Practical arts

Word-Processing Skills

Innovation Skills

Production Skills

Figure 6.1   Essential Life Skills and Concepts

An important question embedded in skills teaching—what constitutes the skill?—is addressed by both content and process standards.

Teaching the skills and concepts of thinking involves two themes: types of skills and concepts students need for the rest of their lives and development of these skills and concepts in the teaching-learning process. The various skills and concepts students require can be broken into two major categories: microskills and macroskills. Once the necessary skills and concepts are identified, they are best taught to students starting at the basic level and moving toward an advanced level, or mastery.

BRAINWAVE #3: MICROSKILLS AND MACROSKILLS

Marzano/McTighe

Microskills comprise discrete skills in the areas of collaboration, thinking, technology, visual and performing arts, mathematical calculation, inquiry in science, historical referencing in social studies, and decoding in literacy. Within those realms, microskills are subcategorized again into such clusters as leadership, critical thinking, and computer graphics. For example, a cluster of skills needed for leadership would include visualizing, motivating, and goal setting. And critical thinking involves microskills such as predicting, classifying, and evaluating.

Macroskills, on the other hand, comprise sets of microskills. Macroskills, or macroprocesses, include problem solving, decision making, communication, research, word processing, innovating, producing, and performing. To use macroskills effectively, learners often call on a series of microskills and abilities. For example, to problem solve, learners may use the skills of brainstorming, organizing, analyzing, prioritizing, and evaluating.

Both microskills and macroskills are used by learners in the brain-compatible classroom.

BRAINWISE STATEMENTS

- Use it or lose it!
- Déjà vu all over again.
- Your brain has been custom made for you.

Braindrops: Strategies

The adage "Use it or lose it!" applies to the brain in terms of the types of skills learned and the ongoing development of those skills. Although there is motor memory that enables one to ride a bike many years after the skill is learned and perhaps abandoned, more complex skills improve over time in relation to the frequency and intensity of use. The more the neural pathways are used, the stronger they become and the easier it is to access them.

In the discussion about the types of skills relevant to today's curriculum, one important question dictates the selections: What do kids need to know 25 years from now?

Microskills

Microskills are human tools that empower learners in the brain-compatible classroom. With competent and proficient use and in combination with other microskills, learners become self-sufficient in the classroom learning environment and throughout life. To make it easier to examine the various microskills, they have been clustered as collaborative skills, thinking skills, academic content skills and concepts, technological skills, and performance skills. Within these clusters, the various microskills are listed. These skills are available for the skillful teacher to use appropriately within the context of classroom activities.

Collaborative Skills

When thinking about what skills students need for the future, the skill area that is often mentioned first is collaborative skills (see Figure 6.2). The number one reason people fail at their jobs is because of lack of social adeptness: they can't get along with their coworkers. Microskills that are included under this collaborative label span the spectrum of social skills within the cooperative learning genre.

Leadership Skills

- Check for understanding
- Encourage others
- Accept responsibility
- Stay on task

Communication Skills

- Wait for the speaker to finish
- Clarify ideas
- Paraphrase concepts
- Sense tone

Conflict Resolution Skills

- Explore different points of view
- Negotiate and compromise
- Reach consensus
- Respect others' opinions; disagree with the idea, not the person

Team Building Skills

- Include others
- Share materials
- Develop guidelines
- Identify with the team

Figure 6.2 Microskills for Collaboration

While the importance of collaborative skills cannot be overstated for the world of work, it's important to note the benefits of cooperation in the school setting also. Now, hear this! Cooperative learning is the number one strategy to increase student achievement and to enhance self-esteem (Johnson, Johnson, & Holubec, 1994). More than 600 studies have focused on cooperative learning in every kind of school setting and group composition, and the results are similar, regardless of the group. Marzano, Pickering, and Pollock (2001) include cooperative learning in their family of best practices, as does Joyce and Weil's (1983) classic, *Models of Teaching.* Cooperative interactions must permeate K–college classrooms.

Students learn in brain-friendly ways in cooperative learning groups because they must restate their thoughts in words that make sense to others. As students try to relate their ideas, they form more solid concepts themselves. Remember, the person doing the talking is probably the person doing the learning. Who's doing the talking in your classroom?

Emotional intelligence is at work here also. Everyone wants to belong. In cooperative groups, students feel like they are part of a group and feel safe; they want to feel that they have meaningful relationships with others, that they are aware of and can control their own feelings. Teachers must help students become productive team members, take on leadership roles of responsibility, and learn how to agree and disagree intelligently with others. Using cooperative learning strategies whenever appropriate in the classroom is part and parcel of skillful teaching. Cooperation and collaboration are skills that foster intense involvement in interactions and investment as a member of the team.

Thinking Skills

The microskills of thinking fall into two distinct groupings: creative and critical (see Figure 6.3). The distinction has to do with the type of processing that occurs in the brain. In creative thinking processes, the mind opens up to ideas and synthesizes information, while in critical thinking processes, the mind closes in on ideas, takes things apart, and analyzes information. In most situations, both processes are intertwined in the course of mindful situations. Students generate ideas, sort the ideas in some way, and then inevitably choose one to use. This process involves one creative microskill (brainstorming) and two critical thinking skills (classifying and prioritizing).

Academic Content Skills and Concepts

Mathematics Skills and Concepts

Proficiency in the skills and concepts that constitute the discipline of mathematics (see Figure 6.4) is one of the most basic academic requirements. Students must have a sense of numbers, patterns, and numerical relationships. They must know, understand, and be able to apply computation skills, problem-solving strategies, and data analysis skills as well as be able to use statistical information to plot probabilities.

Students take a solid understanding of mathematical skills and concepts into every other field of study as they analyze data in the science lab, double a

Creative Thinking Skills: Generative, Productive

- Brainstorm
- Visualize
- Personify
- Invent
- Relate
- Infer
- Generalize
- Predict
- Hypothesize
- Make analogies
- Deal with ambiguity and paradox

Critical Thinking Skills: Analytical, Evaluative

- Compare/contrast
- Classify
- Sequence
- Prioritize
- Draw conclusions
- Determine cause and effect
- Analyze for bias
- Analyze for assumptions
- Solve analogies
- Evaluate
- Discern attributes

Figure 6.3   Microskills for Thinking

recipe in home arts, crunch numerical data on the social studies survey results, and create a tessellation for a promotional poster in art class. Grounded in these skills and concepts, students embrace math. They say things like "Math is easy," "Math is good," "Math is everywhere," and "I'm so glad I studied hard to learn math because I use it all the time."

Science Skills and Concepts

Just as mathematical understandings are applied to a multitude of school and real-world situations, science concepts are integral to various academic areas and are embedded into many situations in life (see Figure 6.4). Students encounter countless situations in which the laws of physics, the concept of chemical compounds, and knowledge of cell structure and DNA are implied or explicitly revealed. They encounter concerns about the ecosystem, earthquakes, and volcanic eruptions.

Throughout their lives, students are fascinated about outer space, the movement of the planets, eclipses, and glorious sunsets. They encounter the mysteries of biochemistry and neuroscience as information mounts on the inner workings of the human brain. To fully appreciate and truly understand ongoing discoveries in science, basic science skills and concepts are critical to a well-rounded academic education.

Mathematics Skills and Concepts

- Number sense: one to one, place value, fractions/decimals
- Computation: add, subtract, multiply, divide
- Problem solving: reasoning, logic
- Geometry: theorems, proofs
- Measurement/time: linear, volume, clock time, calendar time
- Data analysis/probability/statistics: graphing, percentages

Science Skills and Concepts

- Physics: motion, energy and forces, magnetism, electricity
- Chemistry: elements, compounds, reactions
- Biology: evolution, DNA, cell structure, living organisms
- Earth sciences: ecosystem
- Astronomy: universe

Social Studies Skills and Concepts

- Historical: eras, dates, events, leaders
- Economics: supply and demand, currency, investing
- Politics: government, democratic values
- Geography: map and globe skills
- Cultures: ancient to modern civilizations

Language Arts Skills and Concepts

Reading

- Decoding: consonants, vowels, blends
- Fluency: phrasing, pacing
- Comprehension: characters, concepts, mood, setting
- Vocabulary: prefixes, suffixes, derivatives, origins
- Genre: fiction, poetry, drama
- Critical reading: analysis of bias, assumptions, point of view

Writing

- Organization: text organizers, sequencing
- Outlining: main ideas, subheadings, supporting details
- Note taking: paraphrasing, key words, and concepts
- Structure of formats: correspondence, expository essays, creative essays

Speaking

- Language: grammar, syntax, punctuation, spelling
- Conversational/formal English: usage
- Public speaking: presence, rhythm, tone, dialects, inflection
- Persuasive speaking/debate: argument and evidence, demeanor, rebuttal

Listening

- Paraphrasing: using own words
- Affirming: agreement
- Clarifying: be clear
- Testing options: ask questions
- Sensing tone: be aware of undertones

Figure 6.4   Microskills of Academic Content

Social Studies Skills and Concepts

Although the field of social studies is an amalgamation of several areas of study (see Figure 6.4), there is no doubt that students must grasp basic conceptual understandings if they are to function effectively in the world. Students need to be well grounded in historical contexts, including various eras and the people and events that mark those periods of time. Students need a solid foundation in the concepts of economics, such as supply and demand, the role of international markets, various currencies, and basic financial planning skills that involve budgets and simple bookkeeping skills. Students need to know about various types of governments. They need extensive opportunities to grasp the democratic ideals of the country in which they reside. Students need to be skilled in geography, drawing on their map and globe skills, and embrace the concepts of diversity and multiculturalism as they interact with a global society. In short, they need a worldly awareness and deep understanding of the principles of civilization.

Language Arts Skills and Concepts

Reading

Without the skills of literacy—in particular, fluent, flexible, and voracious reading skills—students have a great disadvantage in school and life in general. There is no excuse! All students must learn to read, and to read effectively. Literacy is learning, and there is no real progress in school unless students have adequate, competent, and proficient reading, writing, speaking, and listening skills.

To become proficient readers, students must have extensive experiences with reading and must begin with reading at home in the early years. Folk data revealed by Mem Fox (2001) in *Reading Magic* support the role of early literacy. She states an astonishing truth that emerges from a simple action: if a child learns eight nursery rhymes by the age of four, that child will be a strong reader by the age of eight.

To summarize the seminal point on this idea of the power and impact of early literacy, here is a quick story. During a panel presentation, a parent once asked a reading expert, "Do I have to read with my child every day?" The reading specialist replied, "Oh, no, no! Not every day! Only on the days that you eat." Point made.

Students need specific skill work (see Figure 6.4) in phonemic awareness, phonics, decoding and word analysis, and developing fluency in their reading to comprehend more easily. They need attention to vocabulary development and comprehension skills such as making inferences, summarizing, paraphrasing, and finding the main idea or the hidden meanings of symbols in literature. They need to read widely and taste the flavor of different genres. They need to read critically to ascertain bias, assumptions, and point of view. In brief, students need a whole range of reading competencies to function fully and creatively as intelligent people.

Writing

Companion to the enormous skill set required to be literate in reading is another complete skill set for literacy in writing. Students need a writing vocabulary, spelling skills, skills with text organizers, and hierarchical thinking skills for outlining and note taking. They need to know about language usage, syntax, semantics, and punctuation as well as myriad formats and structures for writing. They need to be able to write expository essays, creative fiction, short pieces, business letters, notes, and e-mails. They need to be able to discern the differences between slang, colloquialism, and formal language as well as when one is more appropriate than the others. In summary, for students to be skillful in written language, they need consistent, continual, and varied opportunities to write, and to write some more, and to write even more. As the saying goes among those who call themselves writers, "Writers write!"

Speaking

Naturally, there are skills and concepts that accompany the literacy function of oral communication (see Figure 6.4). While language is hardwired into the brain, and speaking is the earliest form of literacy to appear, this skill is formalized throughout schooling in more precise and formal ways than in the early learnings of the young child.

Again, students need to learn about language in terms of grammar, syntax, and semantics. They need public-speaking skills that include a sense of presence, rhythm and pacing, tone, intonation, and inflection. They need to understand the art of argument and evidence and the skill of effective, persuasive rebuttal. For students to be literate in listening and speaking skills, they need practice, rehearsal, and repetition as well as rich opportunities to develop their own unique style of public speaking and their own portrayal of themselves in private conversations.

Listening

For students to be skillful in the art of attentive listening (and they are listening 80 percent of the time in some classrooms), they need to practice the PACTS skills: *p*araphrase, *a*ffirm, *c*larify, *t*est options, and *s*ense tone (see Figure 6.4). Good listeners are attentive, skillful listeners who use these techniques to comprehend what they are hearing. They paraphrase the speaker and put ideas into their own words, they affirm understanding by nodding or saying "uh huh," they clarify by asking questions to be sure they understand, they test options by asking about alternative interpretations, and they sense tone by being aware of the undertones that transcend the words being used.

Technological Skills

The terms *technocrat* and *techno idiot* may seem like flippant and insensitive descriptors, but the impact of either 25 years from now could be significant. In the ever-expanding, often exploding field of technology, it is imperative that today's students be technologically literate. In the most basic terms, that means literacy skills such as keyboarding, using spreadsheets and databases, reading technical manuals, and using modems, faxes, e-mail, handheld devices, wireless technology, Web-based learning, and online services. In addition, students should be well versed in graphics programs and in animation and multimedia presentation programs. These are the basic skills in today's society (see Figure 6.5). If children exit schools lacking these essential tools, they are ill equipped to enter the world of work or higher education programs.

Literacy Skills

- Keyboard
- Calculate spreadsheets
- Create databases
- Understand manuals
- Use modems
- Fax
- E-mail
- Use online services

Graphic Skills

- Design
- Animate
- Create multimedia presentations

Figure 6.5   Microskills for Technology

Performance Skills

The most obvious performance skills fall into the realm of athletics or visual, performing, and practical arts. With an understanding of the theory of multiple intelligences (Gardner, 1993) and the idea that humans are multidimensional in their profile of intelligences, the skills associated with the bodily, visual, and musical intelligences take on great importance. These skills are integral to fulfillment and joy in living, to multiple career choices, and to recreational options.

Just to touch on the many areas of skill development, athletics encompass the microskills associated with team sports, recreational sports, and health and fitness regimens. The visual and performing arts include the microskills of painting, drawing, sculpting, and filmmaking, while the performing arts include the microskills of dancing, acting, comedic performing, singing, and playing an instrument. Among the practical arts are the home arts, the industrial arts, and design (see Figure 6.6), as well as the mechanical skills of the building and automotive trades and the fine motor skills required in many age-old crafts. Microskills of performance arts are also integral to the technological skills of various electronic media.

Macroskills

Macroskills, or macroprocesses, include activities such as problem solving, decision making, communicating, researching, and word processing. Each of these macroskills comprises a series of microskills necessary to perform complex tasks. For example, problem solving involves the microskills of analyzing, brainstorming, evaluating, and prioritizing, while communicating involves such skills as listening, speaking clearly, paraphrasing, and summarizing.

To develop macroskills, microskills are often taught first and then strung together in appropriate sequences. Macroskills are, in essence, complex, intricate processes that have layers of microskills built into them. They are at the far end of the developmental path of skill learning, and they are the result of progression in microskills.

Athletic	Visual	Performing	Practical

• Team sports
  ○ Baseball
  ○ Football
  ○ Basketball
  ○ Hockey
  ○ Soccer
	• Painting
	  ○ Watercolors
	  ○ Oils
	  ○ Acrylics
		• Dance
		  ○ Modern
		  ○ Ballet
		  ○ Jazz
		  ○ Ballroom
		  ○ Line
		  ○ Square
			• Home Arts
			• Sewing
			• Cooking
			• Home repairs

Recreational Sports	Drawing	Drama	Industrial Arts
• Golf • Tennis • Sailing • Skiing • Skating	• Pencils • Pen/inks • Charcoals • Pastels	• Stage • TV • Film • Video	• Electrical • Plumbing • Auto mechanics • Carpentry • Welding

Fitness	Sculpture	Comedy	Design
• Walking • Jogging • Running • Stretching • Yoga • Weightlifting	• Clay • Papier-mâché • Pottery	• Stand-up • Slapstick • Situation	• Interior • Industrial • Architectural

Film	Music
• Photography • Movies • Videos	• Vocal • Instrumental

Figure 6.6 Microskills for Performance

Problem-Solving Skills

Recently, a high school student was overheard saying, "If there's one thing you learn in this school, it's how to solve a problem. Everywhere you go in this building, they want you to solve a problem." This seems to be an accurate reflection on student expectations. Yet such a worthy goal is often couched in the aims and objectives of a district. Problem solving, after all, encompasses a realm of situations that range from calculating numerical problems to using problem-based learning or completing semester-long projects. Problem solving stimulates the mind to make meaning and search for patterns. The brain is engaged by challenges. Problem-solving activities increase blood flow, and the dendrites flourish as the brain links new and old neural pathways.

Typical problem solving that occurs in classrooms is encapsulated in activities such as science investigations, math story problems, geometry projects, artistic endeavors, research, essay writing, and foreign language studies. Problems abound in character conflicts in novels, in moral dilemmas in history, and in practical ways in labs and workrooms. To organize learning around problem solving is to honor brain-compatible philosophy.

Decision-Making Skills

Much like problem solving, the macroskill of decision making is of paramount concern in a rigorous curriculum plan. Decision making permeates every aspect of curricular content. Political and economic decisions are made in the study of social studies, character dilemmas require decision making in writing and literature, procedural decisions are part of scientific investigations, program decisions are made in relation to computer technology, and decisions thread through dramatic works, sporting events, and game playing. Decision making is also integral when working with others on collaborative projects and deciding on personal goals and objectives.

Again, as with problem solving, it is imperative that students have multiple and varied opportunities to make decisions if they are to become skilled in the process. Decisions as simple as determining how to prioritize homework assignments or as weighty as justifying a decision to vote for a political candidate offer some insight into the realm of possibilities for decision making in the classroom.

Communication Skills

Without a doubt, one of the most frequently mentioned skills, by business and industry personnel as well as by people working on building and forming relationships, is the macroprocess of communication. Communication means being able to share information effectively with others; to be able to clearly paraphrase, summarize, and pass on information from others; and to be an attentive listener, an articulate speaker, a clear writer, and a critical reader. These are not easy qualities to foster in young people, yet their future success in this information society depends heavily on their abilities in these areas. Fortunately, in today's classrooms, opportunities abound for students to develop communication skills.

Research Skills

Another macroskill of primary importance in the information age is the skill of research. To keep up with the unending stream of data and information available to the learner, research becomes a primary tool of this century. It is neither probable nor possible for the brain to retain the massive amounts of information available today. In fact, with information doubling every few years, with the emergence of online referencing and immediate connections to the great libraries, and with primary sources such as museums, institutes, scientists, and researchers, it is all but impossible even to access all the information that is out there. Remember, the brain is more like a sieve than a sponge. It drops information that is deemed unimportant within nine seconds. It drops information that does not connect to prior knowledge or to some known entity that helps the mind make sense of it. The brain holds onto information that is chunked in some way and quickly loses information that is discrete and unlinked to anything else.

With easy accessibility and the continuing explosion in fiber optics, the information river is flowing at a rapid and ever-increasing pace. Students don't need to know everything; rather, they need to know how to find whatever it is they need at the time. With handheld devices quickly becoming the norm in high school and college classrooms, and with the information highway fast growing into a superhighway, research skills are essential when setting curricular priorities for the brain-compatible classroom.

Word-Processing Skills

Perhaps one of the most urgent skill areas is word processing. To risk an inept analogy, the penmanship skill of yesteryear is the word-processing skill of today. Students are lost in the work or study world if they are unable to manage a word-processing program. It is not a privilege in today's classroom to work on the computer; it is a right of every student. Without the ability to compose, format, edit and revise, design, print, and produce finished documents, students face grave liabilities in their future career options. The introduction of this macroskill cannot come early enough in the schooling process. Computers and word-processing software are essential tools for students from kindergarten to college.

Innovation Skills

Creative ideation is considered one of the most sought-after forms of higher-order thinking. To be creative in any field is to take the given, that is, the known information and move it beyond its present state or form. Creativity is about new ideas; different connections; unusual, sometimes outlandish, often extraordinary, and occasionally novel kinds of things. But innovation is the actual concrete, black-and-white result of the ideation. Innovation is creativity in action. It's the idea realized and manifested in a plausible way.

Students use their microskill sets to create, invent, and innovate. They create poems and pottery, tools and recipes. They invent and reinvent themselves as they try to figure out who they are. They imitate and eventually innovate as they make critical, personal, and unique connections to various content and as they become more expert in skill areas throughout various subjects. No schooling experience is complete without explicit attention to the skills and concepts of innovation.

Production Skills

To discuss the concept of innovation more specifically, there is the macroprocess of production. In this discussion, production relates to a product of some sort. It might be an invention, an authored piece, a puppet, an art object, a musical composition, a new dish cooked up for a special occasion, or simply a letter to a friend. Production of anything requires a set of microskills orchestrated in ways that result in a final product. The product may be valued for its quality, uniqueness, or usefulness, or it may be criticized for its lack of quality, lack of uniqueness, or lack of functionality. But it is there. It exists, and it is a product of someone's imagination. What happens to the product often depends on continued creative thinking. Yet the process of producing has its own inherent rewards. It brings with it a sense of accomplishment and achievement.

Performance Skills

Performances are a similar lot. They represent innovations in the form of an experience. A performance also requires the consolidation of many different skill sets to realize its final form, yet with performance the "proof is in the pudding" of the combined and textured efforts from myriad fields.

Unlike products, performances are categorized as experiences such as an opera or a symphony orchestra presentation, an athletic contest, or a dramatic play. Performances include a cooking experience, a yoga class, or a performance on film or video. They qualify as a macroprocess because of the many and varied skill sets they require. Students need lots of opportunities to perform as they integrate the skills and concepts they are learning.

Habits of Mind

It would be remiss to discuss the concept of macroskills of thinking without mentioning a robust body of work by Costa and Kallick (2000) called *Discovering and Exploring: Habits of Mind.* Envisioned in Costa's (1981) article "Teaching for Intelligent Behavior," Costa and Kallick define, describe, and delineate a quintessential list of thinking behaviors or dispositions. These habits of mind comprise the ultimate in thinking macroskills as they move far beyond the actions of problem solving and decision making and into the realm of attitudinal positions that make other macroskills possible. The complete listing of these 16 habits of mind is as follows:

Persisting

Thinking and communicating with clarity and precision

Managing impulsivity

Gathering data through all senses

Listening with understanding and empathy

Creating, imagining, innovating

Thinking flexibly

Responding with wonderment and awe

Thinking about thinking (metacognition)

Taking responsible risks

Striving for accuracy

Finding humor

Questioning and posing problems

Thinking interdependently

Applying past knowledge to new situations

Remaining open to continuous learning

The habits of mind are ripe fodder for explicit attention in the mindful classroom. In fact, teachers can use particular habits of mind as the focus of their instructional processes.

Brainworks: Activities

Microskill Lesson—Analysis for Bias

This activity illustrates the type of thinking skills students need for analyzing written or spoken words, images, and multimedia bombardment. Use the web from Figure 6.7 to draw possible ideas from three perspectives: viewed from straight ahead, from above, and from below. Think about point of view and how it affects bias. Think of the jury selection process and the particular bias the defense and the prosecutor are looking for in a current newsworthy court case.

Macroskill Lesson—Problem Solving

Use your problem-solving abilities to think about the following question: How would you go about developing a neighborhood watch program? Outline the process you would follow to accomplish the project.

Brainstorms: Applications

In an effort to apply the ideas about the types of skills students need, survey some students, teachers, parents, and businesspeople about how they might prioritize the listings of micro- and macroskills. Ask what other skills they might add to the list as they think of them. Advertise the results; comment on and discuss how bias or their particular points of view might have influenced the survey results.

Braindrain: REFLECTION

Let it all out. Reflect on the types of skills addressed by using the Drop-Down Menu (see Figure 6.8). Learners start at the top of the menu and list all the skills learned, practiced, or used that day. Partners share their lists. If done over time, the highest-priority skills pop out, just like the menu items do with repeated use on computers or handheld electronic devices.

BRAINWAVE #4: DEVELOPMENT OF SKILLS AND CONCEPTS

Posner and Keele/Csikszentmihalyi

Practice makes permanent, not perfect. Skill development causes temporary inconvenience, or a dip in the learning curve, for permanent improvement. Teachers must educate for intelligent performance with rehearsal, practice, and coaching. Therefore, it is appropriate to say that practice makes permanent, not practice makes perfect. With imperfect practice, the neural connections continue to strengthen in incorrect or inaccurate patterns. This results in misconceptions and miscalculations. For example, in earth science, instruction may form misconceptions about the rotation of the earth, and in golf, golfers may develop a bad golf swing, which is "grooved" into their muscle memory. In brain-compatible classrooms, the practice is done with constant, consistent, and specific feedback to ensure practice that is permanent is also correct!

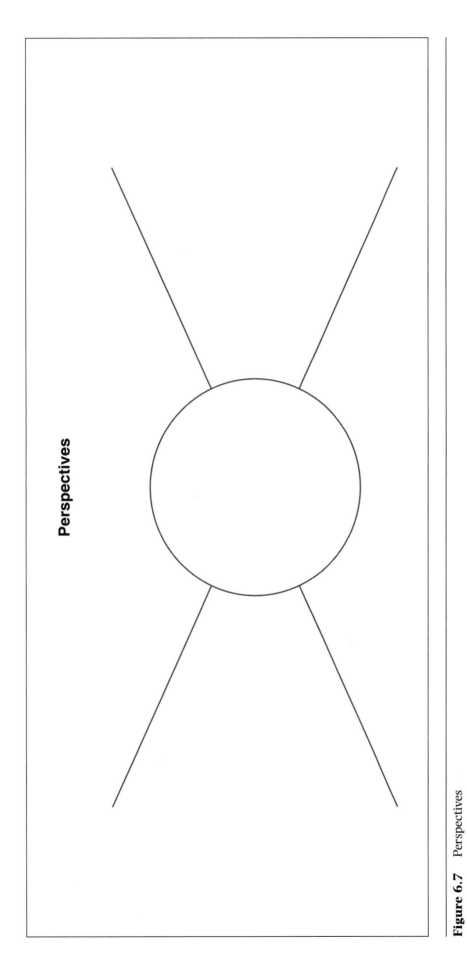

Perspectives

Figure 6.7 Perspectives

Generating Options

Task or Goal:

Menu of Presentation Options

- -

Task or Goal:
Read a biography and present vital information to others in the class.

Menu of Presentation Options

Puppet Show Presentation

Quotations on Tape

Comic Strip

Role-Play

Video Program

Interview Format

Multimedia Presentation

Figure 6.8   Drop-Down Menu

BRAINWISE STATEMENTS

- Practice makes permanent.
- Do what you can with what you have, where you are.
- You can never say "no" to intelligence.

Braindrops: Strategies

The development of life skills centers on two levels of skillfulness: basic and advanced (see Figure 6.9). Ingrained in the development of skills at the basic level are the direct instruction of skills and the developmental path from novice to expert. Embedded in the advanced level of skill development are the ideas of application and peak performance and the concept of reaching a state of flow (Csikszentmihalyi, 2008).

Basic/Apprentice

The direct instruction model, or the traditional Hunter (1982) model of a seven-step lesson design, is basic to comprehensive skill instruction. In turn, knowledge and understanding of the developmental path of skill training is a

---

Basic/Apprentice Level

Direct Instruction Model
- Anticipatory set
- Clear objective
- Input
- Modeling
- Check for understanding
- Guided practice
- Independent practice or application
- Evaluation

Developmental Path
- Novice
- Advanced beginner
- Competent user
- Proficient user
- Expert

Advanced/Master Level

Embedded Application

Peak Performance

Flow
- Set goals
- Become immersed in the activity
- Pay attention to what is happening
- Enjoy the immediate experience

Figure 6.9   Progression of Life Skills

necessary part of the total package of life skills. Both direct instruction and the developmental sequence from novice to expert are brain-friendly or brain-compatible components of the engaged-learning scenario.

Direct Instruction Model

The direct instruction model for lesson design presented by Hunter (1982) comprises seven distinct parts. These are considered essential to a quality lesson and are often incorporated in lesson design models, although they do not always follow in this order:

1. *Anticipatory Set*: The anticipatory set initiates the anticipated learning and encourages students to focus and attend to the learning at hand. It is the hook. To capture the focus of students, teachers use images, sounds, surprising comments, questions, quotes, and anything else they can come up with to grab students' attention.

   For example, a political cartoon on the overhead projector may set the scene for development of the oral skills of speech making. Or the prompt may be a videotaped speech of a politician.

2. *Clear Objectives*: Students are given clear, targeted objectives that set the purpose for the skill. These often include an immediate goal and a long-term goal that give relevance to the learning. Remember, the brain needs an attention grabber, and then it must have meaning, be relevant, and make sense for the brain to tune in.

   Continuing the speech example, the objective statement for learning oral skills might be that learners will demonstrate the essential elements of oral presentation. In turn, the teacher may address students' future needs by suggesting application of the skill when students present themselves for a job interview.

3. *Input*: Often the input is material from the textbook, a lecture, a video, a film, or another form of input that gives students up-front information for their subsequent work. This phase is at the heart of direct instruction, but without the other phases it often can turn into "teacher talk" or one-way broadcasts that are not very brain compatible because they do not foster neural brain activity. It is often too passive a means for the learner to become engaged.

   One example of an input phase for giving a speech or oral presentation is to use a videotaped speech and highlight the critical elements. Then the teacher can create a listing of the elements so that students know what is expected. The list might include eye contact, voice, visual aid, content, and closure.

4. *Modeling*: Modeling entails showing or demonstrating the desired behavior or result. The modeling phase sets a standard for learners and suggests what the learning looks and sounds like. This modeling can be part of the input as illustrated in the previous example.

Another example of modeling is showing completed student artifacts from previous classes (student portfolios) or displaying a teacher-made model of the product or performance.

5. *Check for Understanding*: Feedback is the breakfast of champions! Everyone wants to know how he or she is doing, especially when learning a new skill. Remember, there is a learning curve—when a person is trying something new, things usually get worse before they get better. Feedback from the instructor and from peers is valued. Feedback that is specific and targeted is the most helpful in terms of improving the skill.

   In the speech example, the teacher might provide feedback about the volume or pacing of the voice or the impact of the visual. In each case, the feedback leads to subtle changes by the learner.

6. *Guided Practice*: During this brain-compatible phase, learners are immersed in the experience with step-by-step instruction. In other words, the skill practice is scaffolded, taking one chunk of learning at a time. In this way, learners are guided through the various stages with needed information and coaching.

   For example, when giving a speech, students may be asked to prepare a one-minute talk for their small groups demonstrating all the elements discussed. As the students rotate through their talks, the teacher observes and responds accordingly.

7. *Independent Practice or Application*: In this phase, students practice on their own, incorporating as many of the elements and as much of the feedback as possible. Sometimes this independent practice occurs as homework or as practice outside of the regular class, such as learning a tennis skill or trying a new computing skill. Other times the independent practice may take the form of an actual performance.

   For instance, in the speech example, students may give the speeches in class as independent practice. Or they may practice with partners, then later give the finished speech to the whole class.

Developmental Path of Skill and Content Training

Just as the young swimmer progresses from tadpole to sunfish to dolphin, the developmental path of skill training in the brain-compatible classroom follows a predictable path. The path most often suggested includes these phases: novice, advanced beginner, competent user, proficient user, and expert (Posner & Keele, 1973). The developmental path is sometimes confused with the learning curve. As the learner incorporates the various phases of a skill, the level of skill drops and rises accordingly. Yet the overall path seems to follow a fairly predictable route from awkwardness toward finesse. This path is considered developmental and is observable in skill learning.

1. *Novice*: The novice processes the pieces of the skill under study and may not practice these parts in any special order. For instance, using the

swimming example, the novice may practice the flutter kick, the windmill arm movement, and blowing bubbles under water, when in fact the sequence was introduced as face in water to blow bubbles, flutter kick, windmill arm movement.

2. *Advanced Beginner*: The advanced beginner is characterized by his or her ability to put the skills together in the proper sequence but is more interested in the execution than the results. An advanced beginner asks, "Did I get it right?" Continuing the swimming example, the learner follows the proper sequence: head in water, jellyfish float, dead man's float, flutter kick, rotation of arm movement, alternate breathing.

3. *Competent User*: The competent user cares about the relationship of the skill to the content. In the case of the swimmer, the competent user now tries to execute the stroke systematically across the pool. The swimmer moves back and forth from side to side, aware of his or her body in the water, how it feels, and how it looks.

4. *Proficient User*: Once the user executes the skill with proficiency, he or she is no longer aware of the steps. The proficient user puts the pieces together with grace and ease and uses the skills automatically. In the case of the swimmer, the proficient user glides easily down the length of the pool, working the crawl with style and technique.

5. *Expert*: Beyond proficiency, the expert skips the disparate parts. In fact, sometimes the expert cannot properly explain how the skill is executed and will say, "Let me show you." He or she tends to skip steps and jump to the elegant solution instinctively. The expert swimmer slices through the water with pace and speed, strength and quality, and technique and elegance that are obvious to all.

Advanced/Master

Moving from basic skill development or apprentice level to advanced or master level is achieved when the skill is easily embedded in a relevant application or the performance is considered a peak or exceptional one for the learner, regardless of the skill level. For example, an advanced beginner skier can have a peak performance for that level of skiing and it would be considered expert for the class at that level.

The ultimate level of advanced learner or master is achieved when the learner attains a state of mental harmony called *flow* (Csikszentmihalyi, 2008). Everything is in sync and working at the maximum—everything is flowing.

To teach the skills of thinking in the brain-compatible classroom, the teacher instructs and encourages learners to progress toward the advanced/master levels of skill development. Then and only then are the human tools available and accessible when needed.

Embedded Application

In the development of skills, an initial stage of the advanced level is exemplified in embedded application. This is simply practice or use of the skill within the context of an authentic application. For example, when learning how to recognize and use adverbial phrases, it's one thing to identify the adverbial phrases in a text lesson, and it's quite another to incorporate adverbial phrases in one's own writing. To do the latter, one must learn, comprehend, and internalize the skill with depth of understanding. This is an example of the brain learning parts and the whole simultaneously.

Of course, even in embedded application there are often improper uses and inaccuracies in the early attempts at the new skill. However, embedded application is what transfer is all about. It gives relevance to learning isolated skills, and it anchors the learning of the skill with personal meaning. When this is the case, the skill becomes more and more automatic as the neural pathways of memory and learning become strengthened.

Peak Performance

The concept of peak performance is often mentioned in the context of the elite athlete or star performer. In the case of the legendary Michael Jordan, the former guard for the Chicago Bulls basketball team, the concept of peak performance is what he was referring to when he would say, "I got my rhythm in the second half." That means he gave a peak performance at a certain moment in the overall performance. In a similar example, the renowned phenomenon in the golfing world, Tiger Woods, spoke of having his "A-game going" when he won the Masters for the first time. Others talk of playing in the zone, feeling free, hitting their stride, being on the mark, achieving personal best, or flying high. These are expressions that attempt to describe what happens in a peak performance.

All of us have experienced the feeling of a peak performance, whether it is an unbelievable morning run, a perfect piano rehearsal, or a writing session that wouldn't quit. Peak performances come in other varieties, too. One may experience a perfect sailing day, a magnificent time painting, or an exquisite preparation of a gourmet dish. Children experience peak performances as well. They talk about how they couldn't miss when pitching the baseball game or how they could ride their bike with no hands and move gracefully down the path with obvious ease.

For those who can recall a peak performance, there is no feeling like it. Everything just works! The whole world seems in sync. B. S. Bloom (1981) speaks of peak performance in terms of having deep emotional roots. Bloom's statement supports brain research that suggests that memorable learning experiences are grounded in emotional tie-ins.

Flow

Csikszentmihalyi (2008) describes an immersion in a performance to the extent that a person reaches a state when everything flows. When the learner experiences this state of flow, a creative oasis is reached, and the performer takes great pleasure in encountering the complexities of the task. The performer is free of frustration, fatigue, and futility. In fact, the performer has this feeling of intense enjoyment and joy in the performance of the skill. According to Csikszentmihalyi, flow involves a series of steps. To move toward or achieve a planned state of flow, the performer must do the following:

1. *Set Goals*: Progression toward the attainment of the goal primes the emotional pump for celebration. It is a measurable state and, thus, any

movement in the direction of the goal provides fodder for further joy in the sense of accomplishment.

2. *Become Immersed in the Activity*: To become immersed in a task or project is to see time fly. Literally, time becomes of no concern. The activity is so engaging that other things happening nearby go completely unnoticed.

3. *Pay Attention to What Is Happening*: The performer who attains a state of flow is acutely aware of what is happening during the actual performance. He or she is sensitive to and tuned in to the experience and, at a conscious level, understands that something unusual is happening, similar to the runner's high.

4. *Enjoy the Immediate Experience*: The learner is captured in the moment and relishes the experience as unusual and worthy of conscious and subconscious attention. The performer who attains a state of flow remembers it and earnestly tries to recapture it time and time again.

Brainworks: Activities

Basic/Apprentice

Using the Stair Steps graphic (see Figure 6.10), track your learning of a sport and the skills involved in the developmental path of learning.

Advanced/Master

Recall a moment in your life when you may have experienced a peak performance or actually reached a state of flow. Share these experiences in a journal. Then plan a Future Flow Fantasy. Think about a hobby, activity, sport, career achievement, career change, retirement, avocation, or endeavor that you savor. Then make a plan to follow the steps for attaining a state of flow.

Brainstorms: Applications

Think about instances in the classroom that lend themselves to developing peak performances for students. Design an action plan of informing students about peak performances and attaining a state of flow. Encourage them to think about both and to relate instances when they think they are experiencing peak performances or flow.

Braindrain: REFLECTION

Reflect on the idea of peak performances with the Chain of Events graphic (see Figure 6.11), and track how the experience evolved.

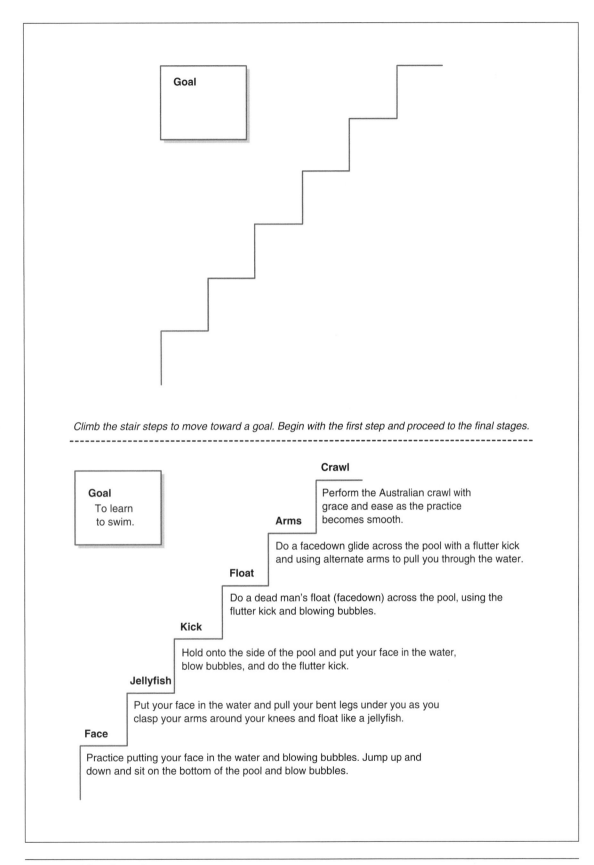

Climb the stair steps to move toward a goal. Begin with the first step and proceed to the final stages.

Goal
To learn
to swim.

Crawl

Perform the Australian crawl with grace and ease as the practice becomes smooth.

Arms

Do a facedown glide across the pool with a flutter kick and using alternate arms to pull you through the water.

Float

Do a dead man's float (facedown) across the pool, using the flutter kick and blowing bubbles.

Kick

Hold onto the side of the pool and put your face in the water, blow bubbles, and do the flutter kick.

Jellyfish

Put your face in the water and pull your bent legs under you as you clasp your arms around your knees and float like a jellyfish.

Face

Practice putting your face in the water and blowing bubbles. Jump up and down and sit on the bottom of the pool and blow bubbles.

Figure 6.10   Stair Steps

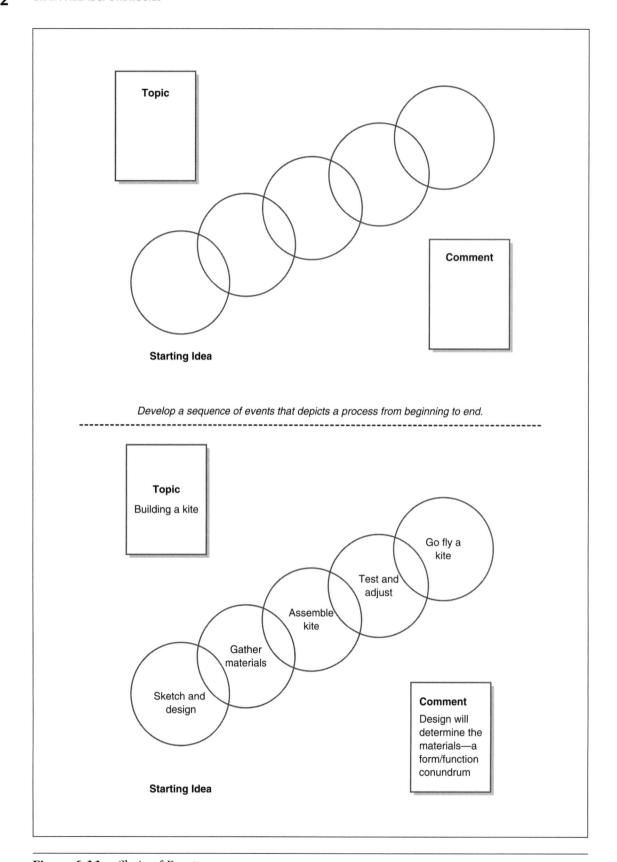

Figure 6.11 Chain of Events

Structuring the Interaction With Thinking 7

We are going to have to find ways of organizing ourselves cooperatively, sanely, scientifically, harmonically and in regenerative spontaneity with the rest of humanity around the earth. . . . We are not going to be able to operate our spaceship earth successfully nor for much longer unless we see it as a whole spaceship and our fate as common. It has to be everybody or nobody.

—R. Buckminster Fuller

In keeping with the constructivist theory of learning, which states that learning is constructed in the mind of each learner as that learner makes sense of new and incoming information, both active/engaged learning and experiential learning are paramount considerations. Active/engaged learning requires the intense, hands-on involvement of the learner; the learner is involved in inquiry, discovery, and exploration and actively interacts and engages with the materials or with others.

Experiential learning, on the other hand, is a total immersion model that involves the learner in more intense and holistic ways. Experiential learning is about field trips, museums, outdoor education, simulations, and role-plays, and it is becoming part and parcel of the learning scenario. It requires authentic, real-world experiences that convert to relevant learning. Learning is a function of experience, and the more experiences that can be orchestrated in the brain-compatible classroom, the more relevant and robust the learning will be.

BRAINWAVE #5: ACTIVE LEARNING

Vygotsky/Ausubel

Active learning is an integral part of constructivist theory of learning, which states that learners construct meaning in their minds. Learners process information in their brains and try to make sense of it by finding patterns and chunking bits of information together. The brain is a pattern-seeking mechanism and is constantly and continually searching for connections that make sense. Active learning facilitates that mental processing and the creation and strengthening of the neural pathways, and this holds the long-term learning.

Thus, in essence, constructivists promote active learning. They believe in intense and interactive methods for students to manage their own learning. The active learning models presented here foster interaction with other people (Vygotsky, 1978) and with information (Ausubel, 1978). Vygotsky's work suggests that learning occurs first during social interaction and then internally in the mind of the learner, while Ausubel's work with advanced organizers makes a case for interacting with the information on hand and representing that information in visual formats that help clarify and illuminate the meanings.

The focus of this active learning section is on using cooperative structures (e.g., think-pair-share, jigsaw) and employing graphic or visual organizers (e.g., mind maps, webbing strategies). The strategies are delineated with discussions and examples. The purpose, of course, is to present a repertoire of ideas to mix and match within the instructional and curricular frames of the brain-compatible classroom. Eventually, once students have been introduced to a spectrum of cooperative strategies and myriad graphic tools, they can take responsibility for selecting and using the tools and techniques themselves. Students can decide which cooperative strategies or graphic tools are most appropriate for the tasks at hand, and they can even create their own graphic organizers to delineate the information they have.

Cooperative learning strategies make thinking and learning audible. Graphic organizers make thinking and learning visible. Both are invaluable tools of the brain-compatible classroom.

BRAINWISE	**STATEMENTS**

- Two brains are better than one.
- Mind over matter.
- Learning is a function of experience.

Braindrops: Strategies

If two heads are better than one, why not practice what the adage so insightfully states? When students interact with each other verbally, the dialogue acts as a rehearsal for their thinking. Just as Vygotsky (1978) hypothesizes, understanding comes first within the context of the social realm, and then it is internalized into long-term memory with deep understanding. An example is when a person verbally tries out an idea on someone else and has difficulty putting her ideas into words. Later, the more she thinks about it, the clearer the idea becomes. And the next time she tries to talk about it, the words come more easily. It is the active conversation with another and the responses and questions that are returned that push the thinking and foster understanding for both the learner and the listener. Cooperative learning groups are natural structures for this kind of verbal exchange. In cooperative groups, learners hear what others are thinking and speak about what they themselves are thinking.

In turn, the use of graphic organizers creates a similar rehearsal for thinking, but in this case the thinking is visually oriented. The cognitive rehearsal is the reason for, and underlies the importance of, structuring social interactions for analyzing and synthesizing information with graphic organizers. Figure 7.1 outlines the active learning strategies discussed in this chapter.

Teacher Decisions for Cooperative Groups

While there are various cooperative learning structures (Kagan, 1992) and groupings to use when they are appropriate to the planned activity, certain decisions permeate every cooperative group activity (see Figure 7.2). The decisions concern the size of the group (two to four people is ideal), the roles and responsibilities of the members, the expectations for the task, the social skills to address (communication, leadership, etc.), the time allowance, the product or result of the learning, and how the teams are to reflect on their teamwork and the quality of their work. The following discussion unpacks these critical decisions in more detail.

Cooperative Strategies

- Turn to Your Partner and . . . (TTYPA)
- Think-Pair-Share
- 2-4-8 Focus Interview
- Cooperative Groups
- Jigsaw
- Expert Jigsaw
- The Three Musketeers
- Cooperative Learning Tear Share

Graphic Organizers

- Seesaw
- Playoffs
- Bubble Quotes
- Comparison Alley
- Starburst
- The Funnel
- Chain of Events
- The Puzzler
- The Tri Pie
- Bridges
- Stair Steps
- Mind Wind
- Brain Drops
- Go to Your Corners
- Drop-Down Menu
- Mind Map
- Venn
- Web
- Flow Chart
- Right Angle

Figure 7.1 Active Learning Strategies

- Size
- Roles and responsibilities
- Task
- Social skills
- Time
- Product
- Reflection process

Figure 7.2   Teacher Decisions for Cooperative Groups

Size

The first decision teachers must make is about the size of the group. In determining the best number, they consider the students, the task, the time, and the goal. For teachers new to cooperative learning, it may be advisable to begin with twosomes. It's hard to drop out of a twosome, and the discipline concerns are lessened when the group size is small.

R. Johnson and Johnson (1982) advocate for groups of three. They feel that three in a group provides for diversity as well as manageability. Threesomes also allow a pair to interact in some way with the third person standing aside from the action, observing and providing feedback to the pair.

Kagan (1992), on the other hand, promotes groups of four as the ideal. Four in a group provides more opportunity for diversity and, according to Kagan, makes it easy to divide the four into partners for various parts of the interaction.

Seldom is it advisable to have a group of more than five. It's just too hard to manage and too easy for one or two of the members to not participate by "hitchhiking" out of the group cooperation.

Roles and Responsibilities

Although it is not necessary to assign member roles for cooperative tasks, doing so communicates explicit expectations and inserts a certain amount of order into the teams' work. Roles often delineate the responsibilities of each member. In addition, assigning roles implies that each member is an important part of the group and encourages individual accountability. Furthermore, this idea ties into the concept of belonging, which is one of the overriding affective benefits of cooperative learning. For a comprehensive listing of suggested member roles, see Figure 7.3.

Task

Teachers usually determine the task required of the cooperative groups, ranging from learning vocabulary words to completing a history project to producing a dramatic performance to executing a lab experiment. Depending on how extensive the task is, teachers also decide how much or how little instructional scaffolding the situation warrants. Of course, the more they use cooperative learning work, the more skilled they become at making these determinations.

General Group

- Task leader: Encourages group in task
- Observer/timekeeper: Observes group process
- Recorder: Writes and records
- Materials manager: Gets what is needed

Mathematics Group

- Calculator: Checks work on calculator
- Analyst: Analyzes strategies
- Bookkeeper: Checks answers and records time
- Inventory controller: Keeps inventories on materials and controls supplies

Writer's Group

- Editor in chief: Tracks progress and sets deadlines
- Publisher: Sets guidelines
- Scribe: Keeps notes
- Author: Supplies the materials

Novel Group

- Discussion leader: Prepares and leads questions
- Vocabulary enricher: Selects enrichment questions
- Literary illuminary: Reads favored passages
- Agent: Gets materials

Social Studies Group

- Presiding officer: Presides over the group
- Parliamentarian: Observes group behavior
- Secretary: Records information
- Sergeant at arms: Keeps the time and gets materials

Science Group

- Scientist: Observes progress and keeps time
- Researcher: Provides guidelines
- Observer: Records information
- Lab technician: Sets up materials and equipment

Primary Group

- Captain: Encourages group
- Umpire: Observes and reports
- Scorekeeper: Writes down information
- Runner: Gets what is needed

Figure 7.3   Cooperative Groups: Suggested Member Roles

Social Skills

A critical element of cooperative learning that sets it apart from other kinds of small-group work is the explicit attention to and instruction in social skills. Teachers continually and consistently target skill development in four distinct areas: leadership, communication, conflict resolution, and teamwork. Within these four areas, the skills are labeled, described, modeled, and practiced with specific feedback from teachers. Over time, the whole range of social skills is taught as part of the process standards or life skills.

Time

There's a saying that the more time students are given to do a task, the more time they take. Based on that belief, and from observation of this very phenomenon, the recommendation is to structure time tightly. Teachers can always do a spot check and add a few minutes to the time allotment if it seems necessary, but if they overextend the time needed, discipline problems may erupt in the groups that finish early.

Product

The expectations for a final product or performance must be clearly understood by each group and each group member. This is the result of the group interaction, the evidence of group learning, and the indicator of the quality of the work produced. The final product or performance provides needed accountability for groups. If they are going to work together, they are responsible for an observable result.

Products range from inventions in science class to relief maps in geography to puppets in language arts to research reports in music. Performances span the spectrum from readings in literature class to lab experiments in chemistry to demonstrations in math. Each product or performance provides the proverbial proof in the pudding.

Reflection Process

Last, but certainly not least, is the decision about how to help students process reflectively the work they've done. This includes processing at several different levels and in several different ways. The levels of reflection include affective processing (How does it feel? What do you like or not like?), cognitive processing (What answers did you get?), and metacognitive processing (How might you connect this to something you already know? How might you use this in the future?).

Processing might occur in the whole group, in a small group, or for an individual. Teachers lead whole-group processing by questioning and sampling responses from the various groups. Small-group processing is structured by teachers, but the discussion occurs and is monitored within the small-group framework. Individual processing is often done through journals, logs, and student portfolios.

BUILD Components/Cooperative Strategies

These cooperative structure decisions have been organized around the BUILD acronym by Bellanca and Fogarty (2002):

Build in higher-order thinking with complex tasks.

Unite teams through a common goal.

Insist on individual accountability within the group work.

Look over, reflect, and discuss the task and the teamwork.

Develop social skills in the context of the group work.

While resources abound in the area of cooperative learning—ranging from Johnson, Johnson, and Holubec's (1986) conceptual work to Kagan's (1992) structures, to Slavin's (1983) work with team tasks and content, to Sharan and Sharan's (1976) work on group investigations—the complementary resource reference here is *Blueprints for Achievement in the Cooperative Classroom,* by Bellanca and Fogarty (2002).

The following selection of group strategies is presented for immediate use in the brain-compatible classroom.

Turn to Your Partner and . . . (TTYPA; Weaver & Cotrell, 1986)

TTYPA is a simple, informal interactive strategy that teachers can use as "pause and think" time during a longer discussion, lecture, film, and so forth. This strategy signals the brain to tune in and think by creating a need for dialogue. In this way, both inner and outer thinking are fostered to illuminate personally developing ideas.

Think-Pair-Share (Lyman & McTighe, 1988)

Students work with partners to think on their own, put their heads together, and share their ideas with each other and other pairs. Sometimes the pair is even required to agree on one idea to share. This is a viable strategy for getting students to think first and then to talk and share their ideas in a safe setting with one other person. It is more formal than TTYPA.

2-4-8 Focus Interview (Fogarty & Bellanca, 1993)

This interview invites interaction, first, between two people, A and B, to talk and listen. Then A and B join two others, C and D, to create a foursome. In the foursome, A tells about B, B about A, and so on. The four people have to listen in the first interaction in order to share in the second grouping. Then the foursome joins another foursome to create a group of eight. Again, in this larger group, no one tells his or her own story, but each instead shares one they have not told before. The 2-4-8 Focus Interview sets the scene for listening to each other and paraphrasing and synthesizing information because as the group grows, the stories get shorter.

Cooperative Groups (D. Johnson, Johnson, & Holubec, 1986)

In cooperative groups, students are formally assigned to groups of three or four. Care is taken to make the groups as heterogeneous as possible—the more diverse the group, the richer the thinking. In addition, roles (recorder, reporter, etc.) and responsibilities are sorted out, either by teacher assignment or through some structured scheme such as drawing a card or number. The task, time, tools, and so on are clarified; the social skill is targeted; and the groups get to work. After completing the task, the groups share their products with each other by sampling ideas or by sharing with one other group. Then they take a moment to reflect about their group work.

Jigsaw (Aronson, 1978)

The jigsaw strategy (see Figure 7.4) is a division of labor in which several students work in a group and each takes one part of the puzzle or task to complete. When the students finish and they have each contributed their part of the

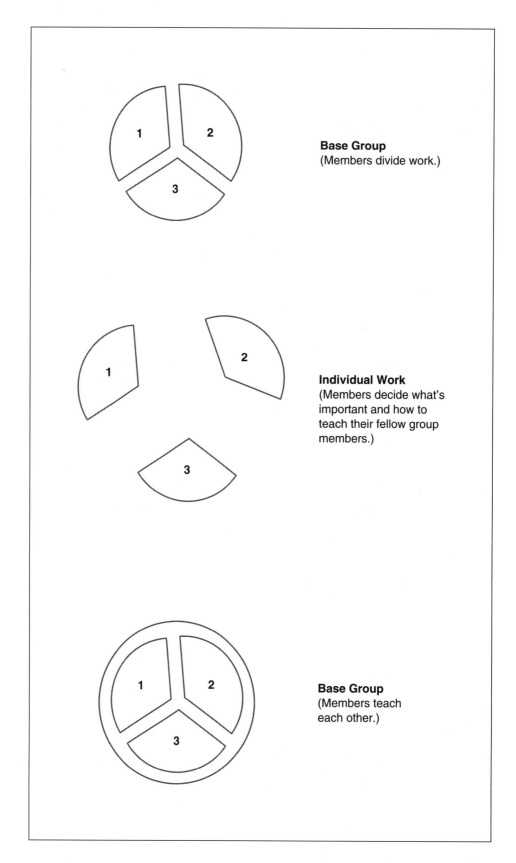

Figure 7.4 Jigsaw

jigsaw, all the pieces of the puzzle come together. In this way, the members of the group must trust each other and be interdependent in achieving their goal.

The key to the jigsaw is when students bring the pieces together. As the saying goes, each one must teach one. Many people know that it is through teaching that the one who teaches truly understands what it is that he or she is teaching. If someone is responsible to teach another, the one doing the teaching really digs in and ferrets out a clear understanding, because it's hard to teach something you don't understand.

However, the key to an effective jigsaw is for teachers to help students focus on two areas: what is important to share about their piece of the puzzle and how students might share that information so that it is memorable. Often, by requiring students to use at least three multiple intelligences in the teaching round with their group members, the teacher fosters effective sharing of the pieces of the puzzle.

Thus, the power in the jigsaw is in helping students decide what they need to share in the jigsaw and how they can share it so that every group member understands it. The jigsaw is a somewhat sophisticated strategy and may need a lot of scaffolding by teachers.

Expert Jigsaw (Aronson, 1978)

Just like the jigsaw, in the expert jigsaw the work is divided among the base group members. However, in the expert jigsaw (see Figure 7.5), members from each base group who have the same part come together as experts on that one part. Together, the expert group works to decide what is important to take back to the base groups and how the members will share that information.

For example, if the base groups jigsaw three parts (ones, twos, and threes), the ones from all the base groups meet, as do all of the twos and all of the threes. After doing preliminary work in the expert groups, the members return to their base groups to do the teaching rounds. In this way, the base group members have the advantage of collaborating on each of their jigsawed parts.

The Three Musketeers

This is a cooperative learning strategy to form small groups quickly. The students are asked to put one hand in the air, find two other students, and form a teepee with their raised hands. Once they are in the threesome, they put their hands down and get ready for the task. At this point, the teacher asks students to discuss the focus topic or theme. For example, the teacher might ask them to discuss the hardest problem in their homework or the one thing they remember from yesterday's lesson.

Cooperative Learning Tear Share

In groups of four, all members read and write answers to four questions; then they jigsaw summaries of each of the questions. This is the most engaging cooperative learning activity that can be modeled in a professional development setting. In teams of four, count off 1, 2, 3, and 4. Each member has an 8" × 11" sheet of paper, folded into fourths and with the corners numbered 1, 2, 3, and 4.

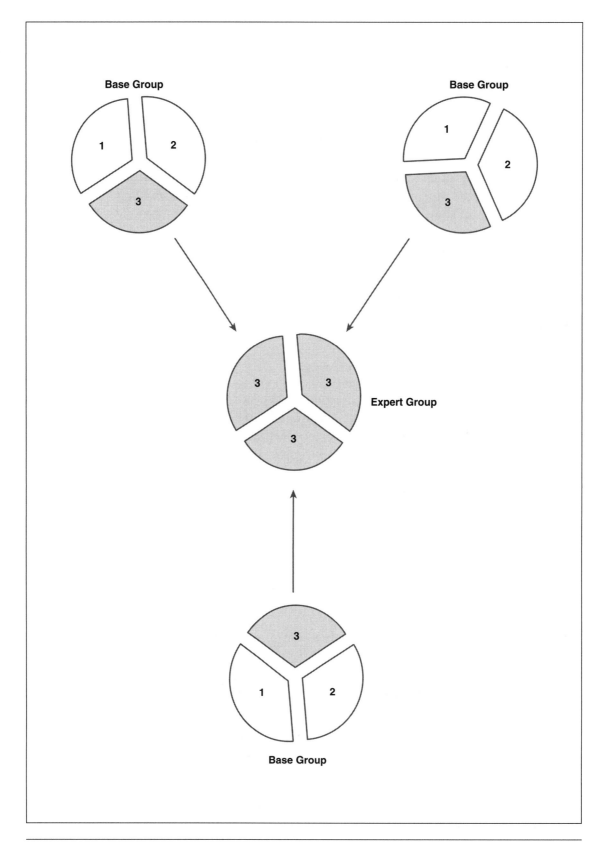

Figure 7.5 Expert Jigsaw

In each corner, write one of the four questions from the board, which are related to the reading to follow. Then, all four members read an article or passage from a text (not too much reading, three to four minutes) and gives written answers to all four questions. When done answering the questions, they tear their papers into four corners and pass all of the 1s to Member #1 and so on.

Member #1 has four pieces of paper with answers to Question #1.

Member #2 has four pieces of paper with answers to Question #2.

Member #3 has four pieces of paper with answers to Question #3.

Member #4 has four pieces of paper with answers to Question #4.

At this point, all members take a minute to read over the answers and prepare an oral summary of the answers. When all members of the group are ready, Member #1 gives an oral summary of the four answers to his or her question, and the process continues until all have shared. For example, Shel Silverstein's (1974) poem "Smart" is perfect to use for the Tear Share. Participants read the poem, answer four higher-order questions (e.g., Do you agree or disagree with the title of the poem? What inference can you make from the last line?) and summarize their group of answers.

Graphic Organizers

The use of graphic organizers is a strategy often seen in today's classrooms. Graphic organizers are the interaction with information that makes the thinking visible to students. The organizers most common among the available spectrum are the concept map (or mind map), the web, the Venn diagram, the sequence or flow chart, and the right-angle thinking model. Students are familiar with these and are often expected to use them in their cooperative group work. When they use them in small groups, they may draw the graphics on large newsprint and create a model for the group to work with. Because the drawing is large enough for everyone in the small group to see, the activity invites participation by all members. It also gives them a tool to use as they do their thinking.

While teachers often are the ones to assign a particular graphic, eventually, after the students have been introduced to a repertoire of graphic organizers, the groups should decide on the most appropriate organizer to use to represent the information at hand. This empowers students to consider how they want to represent their thinking.

There are 24 graphic organizers presented in Figure 7.6. They are then presented individually in Figures 7.7–7.30 for teachers and students to play around with and, hopefully, to spark further ideas for students to generate original graphics to suit their needs. Figures 7.7–7.30 each show a completed example as well as a blank graphic for duplication or reproduction on large paper.

(Text continued on page 159)

Figure 7.6 Overview of Graphic Organizers

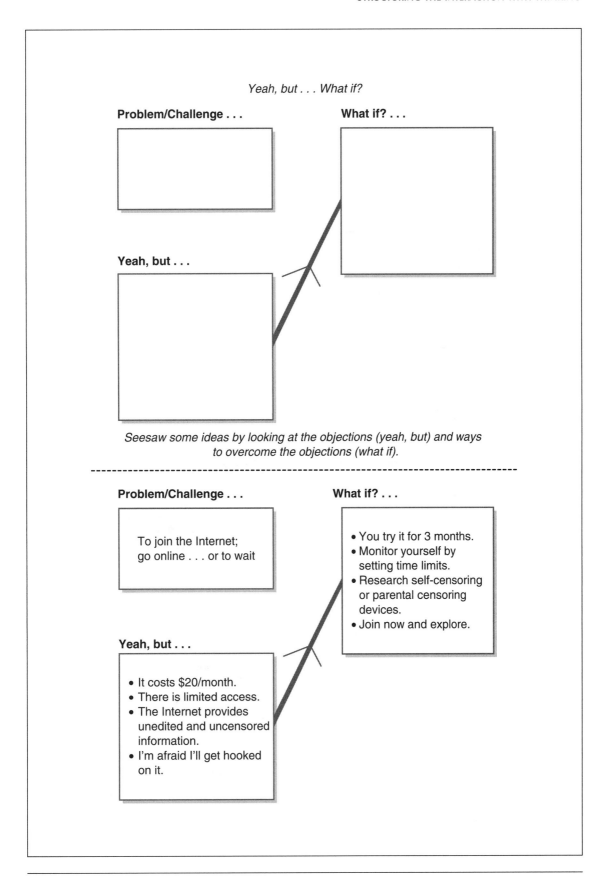

Figure 7.7   Seesaw

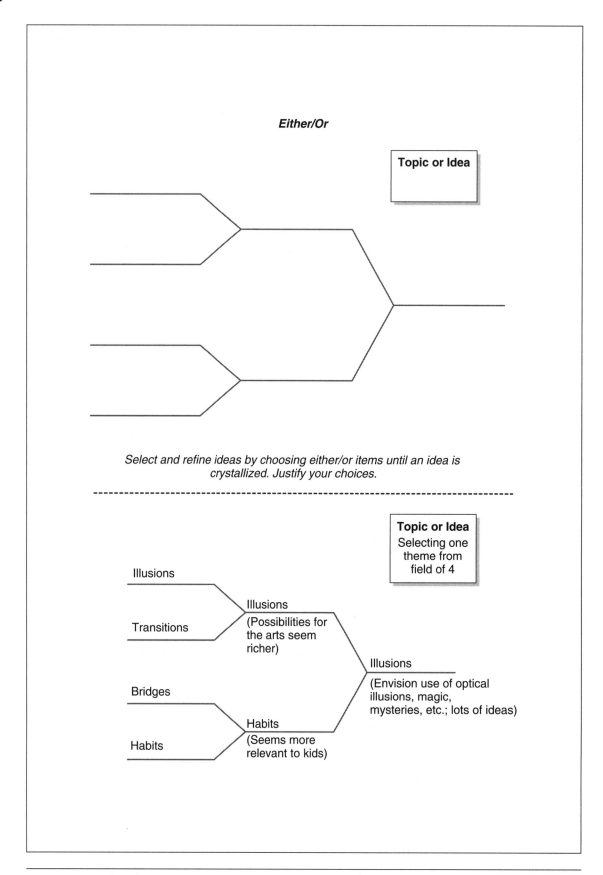

Figure 7.8 Playoffs

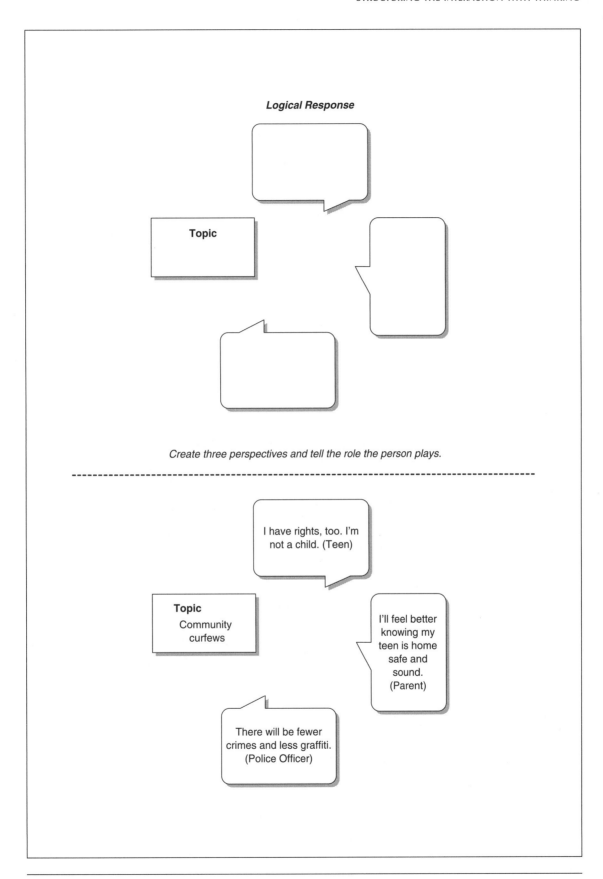

Figure 7.9   Bubble Quotes

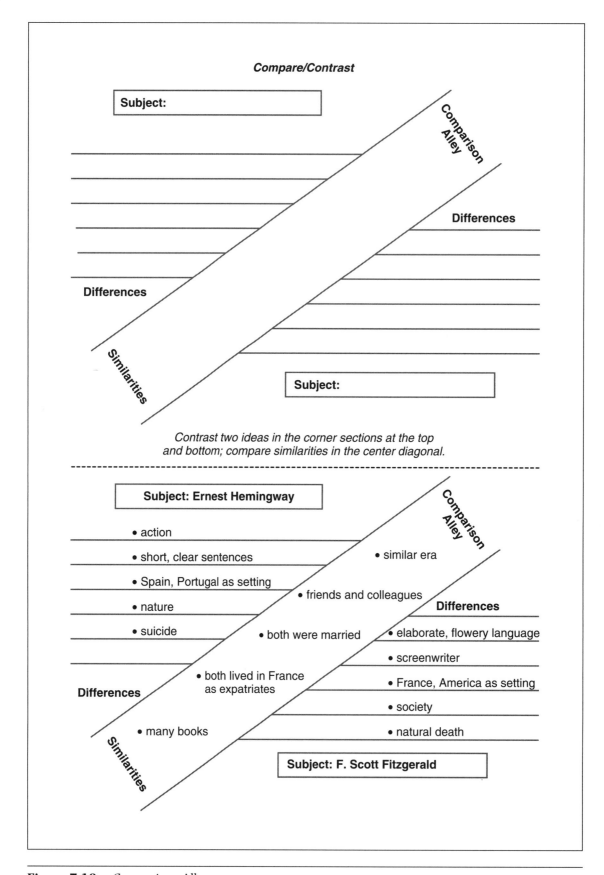

Figure 7.10 Comparison Alley

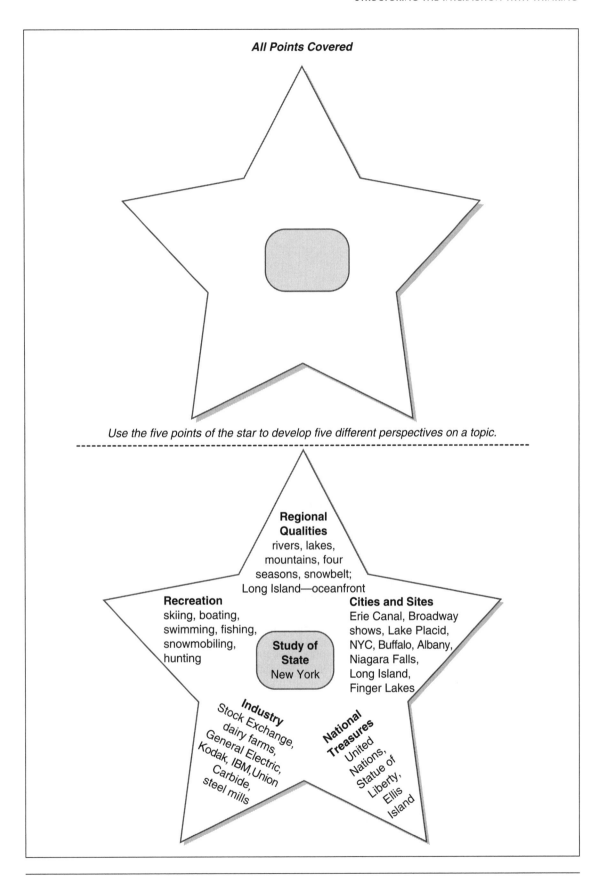

All Points Covered

Use the five points of the star to develop five different perspectives on a topic.

Regional Qualities
rivers, lakes, mountains, four seasons, snowbelt; Long Island—oceanfront

Recreation
skiing, boating, swimming, fishing, snowmobiling, hunting

Cities and Sites
Erie Canal, Broadway shows, Lake Placid, NYC, Buffalo, Albany, Niagara Falls, Long Island, Finger Lakes

Study of State
New York

Industry
Stock Exchange, dairy farms, General Electric, Kodak, IBM, Union Carbide, steel mills

National Treasures
United Nations, Statue of Liberty, Ellis Island

Figure 7.11   Starburst

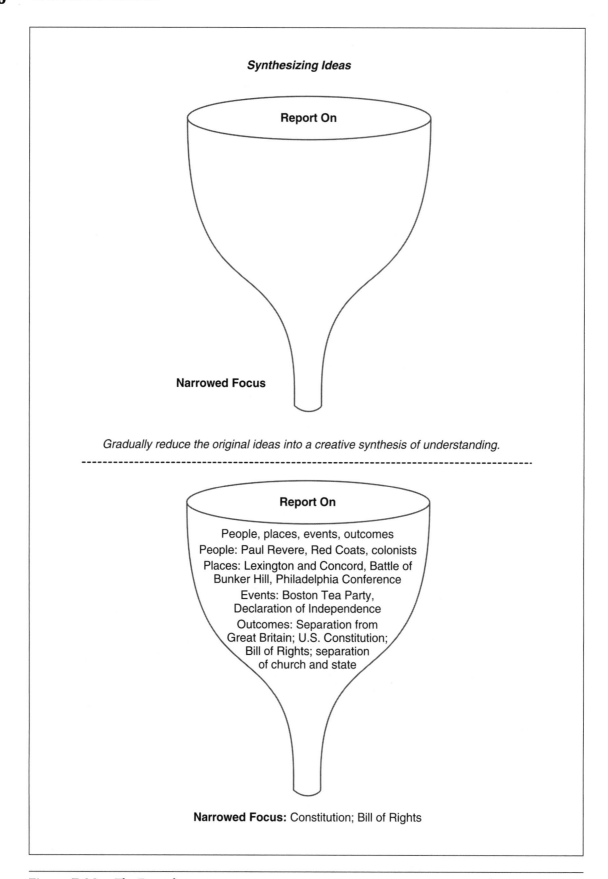

Synthesizing Ideas

Report On

Narrowed Focus

Gradually reduce the original ideas into a creative synthesis of understanding.

Report On

People, places, events, outcomes
People: Paul Revere, Red Coats, colonists
Places: Lexington and Concord, Battle of
Bunker Hill, Philadelphia Conference
Events: Boston Tea Party,
Declaration of Independence
Outcomes: Separation from
Great Britain; U.S. Constitution;
Bill of Rights; separation
of church and state

Narrowed Focus: Constitution; Bill of Rights

Figure 7.12   The Funnel

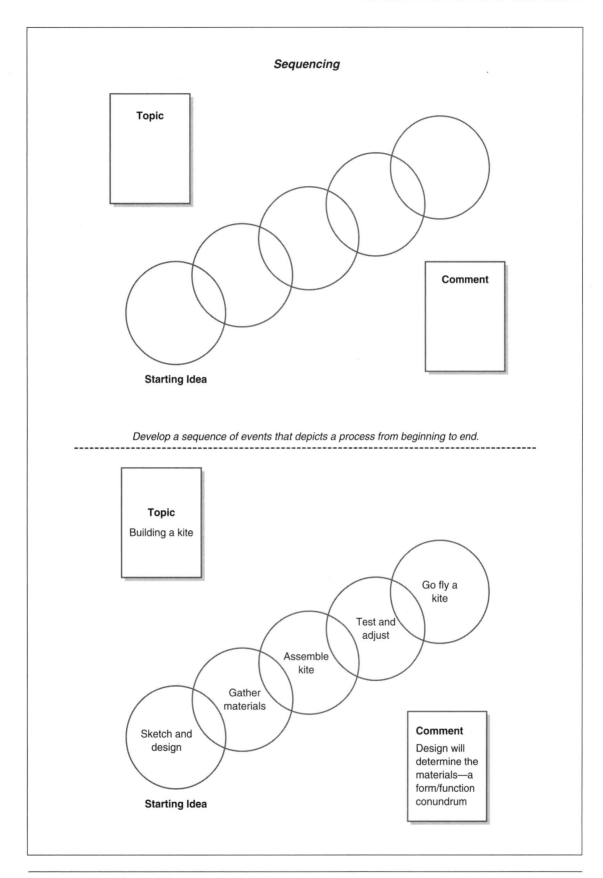

Figure 7.13 Chain of Events

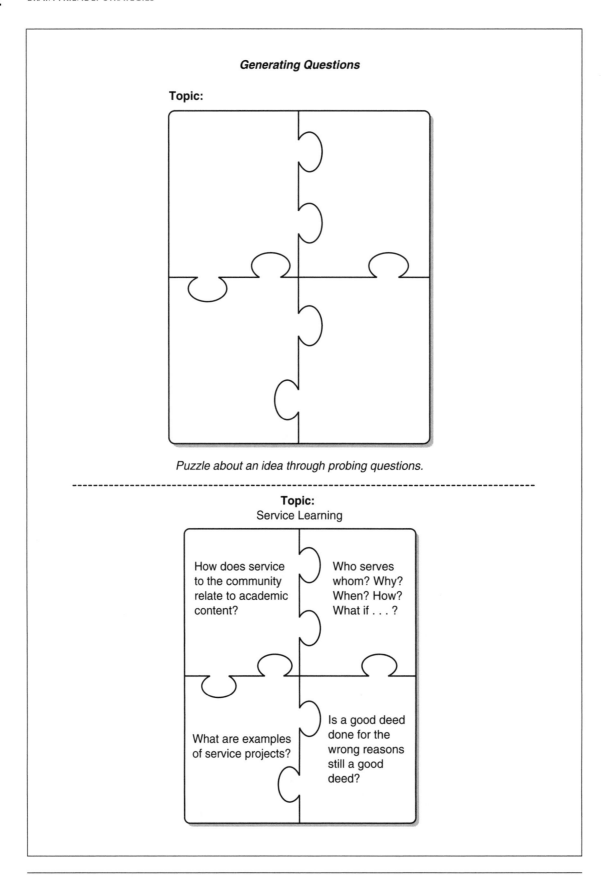

Generating Questions

Topic:

Puzzle about an idea through probing questions.

- -

Topic:
Service Learning

How does service to the community relate to academic content?

Who serves whom? Why? When? How? What if . . . ?

What are examples of service projects?

Is a good deed done for the wrong reasons still a good deed?

Figure 7.14 The Puzzler

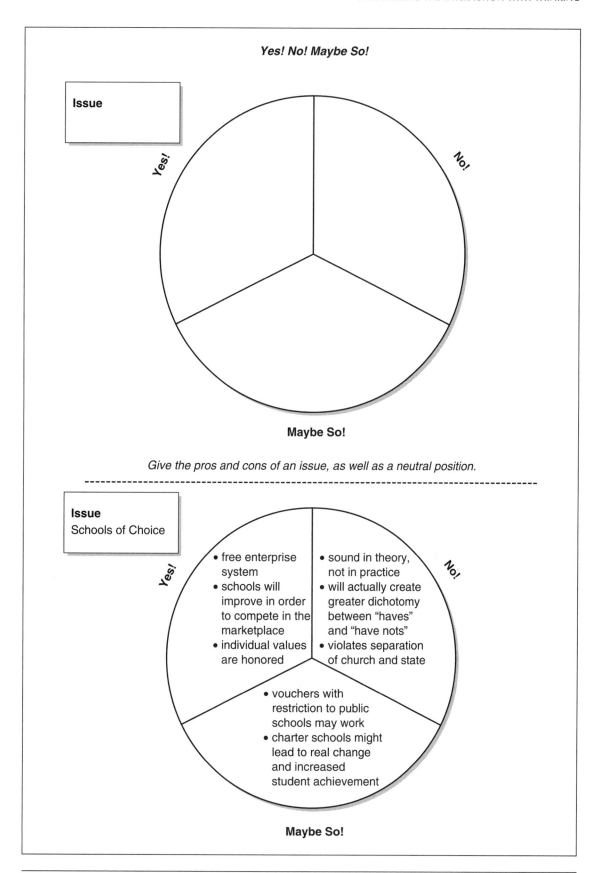

Figure 7.15 The Tri Pie

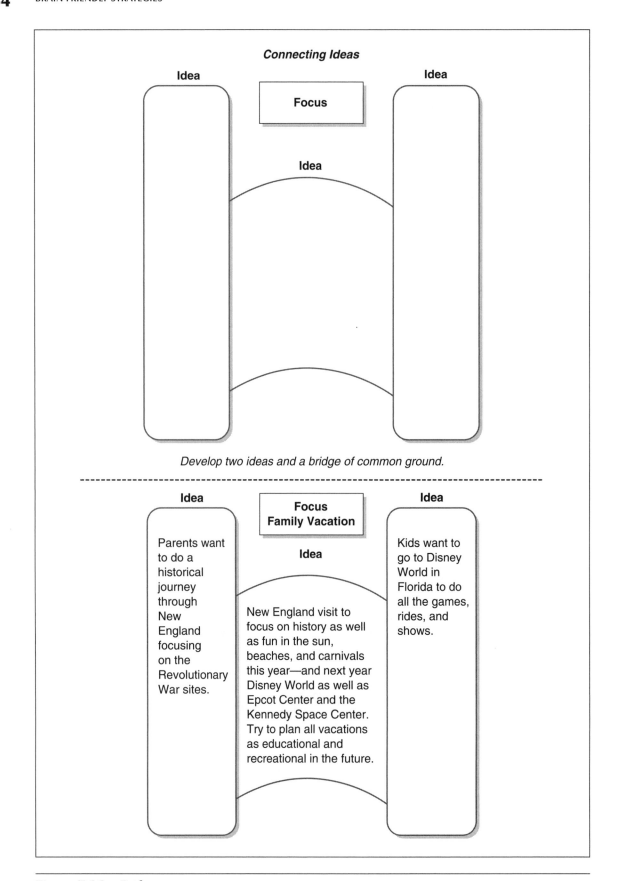

Figure 7.16 Bridges

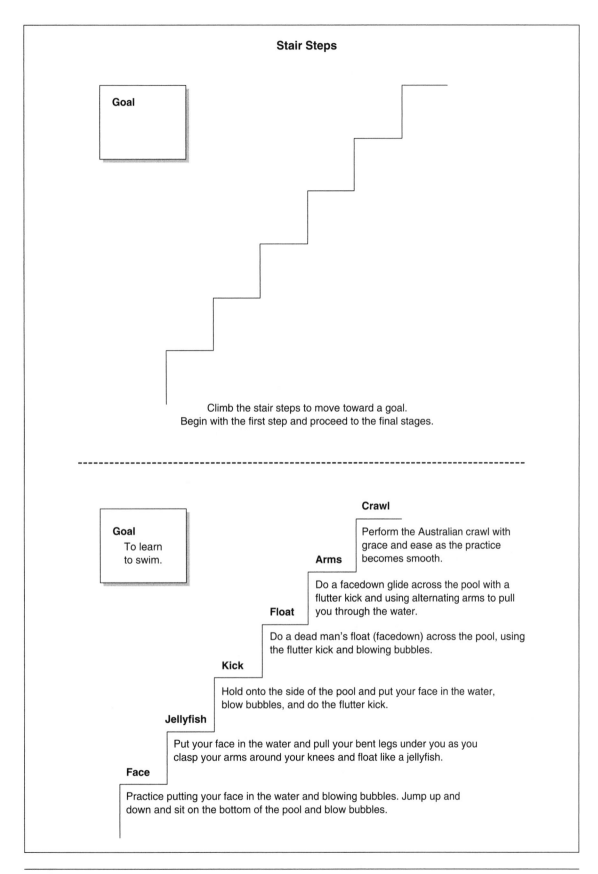

Figure 7.17   Stair Steps

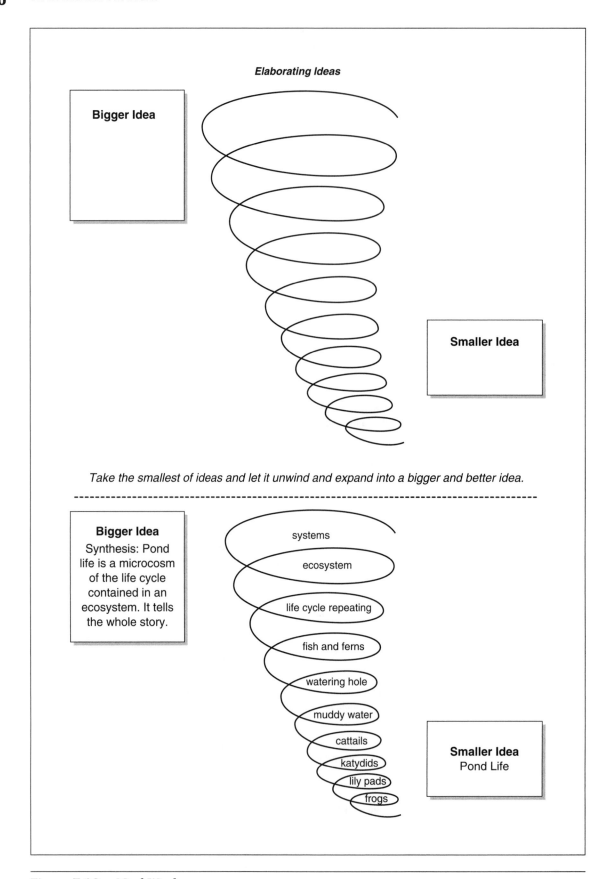

Figure 7.18   Mind Wind

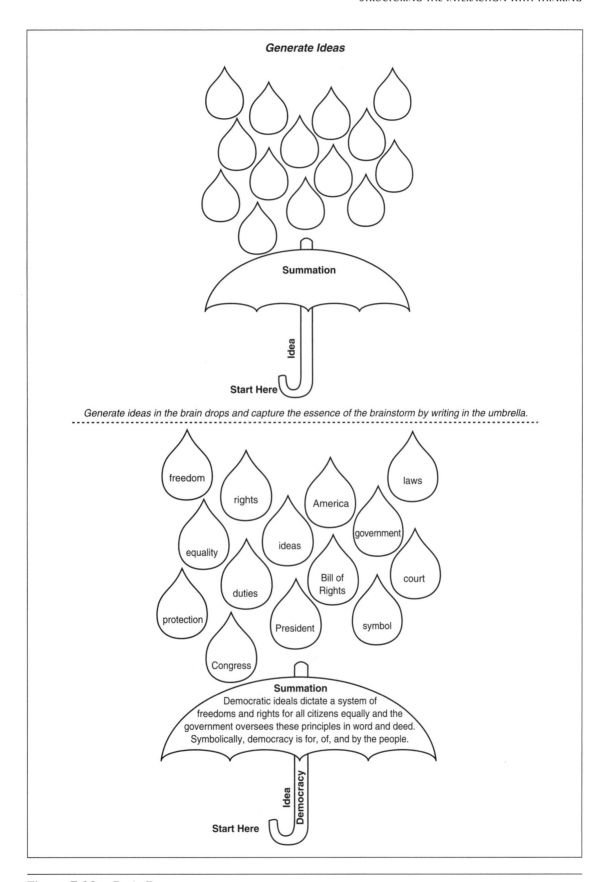

Figure 7.19   Brain Drops

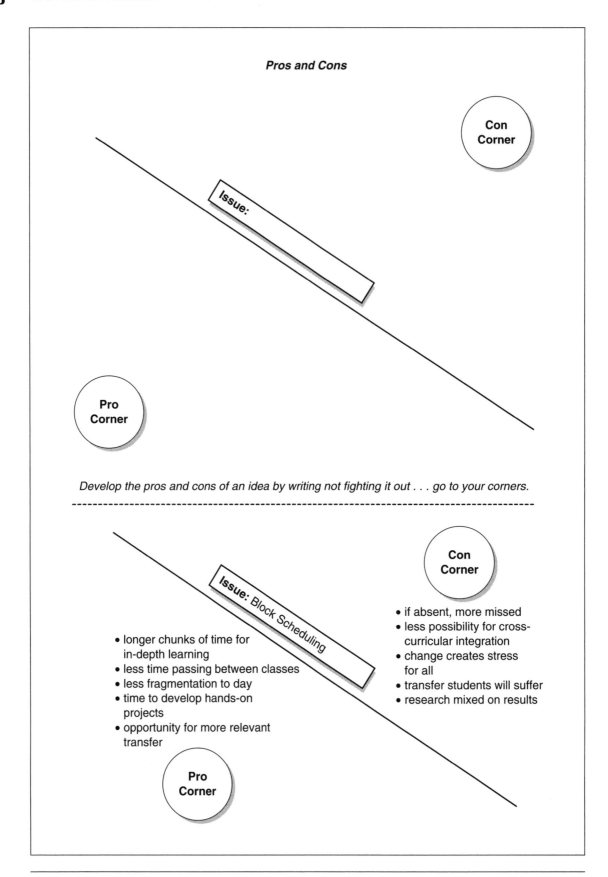

Figure 7.20 Go to Your Corners

Generating Options

Task or Goal:

Menu of Presentation Options

- -

Task or Goal:
Read a biography and present vital information to others in the class.

Menu of Presentation Options

Puppet Show Presentation

Quotations on Tape

Comic Strip

Role-Play

Video Program

Interview Format

Multimedia Presentation

Figure 7.21   Drop-Down Menu

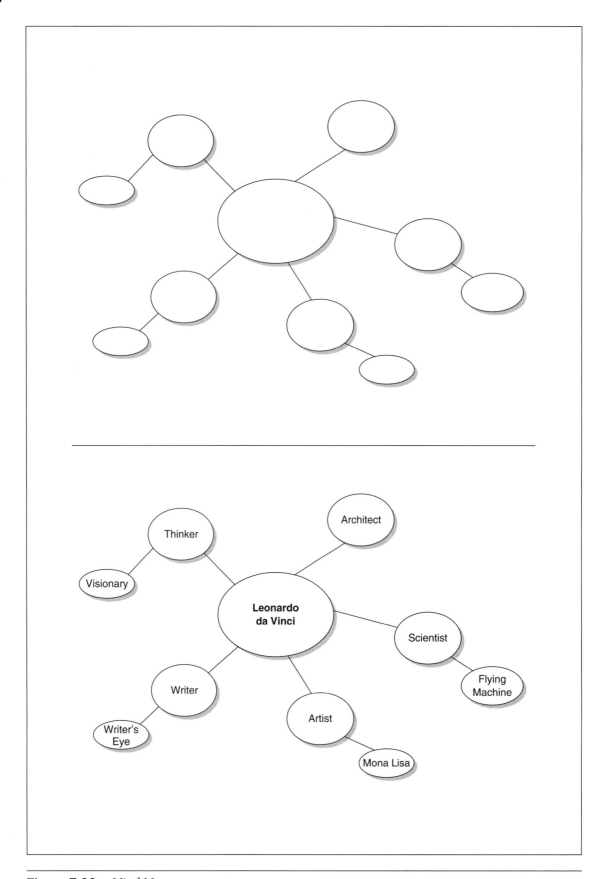

Figure 7.22 Mind Map

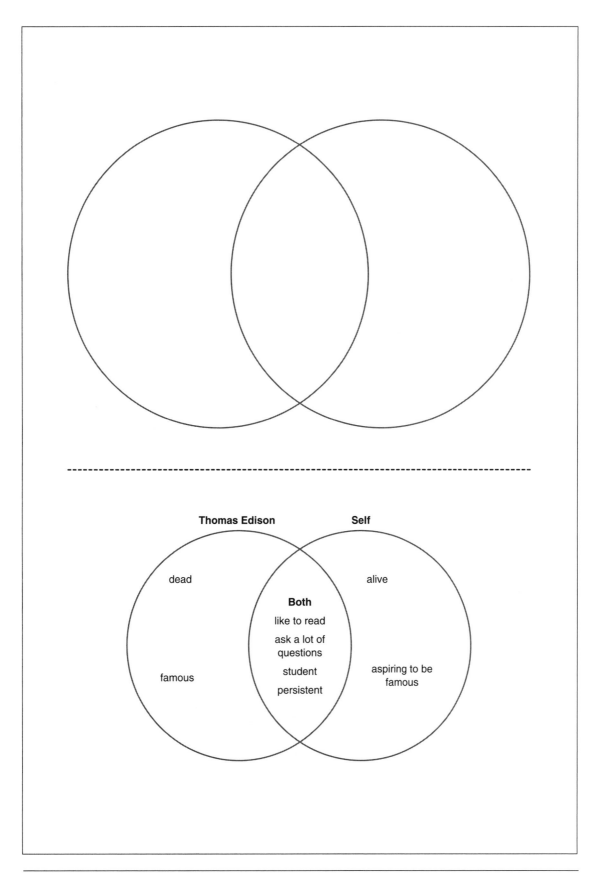

Figure 7.23 Venn

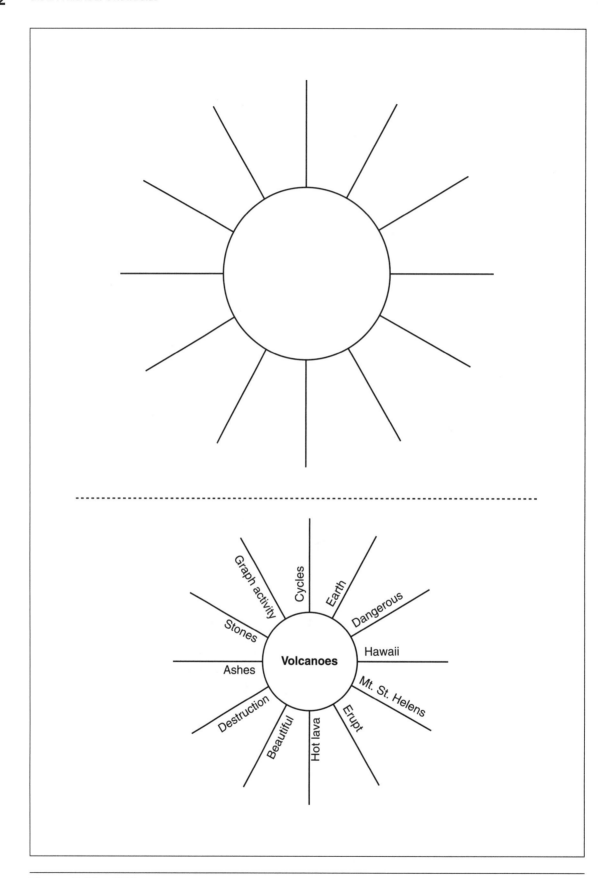

Figure 7.24 Web

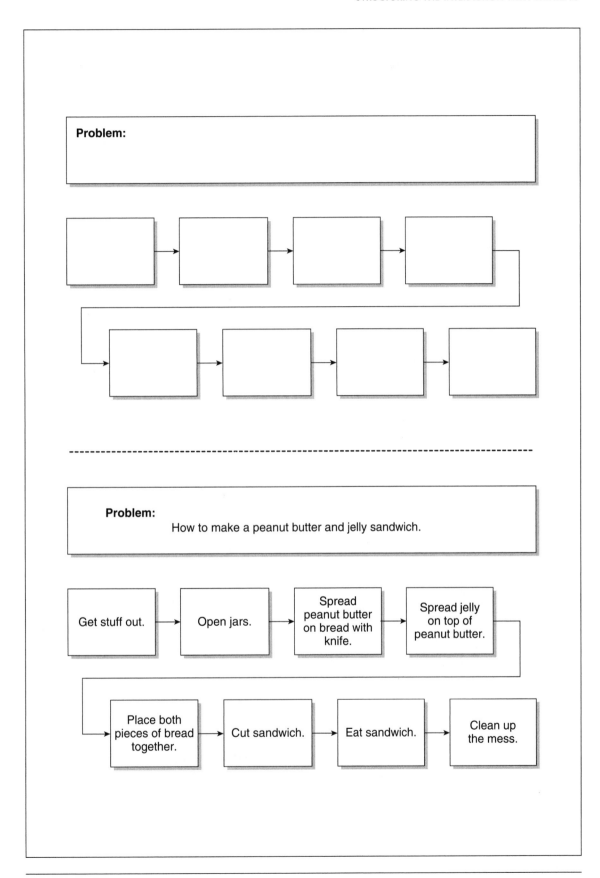

Figure 7.25   Flowchart

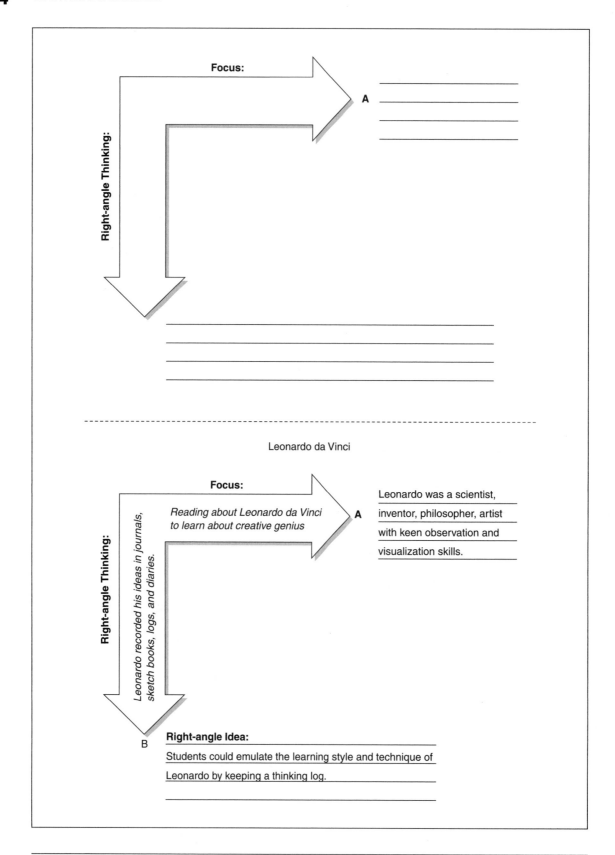

Figure 7.26 Right Angle

NOTE: The right angle idea is a serendipitous thought that you want to capture for later scrutiny.

Brainstorming

Topic:

A	N
B	O
C	P
D	Q
E	R
F	S
G	T
H	U
I	V
J	W
K	X
L	Y
M	Z

Brainstorm by matching each letter of the alphabet with a word that describes the topic.

Comprehension

Asking questions	**N**ow I get it!
Beautiful Mind	**O**pinion
Can apply	**P**aying attention
Describe	**Q**uestions
Explaining	**R**eview
Facts	**S**ort facts
Grasp	**T**he "gist"
How to do it	**U**nderstanding
Inquiry	**V**ocabulary
Just get it	**W**ords
Knowing	**X**cellent!
Listening	**Y**ou know!
Make sense of	**Z**estful

Figure 7.27 ABC Graffiti

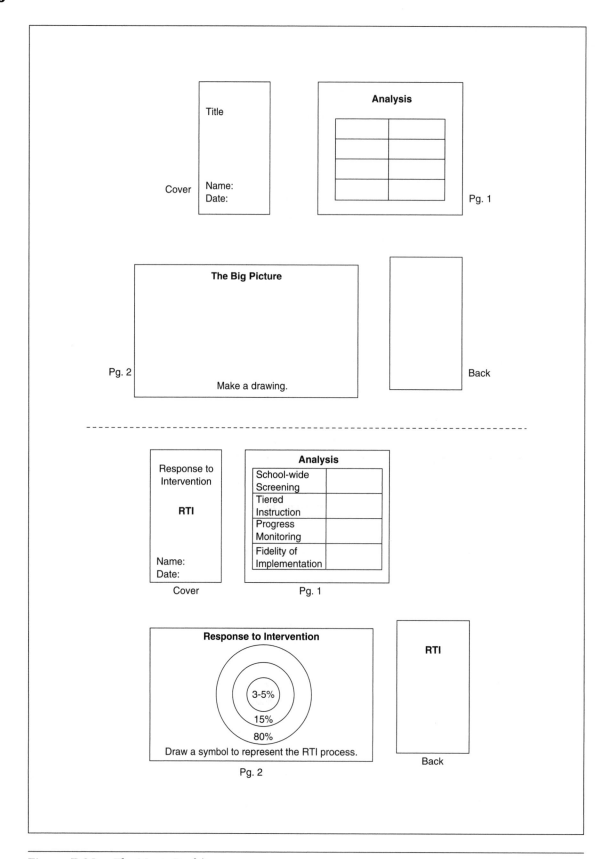

Figure 7.28 The Magic Book*

*For complete instructions on making the Magic Book, visit www.robinfogarty.com

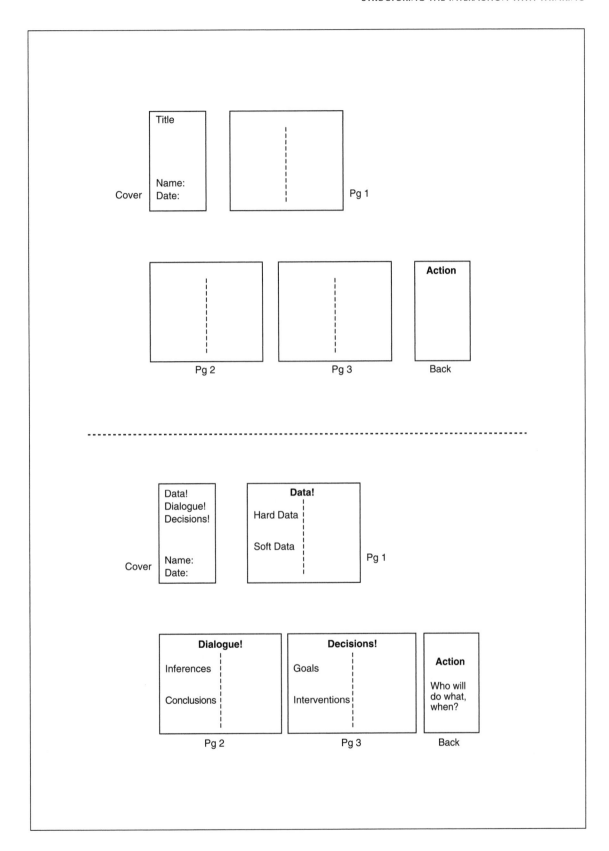

Figure 7.29 The Little Book*

*For complete instructions on making the Little Book, visit www.robinfogarty.com

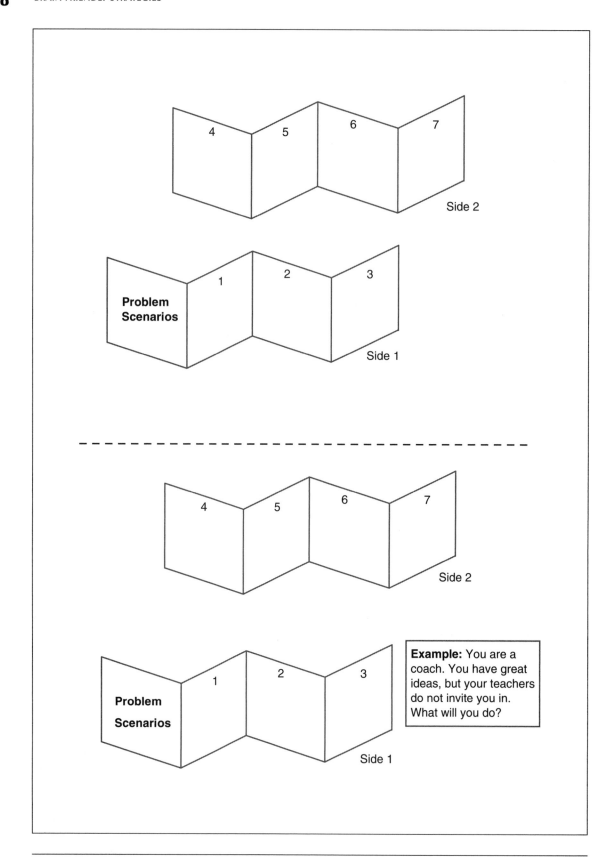

Figure 7.30   The Accordion Book*

*For complete instructions on making the Accordion Book, visit www.robinfogarty.com

ABC Graffiti

Using the alphabet as the graphic or advance organizer, teams focus on the designated target word or concept and brainstorm phrases, synonyms, or connections for each letter of the alphabet. The paper that they use (see Figure 7.27) is folded into two columns, and each column has an alphabetical listing from A to Z. With this structure, teams can brainstorm freely. They do not have to complete the list in alphabetical order; they just need to be sure to complete the full list of 26.

Magic Book

The Magic Book (see Figure 7.28) is also a foldable and can be used to both analyze and synthesize information with higher-order thinking strategies. The inner "hidden" panels help students take ideas apart, while the hidden magic page is large enough to synthesize the big picture. The magic, of course, is in the hidden pages that magically appear as the folds are manipulated. Here are the directions for creating the Magic Book:

1. Each person needs two single sheets of paper.

2. Fold the first sheet in half like a hamburger bun, and tear it in half.

3. Save one half and tear it in half again, making two strips of equal length and width. Save the two strips and put the other half aside.

4. Take the second whole sheet of paper, and fold it in half like a hamburger bun.

5. Fold both sides back toward the center fold, creating "wings" or the letter W if you look at it from the end.

6. Grasp the middle section of the same piece of paper between the two wings, and mark off two spots to create thirds.

7. Tear the two marked spots through the fold to the mark. When you are done, the paper should look like three teeth of the jack-o-lantern.

8. Open the torn paper, lay it flat like a mat, and weave the two strips through the cut sections. Be sure that one strip goes under the middle section and the other goes over the middle section.

9. After the weaving is done, refold the book together with the six sections in the middle, pressing it to get the puffiness out of it.

10. Carefully find the middle fold, and using your two thumbs, tug the two sections apart as you open to the six sections. Close it again.

11. Carefully find the two edges or wings beneath the six-sectioned middle, and pull those far edges out. As the pages flip, you will see the big magic page hidden behind the six sections.

12. The Magic Book is ready for the note-taking activity.

Little Book

This "foldable" also is used as the graphic or advance organizer. The Little Book (see Figure 7.29) can be used in the classroom to capture ideas and to mark key points and the organization of those points. Here are the directions for creating the Little Book:

1. Fold a sheet of paper in half the short way (a hamburger bun or a taco fold). Then fold it in half again, and fold it in half one more time. When you open the paper, it will have eight sections.

2. Fold the paper again as in the first part of Step 1. Keep the fold at the top, and tear along the center vertical through the fold to the horizontal mark halfway down. If you do this correctly, when you unfold the paper there should be a hole in the middle that you can look through.

3. After the tear has been made, refold the paper the long way, like a hot dog bun or burrito. The fold and the hole will now be on the top.

4. Hold both ends of the hotdog fold and push the ends toward the center (your hands are pushing toward each other) until all four sections touch. It looks kind of like a pinwheel.

5. Gently fold the pages around to form a little book with a cover and seven pages.

6. Put the ragged edges on the bottom, and you are ready to make a cover.

Brainworks: Activities

Dealing With Paradox

Lead students through three distinct levels of the activity presented below, moving from the concrete to the representational to the abstract. Use small groups and graphic organizers to develop the active learning experience.

Concrete

Organize students into small groups. Have one student in each group put on a vest and a sport jacket over the vest. Challenge the groups to problem-solve a way for the subjects to remove the vest without removing the jacket. This is an example of a concrete paradox in which the vest on the bottom layer can literally be taken off without disturbing the coat on the top layer.

Afterward, have each group create Möbius strips by making a loop from a long strip of paper and putting one twist in the paper before fastening the ends of the loop.

Have students write this message on the Möbius strip: "The beginning is the end. The end is the beginning." Have students discover the paradox of the Möbius strip. Encourage investigations and comparisons of the vest exercise and the Möbius strips, and introduce the concept of paradox.

Representational

Present a number of well-known optical illusions (face/vase; old woman/young woman) to students and help them adjust to both perspectives of the optical illusions. Discuss the relationship to paradox and ambiguity using the Bridges graphic (see Figure 7.16). Ask why paradox and ambiguity might be relevant. Lead students to connect the ideas of divergence and lack of closure to something in life.

Abstract

Lead students into an investigation of oxymorons and compressed conflicts or seeming contradictions such as "youthful aging." Have them use the Mind Wind graphic organizer (see Figure 7.18) and brainstorm a spiral of phrases such as "silent shouts" (T-shirts and bumper stickers), "peaceful protest" (marches, sit-ins, blue flu), and "icy hot" (lipstick name).

Brainstorms: Application

Apply the concept of paradox and ambiguity appropriately to the classroom, incorporating any of the above experiences, and then relate paradox to literature or social studies or in other ways that are meaningful to the curriculum.

Braindrain: REFLECTION

Reflect using the Puzzler graphic (see Figure 7.14), and place these questions in each of the pieces as students think about paradox and ambiguity:

1. Is a good deed done for the wrong reasons still a good deed?

2. Is an unanswered prayer a "no"?

3. Does the falling tree make a sound if no one is there to hear it?

4. Which came first, the chicken or the egg?

Ask students to think about how group work helps in the lesson. Compare the two graphic organizers that were used in the lesson (bridges and mind wind).

BRAINWAVE #6: EXPERIENTIAL LEARNING

From the other perspective of structuring the interaction, *experiential learning* is the term used for immersion in the unit of study. The one immersed in the experience is the one learning, implicitly and explicitly, from the experience. For example, if a teacher wants to teach students how to use a computer but only demonstrates all the skills, how much will the students learn? The students probably won't really start to figure things out until they put their hands on the keyboard and experience the act of keyboarding and computing.

Experiencing the learning as authentically as possible stimulates the brain activity that leads to deep understanding. If students are invited, instructionally, to use multiple ways of knowing about an idea with their many multiple intelligences, they are more likely to grasp the idea with real understanding. And if they are exposed to integrated thematic units of study, in which ideas are connected under an umbrella theme or are interrelated through a problem base or case study, then the learning is facilitated in connected ways.

In terms of the experiential learning advocated by Dewey (1938), the two areas of concern are experiencing the learning through multiple intelligences (Gardner, 1983) and experiencing the learning in coherent and connected ways through integrated curriculum models (Fogarty, 1991). The multiple intelligences theory offers sound instructional practice, while integrated, authentic learning provides holistic curricular models that are robust and relevant to students. Thus, the discussion on structuring interaction with thinking presents multiple ideas for thoroughly engaging students in learning with proven brain-compatible methods.

BRAINWISE STATEMENTS
• I hear and I forget; I see and I remember; I do and I understand.   • It's not how smart you are, but how you are smart.   • The one who is immersed in the experience is the one who is learning.

Braindrops: Strategies

Experiential learning is integrally related to the use of multiple intelligences (Gardner, 1983) and the incorporation of integrated curricular models. The multiple intelligences approach is a natural way to involve all learners holistically in the moment, and integrating the curriculum fosters immersion in an idea either through umbrella themes or threaded ideas.

Multiple Intelligences

- Visual-Spatial
- Verbal-Linguistic
- Logical-Mathematical
- Musical-Rhythmic
- Interpersonal-Social
- Intrapersonal-Introspective
- Bodily-Kinesthetic
- Naturalist-Physical World
- Existential-Spiritual (hypothesized)

Integrated Curriculum

- Performance tasks
- Themes
- Problem-based learning
- Projects/service learning
- Case studies

Multiple Intelligences

Gardner's multiple intelligences theory first appeared in 1983, but its impact in schools today is reaching new heights as teachers strive to differentiate learning to meet the needs of a diverse learning population. Interestingly, the idea of multiple intelligences provides a natural framework for instruction, curriculum, and assessment decisions. Learners have unique profiles of intelligences, and while they are endowed with some bit of intelligence in the many identified areas, they have peaks and valleys in their profile—jagged profiles of strengths and weaknesses. To address these many kinds of minds, differentiated learning is front and center in the classroom.

More specifically, to meet these diverse learner profiles, Gardner (1983) identifies areas of brain processing that he labels *intelligences:* visual-spatial, verbal-linguistic, logical-mathematical, musical-rhythmic, bodily-kinesthetic, interpersonal-social, intrapersonal-introspective, and naturalist-physical world. A closer look reveals an emergent literacy in each intelligence that fosters problem solving and production. In fact, the intelligences are defined as such by Gardner. In addition, he discusses the idea of the multiple intelligences as entry points for learners. Each learner has certain entry points that facilitate the learning in the beginning. Some learn best through reading, others through a hands-on approach, and still others through music.

The intelligences also embody the concept of end states or authentic assessments of learning. Some learners express best what they know and are able to do through written artifacts, others through artistic endeavors, and still others through interpersonal dialogue and conversation. To embrace the multiple intelligences theory is to embrace multiple ways of knowing and expressing.

Armed with this theory of multiple intelligences, the brain-compatible classroom becomes a laboratory for experimenting with many ways of knowing and expressing what one knows. The goal is not to teach a lesson in several different ways, although that may be a way to start, but to design learning in authentic ways that naturally tap into the various intelligences. By utilizing the multiple intelligences, which work together as a complex ecosystem, the profile becomes strengthened and more balanced. Thus, it seems much more prudent to engage the choir of them rather than to artificially engage just one.

For example, when engaged in essay writing, students tap into the verbal-linguistic intelligence, of course, but they must also use their logical-mathematical intelligence to organize their thinking and their visual-spatial intelligence to format and design the final product. When planning a dramatic play, students use the bodily-kinesthetic and verbal-linguistic intelligences for acting, the visual-spatial intelligence for the scenery, the musical-rhythmic intelligence for accompanying sound or music, the interpersonal-social intelligence for working with other actors and crew, and even the intrapersonal-introspective intelligence in taking on the roles of their characters.

In short, when curriculum and instruction are designed with complexity and rigor, many of the intelligences come into play. This is the power of using multiple intelligences as tools in the classroom. To introduce multiple intelligences more fully or to awaken ideas about intelligences that one might already know, the following definitions and examples are given. The applications for the creative teacher who knows about multiple intelligences are unending.

Visual-Spatial Intelligence

This intelligence comprises one's abilities to visually depict and appreciate information and ideas. The skills of visual intelligence are found in imagining, visualizing, and seeing in the mind's eye. Visual representations such as maps, drawings, paintings, cartoons, architectural blueprints, film, and video are the media that tap this intelligence.

Verbal-Linguistic Intelligence

Embedded in this intelligence is the gift of language and literacy. Reading, writing, speaking, and listening; the print-rich environment of books, magazines, newspapers, poetry, and essays; and speeches, dialogues, and conversation are ways that tap this vital intelligence.

Logical-Mathematical Intelligence

This intelligence houses the abilities to reason and think in abstractions. It is served through the skills of debating, calculating, computing, and concluding. This intelligence is tapped through mathematical problem solving, logical arguments and justifications, theory, principle, and proof.

Musical-Rhythmic Intelligence

This intelligence gives one the sense of melody, rhythm, and rhyme. It lets one feel the beat of the music. This is the intelligence that moves people emotionally through the sound of songs and symphonies. While vocal and instrumental performances are embedded in this intelligence, exposure to and appreciation of music, while not actual performances, also tap into it.

Bodily-Kinesthetic Intelligence

This intelligence is manifested in the body's muscle memory. The skills of the athlete and the dancer are expressed in this intelligence, as are the talents of the craftsperson, the carpenter, and the car mechanic. To tap this intelligence, hands-on learning, math manipulatives, labs, and practicums are avenues to pursue.

Interpersonal-Social Intelligence

The charismatic leader, the sympathetic counselor, and the empathic social worker epitomize the interrelational character of this intelligence. The skills of caring, comforting, collaborating, and communicating bring this intelligence into being, and small- and large-group activities, team tasks, and partner work awaken and develop it.

Intrapersonal-Introspective Intelligence

This intelligence is found in the inner nature and soul of the person. It is the inner thought—the reflective self. The skills of the intrapersonal intelligence are seen in the abilities to be self-aware, self-regulating, and self-assessing. Learning logs, response journals, goal setting, and personal portfolios are tools of the trade to tap this intelligence.

Naturalist-Physical World Intelligence

The intelligence of the naturalist can be realized in the ability to discern the differences in species of flora and fauna, in the ability to understand the interrelatedness of things in nature, and in the survival instincts all people possess. The skills of the naturalist lie in the realm of knowing about and being able to classify forms of wildlife, including all the various species of plants and animals. The skills of the naturalist are tapped through nature walks and rooms filled with living organisms such as plants and flowers, animals, rocks and fossils, and seashells.

Existential-Spiritual

This intelligence is still not officially recognized, although Gardner himself has written and talked about it. This hypothesized intelligence addresses the processes used when considering the unanswerable questions of life and the universe, such as: Who am I? Am I just a speck in the universe? What happens when we die? Is there a God? What is beauty? What is evil? These are the "big" questions of life that reside in the philosophical arenas of the mind. Ways to promote this intelligence are open-ended exercises that cause students to think deeply about profound ideas. One simple exercise that opens the door to this kind of phenomenon is to have students write a letter to themselves and create an envelope addressed in this manner:

Name

Number

Street

Town

State

Country

Continent

Planet

Galaxy

Universe

Integrated Curriculum

The brain seeks connections, patterns, and chunks of information that fit together (Caine & Caine, 1991, 1993). By structuring learning around authentic designs such as projects, problems, and real-life dilemmas, the connectedness and relevance are inherent in the learning. When students are building a model, solving the problems that accompany a mock election, or deliberating about the ethics of the media, the learning is both purposeful and meaningful. The learning is also contextual, tying the ideas together within the fabric of the key understandings (Fogarty & Bellanca, 1993).

Often the projects and events that are considered extracurricular are the authentic kinds of experiences that integrate skills and concepts from within and across the disciplines. Publishing a school newspaper, developing the yearbook, producing the musical or school play, orchestrating a spaghetti dinner as a fundraiser, or synchronizing and choreographing the marching band for the football game—these are the experiences that pull the threads of learning together.

Now, that is not to say that all learning must be integrated or interdisciplinary in nature. In fact, the opposite is probably closer to the ideal. Learning that is discrete within a discipline develops the literacy (and the lingo) of the discipline in a pure way, a way that is inherent to the particular rigors and expertise of the discipline. For example, to learn to conduct a scientific investigation through the time-honored techniques of the scientific method is to learn science as a scientist. To study genre through the treasured literature of the ages is to learn literature in the style of the classicists. To learn computer literacy such as multimedia presentations in the manner of the technology wizards is to learn in the context of a computer programmer.

Yet to learn within the discipline and not apply the learning to the context of real-life situations is to short-circuit the process. The glory and real value of an integrated curriculum are to give relevance and purpose to the skill and concept of learning that occurs within the realm of the disciplines as we know them. Thematic units, authentic projects, case studies, and problems that replicate real life lend credence to the disparate skills and concepts learned within the parameters of a discipline.

When teachers move the learning into more integrated contexts, the brain is better able to chunk the information, see patterns, and link ideas to one another. Thus, it is imperative in the brain-compatible classroom to strive for both learning within the discipline and application beyond the discipline—integrated with and connected to real-life events. The discussion that follows suggests five types of integrated applications: performance tasks, themes, problem-based learning, projects/service learning, and case studies. While there are many more models that foster relevant, purposeful learning, these illustrate the idea.

Performance Tasks

As part and parcel of designing curriculum based on core content and state or national standards of learning, performance tasks play a critical role. There are three parts to the curriculum design piece: target standards of learning, create authentic learning experiences, or performance tasks, and assess the quality of the performance with scoring rubrics. In short, it's

One! Goals! (standards of learning)

Two! Evidence! (performance tasks)

Three! Rubrics! (judgment)

For example:

One! A fourth-grade teacher targets core science curriculum that deals with motion and force. In addition, the teacher delineates several other science standards by adding simple machines and the scientific method. Finally, he adds some of the process standards of teamwork, social skills, higher-order thinking, problem solving, model building, and written and oral communication skills.

Two! After the standards are targeted and clustered, the teacher crafts a performance task that gives a stakeholder role to the students: "You are a patent attorney reviewing an application for a new device. You will investigate the parameters of pending patents."

Three! A scoring rubric is developed to set criteria for the quality of work. Criteria might include organization, completeness, content, and presentation, with four levels of quality indicators for each criterion. Performance tasks are rigorous and require real evidence of learning.

Themes

Using an umbrella theme (Fogarty & Stoehr, 2008) to cover overlapping skills and concepts from various content is both appropriate for and invitational to student learning. The big ideas that override different content provide obvious, visible, and known connections from one subject area to another. These ideas become recursive in the learning and create strong neural pathways.

The idea of a tapestry and the overarching impact it has for many disciplines offers a good metaphor. Some examples are the tapestry of the novel, painting, investigation, or culture; the tapestry of geometry, algebraic notation, or computation; the tapestry of nature or research; and the tapestry of a foreign language. In its broadest sense, such a tapestry provides an integrative theme for learning that has great appeal to students of any age.

To use thematic instruction, teachers brainstorm a number of themes, select one to use, and then develop essential questions that provide depth in the thematic investigations. If activities align to the target goals represented in the various core content standards, the theme develops naturally and the process goals or life skills are automatically embedded in the unit of activities. Themes need to change often enough to keep students motivated and energized about the learning.

Problem-Based Learning

Problems provide great fodder for the brain. They stimulate brain activity in various ways. The brain becomes a pattern-seeking, sense-making, connection-finding mechanism, functioning efficiently and effectively as it tries to bring harmony to the dissonance it is sensing. The more complex the problem, the more complex the brain activity becomes. In fact, problem solving relates to the idea discussed earlier in this book about how challenge engages the intellect.

An emerging model for the classroom comes from the medical model of interns, in which a patient's problem is presented and the students, with guidance from experts, work to diagnose and prescribe. Now, the model that is evolving in schools takes a slightly different form (Fogarty, 1997). Students are presented with an open-ended situation, an ill-structured problem. Then, using their questioning and research skills, they attempt to zero in on the primary problem, gather the necessary data, generate alternatives, and recommend a viable solution. The key to this authentic learning model is that students take on the role of one of the stakeholders; therefore, they tend to become invested in the solution. In addition, the goals of the problem-based unit are aligned to the goals of the class, so the experience has a definite academic plan.

A specific example of a problem-based learning unit is one in which students tackle the graffiti problem in the neighborhood surrounding the school. They take on the roles of citizens who own property in the area and live in the neighborhood. Their responsibilities as problem solvers are to gather data, compile ideas, and recommend action to the local citizenry. Naturally, their investigation leads them to local news articles and media reports, various civic groups, and interviews within the neighborhood. The authenticity of the learning is based in the problem, thus, problem-based learning.

To develop problem-based learning scenarios, teachers often collaborate and collect a stock of possible situations. Then each teacher or teacher team revises and refines the problem scenarios appropriate to academic goals and the ages and stages of the learners involved. The problem-based unit unfolds with students taking the lead. The learning, of course, is monitored by the teacher, and minilessons or instructional interludes occur as necessary.

Projects/Service Learning

As most teachers know, projects of any sort garner the intense interest and earnest efforts of students. Students love projects because they enjoy digging in, messing around, and figuring things out. They can become as interested in constructing a kite as they are in creating scenery for a play. They have as much energy for inventing electrical wizardry as they do for reenacting historical events.

Student projects are unlimited in number, type, and scope. The learning is natural, and projects are compelling to students and easily integrated with various aspects of the instruction, curriculum, and assessment cycle (Berman, 1997, 1999). Projects can kick off a unit of study: students make models of pyramids as they begin their study of Egypt. Projects can become the heart of the unit of study: students incorporate simple machines in their working models of dragons. Or projects can be used to culminate a unit: student teams demonstrate their solar energy cars as part of their performance assessment for the science unit on alternative energy sources.

Service learning is another form of project learning that has a civic focus. It often involves a partnership with a community agency.

Incorporating more projects into learning is the goal of the brain-compatible classroom. Teachers working in grade-level or department teams or interdisciplinary clusters can easily find appropriate projects that make learning more genuine for students.

Case Studies

The study of a specific case scenario offers a viable curricular model similar to problem-based learning. The case study begins with a problematic situation, which in this instance is referred to as a dilemma. In fact, the case study model taps into the moral intelligence that Coles (1998) emphasizes. Students are presented with a sticky situation, and through Socratic questioning, their goal is to unravel the situation. In the rigor of the questioning and dialogue that ensue, students are led to examine their own values and beliefs.

Case studies are written around moral and ethical issues such as telling the truth and caring for and respecting elders. With older students, issues such as gay rights, human rights, or the medical dilemma of life-support systems may provide possible case studies. In all of these cases, the research, discussions, and related activities are aligned to predetermined curricular goals.

To use the case study model in the classroom, many teachers find that if they write the cases themselves, key academic areas are more easily targeted. For example, one teacher used the issue of censorship and created a case around censorship on television. The student research, however, stretched into the realm of the V-chip and even censorship on the Internet, which was also a current concern to the local Board of Education. The teacher was then able to tie into the class the media unit and technology research.

In this way, the teacher determines the issues and can readily design related activities to fuel in-depth discussions and debriefing sessions following the case study. As in other authentic models, learning is compelling for students. They can barely stop talking about the issues because they are relevant to the students. Naturally, all sorts of reading and writing as well as communications activities and student-generated projects result.

Brainworks: Activities

Curriculum Corners

Post signs listing the previously discussed five types of authentic learning around the room. Then allow students to form small groups next to each of the signs. Have students create appropriate lists for each sign: performance task ideas, possible themes, ideas for projects/service learning, problems, or issues for cases. Once the lists are developed, have the groups select one idea from their lists to work with. Let groups proceed accordingly:

Performance tasks: Design a performance task.

Themes: Develop essential questions.

Problem-based learning: Describe the problem scenario and stakeholder role.

Projects/service learning: Develop procedures and guidelines.

Case studies: Write a case study around the selected issue.

Using the multiple intelligences grid in Figure 7.31, have each group brainstorm appropriate activities. As the grid fills up with ideas, designate specific challenging learning experiences as possible assessment pieces. For example, identify items for a student portfolio and for student performance assessment.

Brainstorms: Application

Develop a multiple intelligences approach to an active learning lesson using the Web graphic in Figure 7.24.

To apply the ideas about experiential learning, select one of the curriculum models and create a personally relevant grid, working with one other teacher who teaches in a similar situation.

Braindrain: REFLECTION

- Reflect on the ideas of multiple intelligences or integrated curriculum by using the pro-and-con approach.

MULTIPLE INTELLIGENCES PROJECT/PERFORMANCE							
Verbal	Visual	Logical	Musical	Interpersonal	Intrapersonal	Bodily	Naturalist

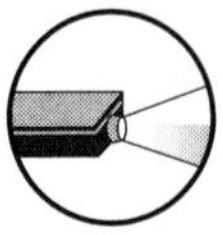

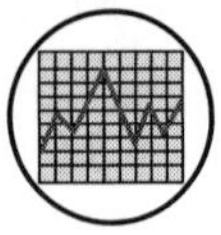

Figure 7.31   Multiple Intelligences Grid

Thinking About Thinking **8**

Neurons that fire together wire together.

—Pat Wolfe

Metacognitive reflection, or the mind watching itself, is essential to the learning process. In the metacognitive moment, learners plan, monitor, and evaluate their own thinking and learning. The reflection is the pause in the act of learning that deepens understanding and gives meaning to the learning. In metacognitive processing, or reflecting, learners are, first, self-aware and, second, self-regulatory. Mature learners know that to really know, to fully comprehend something, involves a moment when they are aware of what they are learning and how well they are learning it. This awareness and control over one's thinking and learning is the key to learning that has breadth and depth for future use.

Implied in the realm of metacognition, or the moments of thinking about one's thinking, are two arenas to consider: the reflection of the learning and the assessment of that learning. Both are of utmost importance in the brain-compatible classroom. For in the reflection, the mind makes meaning of the learning and is then able to generalize the learning for transfer to similar and novel situations. In the assessment of the learning, there are summative measures and dynamic data, both lending credence to the extent and quality of the learning. An integral part of the assessment is in the self-assessing techniques of the student. These involve awareness of and control over one's own learning and are extremely metacognitive in nature.

Both the reflective phase and the assessment phase of the metacognitive process are addressed in this final chapter on the four-corner framework for brain-compatible classrooms. The discussion about reflection focuses on making meaning of the learning and transferring the learning to relevant applications. On the topic of assessments, the discussion compares and contrasts traditional measures to dynamic, fluid ones.

BRAINWAVE #7: REFLECTION

The mind is like a mirror that reflects images of the learning for a somewhat silent and prolonged look. The reflection sometimes gives the mind quite an accurate image, and other times the reflection is distorted by emotional baggage or other forms of interference. Yet without the benefit of reflection, much of the initial learning may be lost. Reflection gives students time to scrutinize, observe, and question. In the reflective phase of learning, the mind sorts and synthesizes, rearranges and reconnects. This is when transfer takes place. This is the phase of the learning cycle that moves inert knowledge to relevant application.

In this reflective phase, the mind literally rewires itself based on new experiences and new learnings. This rewiring of the neurons through new dendrite connections is the way the brain links new ideas to other ideas already in the brain. These linkings are, in essence, the way the brain makes meaning of the information for future transfer, application, and purposeful use. Therefore, "neurons that fire together wire together" (Wolfe, 1996).

BRAINWISE STATEMENTS

- The human mind, once stretched to a new idea, never goes back to its original dimensions.
- An intellectual is someone whose mind watches itself.—Camus
- Our rewards come not from having brains but from using them.

Braindrops: Strategies

This discussion delineates five aspects of the meaning-making processes in the mind and other elements that lead to transfer of learning (see Figure 8.1). The areas investigated in terms of making meaning are understanding that it is inextricably linked to personal relevance, constructing knowledge, fostering deep understanding, extrapolating generalizations, and engagement. The transfer of learning specifically covers strategies to promote transfer, including cognitive mediation, metacognitive reflection, and direct application. Also outlined are different levels of transfer and ways to enhance transfer.

Making Meaning	Transfer of Learning
Personal relevance	Cognitive mediation
Knowledge construction	Metacognitive reflection
Deep understanding	Direct application
Generalizations	Transfer levels
Engagement	Enhancing transfer

Figure 8.1   Reflection Strategies

Making Meaning

The idea of making meaning is at the heart of constructivist theory, which basically states that learning is constructed in the mind of the learner. In this sense, learners take information into their own schemata or mental organizational system and try to make sense of it by fitting it into an existing chunk or pattern. When the learning has personal relevance, knowledge is constructed more easily, generalized ideas are formulated, and deep understanding results. In the brain-compatible classroom, learners are given opportunities to internalize ideas and make meaning in their own time and in their own way.

Personal Relevance

For the brain to attend to an idea—to instantly decide that it wants to hold onto the information flowing through the neural pathways at the rate of 250 miles per hour—the information has to have an emotional hook, personal relevance, or discernible meaning. The emotional hook is easy. The limbic system automatically enacts (see Chapter 1), and the hook is in. The link to personal relevance is sometimes less obvious. The idea may at first seem to have no personal connection, but then a mere glimpse of something makes the needed connection. For example, a person reads a headline in the paper about a child who is missing from a neighboring town. At first, this person passes over the article but then notices a familiar word, such as the name of the town. Then he or she reads on because the information now has a relevant link.

Teachers must foster neural linking in the brain, encourage the brain to label the information relevant, and help the brain receive the signal to pay attention. Teachers should try to make an explicit statement about why students need to take notice, should elicit from students possible uses for an idea, or should link someone's name to an idea and awaken the brain to an important incoming thought.

Knowledge Construction

The most elemental stage of learning is acquiring a knowledge base. In the early learning stages of any number of situations, what do people learn first? The answer is vocabulary—words that allow people to identify things and talk about them. This is true of a basic writing class, French I, beginning computing, general science, or even a beginner ski class.

Once students are empowered with the language, the knowledge base grows around the terminology. Yes, the brain literally grows dendrites that connect around a particular set of neurons—becoming more and more interconnected. For example, as one is learning about online services, words and phrases such as *e-mail, sign on, Web site, home page, server, chat room,* and *links* are logged into the knowledge base. This vocabulary allows the learner to continue to talk and read about online research and related issues. Without that initial knowledge base, learning is short-circuited because there is nothing to which the learner can attach the new learning.

To develop a knowledge base, deductive approaches such as direct instruction, mentoring models, coaching, and internships are expedient ways to learn the initial information. In addition, more natural, inductive methods such as inquiry learning, hands-on discovery learning, and group investigations can provide an initial foundation of knowledge to build on.

Deep Understanding

To teach for deep understanding is to teach with rigor and vigor over time. Deep understanding seldom happens quickly. It is a layering process that builds idea upon idea, concept upon concept, and skill upon skill. To achieve this, one goes beyond a genuine knowledge base. Deep understanding requires factual information, relevant associations, and conscious thought about its meaning and the implications of that meaning.

Deep understanding occurs only when students know enough about something to know that they in fact know very little. The paradox is that a little knowledge opens the eyes to the larger field of study. As the saying goes, a little knowledge is dangerous. When a student has superficial information or surface knowledge without the deep understanding to ground the learning, action may be taken with little insight or forethought for implications and consequences of the action.

To teach for deep understanding, a major revolution in thinking about curriculum must occur. The concept of curriculum coverage must be replaced with that of curriculum priorities. Schools cannot continue the race to cover the content in every subject area. There is simply too much content to cover. Instead, the content of every discipline must be examined for essential conceptual learnings. Once curricular priorities are set, skillful, authentic designs, such as problem-based learning and case studies, are implemented to foster deep understanding for long-term learning.

Generalizations

One of the foremost reflective strategies for making meaning is in the ability to generalize the learning. Through generalizations, principles are founded and concepts are organized and affirmed. Ideas move from the concrete to the abstract, and generalizable bits of information are linked appropriately in a spectrum of related realms. An example of the power of generalizations in making meaning of new information is learning about the concept of weather and all the data and information that is compiled to make a forecast. From generalizations about recurring cloud patterns, the flow of the jet stream, or the impact of barometric pressure on the weather, accurate forecasts are formed.

To take the generalizations a step further, if one extrapolates the process for predicting the weather, a similar process may lead to other kinds of predictions that are also accurate. For instance, if gathering data from multiple sources, searching for patterns of reliability, and tracking trends over a period of time lead to accurate forecasts in weather, perhaps appropriate procedures coupled with a similar process might lead to accurate predictions for the stock market. The ability to generalize, although simplified greatly in this brief discussion, is a primary strategy for reflecting on learning and making meaning of that learning.

To foster the skill of generalizing, teachers can ask three questions: Have you ever seen anything like this before? How does this connect to something else you know? How might you use this idea again? When teachers push for connections to prior knowledge and future application, learners are forced to find the big idea to the generalizable idea in the learning.

Engagement

To foster meaning making, students need time to engage in mindful ways. In addressing the idea of engagement, there is a discernible difference between active learning and engaged learning. In active learning, teachers facilitate experiences and interactions through cooperative tasks, small-group collaborations, and hands-on learning investigations that involve lab work, manipulatives, and bodily-kinesthetic activities. Students are actively involved in the learning. They try things out, mess around, and move things and themselves around and about.

By contrast, engaged learning often accompanies the activity part of active learning. That is to say, when students are actively working with things and ideas, they often move into a state of mindful engagement during which they experience more internal dialogue, evidenced by moments of silence and moments of insight. Students think, question, converse, and truly engage in thinking about what is going on. They internalize the ideas and make critical connections that are personally relevant to their particular cognitive schema.

The goal of the skillful teacher is to move learners from active learning to mindful engagement as often and as purposefully as possible. For it is the engaged mind that makes personal meaning and builds concepts and skills in learners.

Transfer of Learning

All learning is for transfer. The goal of all learning is to make information portable so the learning travels with the learner to new locations. In the new locations the learning is transferred and applied in novel, interesting, and innovative ways. This is the phenomenon referred to as the transfer of learning. Think of some learning you carried from one situation to the next. Perhaps it was something you learned about managing a classroom in your first year of teaching. Notice how you are still implementing some of these early learnings today.

But how is transfer fostered? How can teachers promote the transfer of learning so it moves from one context to another? What are the elusive elements of transfer that need explicit attention? In the ensuing discussion, transfer of learning is related to the brain-compatible classroom as a critical strategy that enhances learning—not for a test, but for a lifetime. Strategies that promote this are cognitive mediation, metacognitive reflection, and direct application. Cognitive mediation is teachers leading students to self-reflection or thinking about their own thinking; metacognitive reflection is student-initiated self-reflection; and direct application is learner awareness of the self-reflective process through purposeful use. Included in this discussion are the various levels of transfer and ways to enhance transfer.

Cognitive Mediation

The concept of cognitive mediation (Feuerstein, 1980) means that learning can be mediated or facilitated—that human intervention in the learning, at the right time and in the right way, can help learners in the learning process. In fact, cognitive mediation not only facilitates the learning, but also deepens it for future transfer and use. It is explicit intervention by teachers to guide students' thinking and reflection. In brief, cognitive mediation occurs when teachers mediate the learning.

The principles of cognitive mediation (Feuerstein, 1980) involve several interrelated components. These critical elements are intentionality and reciprocity, meaning, and transcendence. A closer look at these terms reveals insight into the transfer process.

To have intentionality, teachers deliberately guide the learning in a specific direction, and reciprocity occurs when there is an indication that learners are receptive to the mediation or guided learning. To have meaning, mediators emphasize the significance and purpose of the learning and elicit an understanding of why the activity is important. Finally, the mediators promote transcendence by taking the learning beyond the immediate situation and into the realm of proven principles, concepts, and strategies for use in other circumstances.

While the elements of meaning and transcendence are similar to the ideas in the section on making meaning through relevance and generalizations, cognitive mediation is much more direct and intentional. In fact, cognitive mediation as it is represented here is explicitly designed to extract certain key learnings. It goes beyond the push for finding personal relevance and seeking generalizations.

The easiest and most direct way to mediate the learning is to be clear and explicit about the purpose, elicit some response from learners to indicate their ownership in the process, extract meaning from them through probing questions and personal comments, and push the transfer by getting learners to think of opportunities to use the idea again.

Metacognitive Reflection

To speak of transfer without discussing metacognition would be like rowing a boat without the oars. Metacognition moves the transfer boat, and without it the boat would be adrift at sea. In other words, metacognition—the ability to think about one's own thinking, to be aware of the learning, and to control the learning—is the key to effective and skillful transfer.

An examination of metacognitive activity suggests that this is thinking beyond—about, around, and outside—the cognitive focus. That is to say, metacognitive behavior is the thinking that is done when one plans, monitors, or evaluates one's own learning. It is thinking beyond the immediate situation, similar to looking through a window at oneself and knowing what one is doing and how one is doing it.

For example, a teacher is giving a lesson on fractions. The teacher is about to finish the demonstration on the board when she becomes aware that the students' eyes are glazed over. They don't get it. This sudden awareness of the circumstances surrounding the cognitive lesson being taught, the cue that the lesson is not connecting, is metacognitive monitoring on the part of the teacher.

Likewise, metacognitive reflection might come in the form of planning, monitoring, or evaluating the lesson. Again, the thinking is about, around, and outside of the actual teaching. It is reflective thinking before, during, or after the action takes place. It is the time when the teacher is anticipating what might happen, recognizes what is happening, or evaluating what did happen (see Figure 8.2).

To foster the metacognitive thinking in students, planning time is built in for groups to predict what might happen, strategies are included that force them to self-monitor their progress, and self-evaluation tools are employed to foster reflective analysis after the fact.

Swartz and Perkins (1989) elaborate on the concept of metacognition by describing four distinct levels of thinking: tacit, aware, strategic, and reflective. Each level has a specific mode.

Tacit Level of Metacognition

This level of metacognition is evidenced when a behavior is repeated because it is working. However, this level implies that there is no real awareness

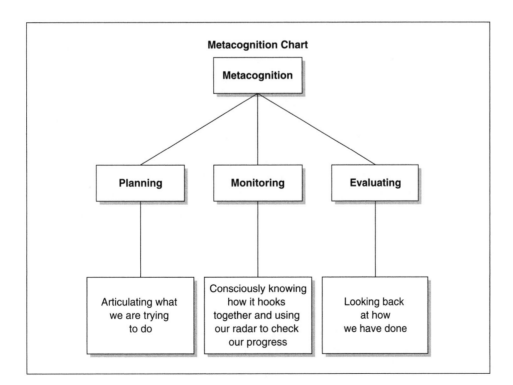

Figure 8.2   Metacognition Chart

that the behavior is working, but it is tacit or automatic—not with conscious awareness. For example, a writer might always write at the kitchen table with the radio on in the background. It works; therefore, the writer continues but never really analyzes the process.

Aware Level of Metacognition

To move to the level of awareness, the behavior must be consciously noted. The learner must become aware of the behavior and think about it explicitly. If the ingredients of awareness are added to the writer from the previous example, the writer now notices that he always sits at the kitchen table with the radio on in the background. He may even comment on this to someone. He is aware.

Strategic Level of Metacognition

At the strategic level of metacognition, the learner not only is aware of his or her specific behavior but actively strategizes to repeat the behavior. Continuing the example, the writer is not at home, so he is not able to sit at the kitchen table. However, he strategically recreates the situation to resemble his favorite mode. He finds a table or desk and sets a radio nearby, thus creating a familiar atmosphere for writing.

Reflective Level of Metacognition

The reflective level of metacognitive behavior moves beyond the strategic level; there is deliberate thought about the best or easiest way to do something. This level implies that there is true reflective thought guiding the action. Therefore, the writer not only sits at the kitchen table with the radio on in the background but gingerly selects the right station. He reflects on the effects of different kinds of music and chooses accordingly.

Specific tools for transfer that have classroom appeal include Mrs. Potter's questions (see Figure 8.3); the Plus/Minus/Interesting evaluation chart (see Figure 8.4); a reflective schemata that elicits What? So what? Now what? (see Figure 8.5); the KWL strategy to determine what one knows, wants to know, and has learned (see Figure 8.6); and learning logs with lead-ins such as "I wonder . . ." and "My problem is . . ." (see Figure 8.7).

- What were you expected to do?
- In this assignment, what did you do well?
- If you had to do this task over, what would you do differently?
- What help do you need from me?

Figure 8.3 Mrs. Potter's Questions

SOURCE: Bellanca & Fogarty, 1991.

Figure 8.4   Plus/Minus/Interesting

Metacognition
What?
So what?
Now what?

Figure 8.5   What? So What? Now What?

Strategy Sheet		
What we Know	What we Want to Find Out	What we Have Learned

Figure 8.6   KWL

Lead-Ins That Promote Thinking at Higher Levels

Analysis

Compared to . . .

The best part . . .

On the positive side . . .

An interesting part is . . .

Take a small part like . . .

A logical sequence seems to be . . .

On the negative side . . .

Similarly . . .

By contrast . . .

Synthesis

Suppose . . .

Combine . . .

Possibly . . .

Imagine . . .

Reversed . . .

What if . . .

I predict . . .

How about . . .

I wonder . . .

Evaluation

How . . .

Why . . .

It seems irrelevant that . . .

One point of view is . . .

It seems important to note . . .

The best . . .

Application

Backtracking for a minute . . .

A way to . . .

I want to . . .

A connecting idea is . . .

A movie this reminds me of is _____ because . . .

If this were a book I'd title it . . .

I think this applies to . . .

Does this mean . . .

Problem Solving

I'm stuck on . . .

The best way to think about this . . .

I conclude . . .

I'm lost with . . .

I understand, but . . .

I'm concerned about . . .

My problem is . . .

A question I have is . . .

Decision Making

I disagree with _____ because . . .

I prefer _____ because . . .

If I had to choose . . .

I believe . . .

My goal is . . .

I hate . . .

Lead-Ins That Promote Different Styles of Thinking

Visual Representations	Verbal Presentations
Try to visualize	Another way of saying this is . . .
My picture of this	I learned . . .
A diagram of this idea looks like	I discovered . . .
I feel like	A quote that seems to fit is . . .
A chart	I want to read ___ because . . .
I'm ___ like ___ because	I want to talk to ___ because . . .

Figure 8.7   Log Lead-Ins

Direct Application

Direct application, or purposeful use, is highly metacognitive because it demonstrates concrete transfer of the learning from one context to the next. The application may be implicit or explicit, yet some self-reflection has to occur for the transfer to take place.

The surest way to foster transfer is to create a need for immediate use. The sooner the learning is actually applied and used, the greater the chance for permanence. That is to say, when the learning is purposefully applied by the learner, it becomes anchored in the mind. It is attached and held in the mind within a meaningful context. Thus, the learning is likely to be placed in long-term memory.

Hopefully, the learning can be authentically used in a meaningful application, such as incorporating more adverbial phrases in a draft of writing after a lesson on adverbs. But even if the application is somewhat contrived, such as playing a game in which the adverbs are used or creating cartoons based on adverbial phrases, the application is still of value and helps foster transfer.

Transfer Levels

Transfer extends learning, bridges the old and the new, and leads students toward relevant application across academic content and into real-life situations. In some cases, the transfer of learning is obvious because the learned skills seem close to the skill situation in which they are used or transferred. For example, when teaching "supermarket math" (price comparisons, making change, etc.) the learning situation "hugs" the life situation. The transfer is clear. This is called *simple transfer.*

In other instances, the learning in the school situation seems far removed or remote from the transfer across content or into real life. For example, a high school student spends a great deal of time and energy staring at, memorizing, and using the periodic table of elements. However, unless the student is destined for a scientific career in which frequent reference and deep understanding of the periodic table is essential, it is difficult for the student to feel that the learning is really useful. The student wonders if he or she really needs to know that Au is gold.

Most students do not see how this learning is useful. The transfer is complex. They miss the connection between the rigors of learning the elements and the similar rigors of visualizing, practicing, and memorizing other material. Few students note that the analytical skills used in reading the periodic table are similar to the critical thinking skills used in analyzing other charts or graphs. Seldom are students aware that the patterns evident in the periodic table set a model for searching for patterns in other phenomena or constructing similar matrices or grids. The transfer here is remote; it is obscure. The student needs explicit instruction in making these and other connections. In a situation such as this, teachers can help students make relevant transfer through mediation or bridging strategies.

The six transfer strategies illustrated in Figures 8.8–8.10 require explicit instruction with students to help them make application—in other words, to help students transfer learning.

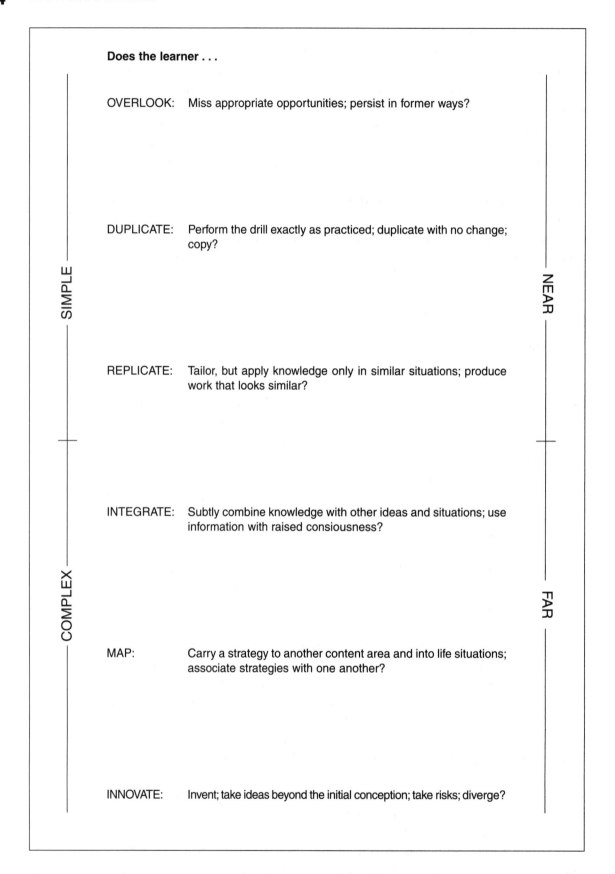

Does the learner . . .

OVERLOOK: Miss appropriate opportunities; persist in former ways?

DUPLICATE: Perform the drill exactly as practiced; duplicate with no change; copy?

REPLICATE: Tailor, but apply knowledge only in similar situations; produce work that looks similar?

INTEGRATE: Subtly combine knowledge with other ideas and situations; use information with raised consiousness?

MAP: Carry a strategy to another content area and into life situations; associate strategies with one another?

INNOVATE: Invent; take ideas beyond the initial conception; take risks; diverge?

SIMPLE — COMPLEX

NEAR — FAR

Figure 8.8   Situational Dispositions Toward Transfer

TRANSFER OF LEARNING

Model	Illustration	Transfer Disposition	Looks Like	Sounds Like
Ollie the Head-in-the-Sand Ostrich		Overlooks	Persists in writing in manuscript form rather than cursive. (New skill overlooked or avoided.)	*"I get it right on the dittos, but I forget to use punctuation when I write an essay."* (Knows, but not embedding or applying.)
Dan the Drilling Woodpecker		Duplicates	Plagiarism or copying the example exactly. (Uses in rote way; does not personalize.)	*"Mine is not to question why —just invert and multiply."* (When dividing fractions.) (Some understanding of what she/he is doing.)
Laura the Look-Alike Penguin		Replicates	"Bed to Bed" or narrative style. "He got up. He did this. He went to bed." or "He was born. He did this… He died." (Student has groomed a method and uses it over and over.)	*"Paragraphing means I must have three 'indents' per page."* (Tailors into own story or essay, and uses "the mold" somewhat mechanically and somewhat successfully.)
Jonathan Livingston Seagull		Integrates	Student writing essay incorporates newly learned French words. (Applying: weaving old and new.)	*"I always try to guess (predict) what's gonna happen next on TV shows."* Connects to prior knowledge and experience; relates what's learned to personal experience.)
Cathy the Carrier Pigeon		Maps	Graphs information for a social studies report with the help of the math teacher to actually design the graphs. (Connecting one subject to another.)	Parent-related story: *"Tina suggested we brainstorm our vacation ideas and rank them to help us decide."* (Carries new skills into other content areas and into real-life situations.)
Samantha the Soaring Eagle		Innovates	After studying flow charts for computer class, student constructs a Rube Goldberg–type invention. (Innovates: invents; diverges; goes beyond and creates something novel.)	*"I took the idea of the Mr. Potato Head and created a mix-and-match grid of ideas for our Earth Day project."* (Generalizes ideas from experience and transfers creatively.)

Figure 8.9 Transfer of Learning

Overlooking

Think of an instance where the skill or strategy would be inappropriate.

"I would not use _____ when _____ ."

Duplicating

Think of an opportunity passed when you could have used the skill or strategy.

"I wish I'd known about _____ when _____ because I could've _____ ."

Replicating

Think of an adjustment that will make your application of _____ more relevant.

"Next time I'm gonna _____ ."

Integrating

Think of an analogy for the skill or strategy.

" _____ is like _____ because both _____ ."

Mapping

Think of an upcoming opportunity to use the new idea.

"In _____ , I'm gonna use _____ to help _____ ."

Innovating

Think of an application for a real-life setting.

"Outside of school, I could use _____ when _____ ."

Figure 8.10   Transfer Strategy for Making Connections With Questions

Enhanced Transfer

Application, use, and meaningful transfer are facilitated in five distinct ways: decontextualizing learning through generalizations, crystallizing learning for deep understanding, recontextualizing learning for purposeful use, energizing learning with active involvement, and personalizing learning for internalization.

Decontextualized Learning: What's the Big Idea?

When process instruction becomes the content of instruction, transfer is enhanced because learning is decontextualized (Feuerstein, Rand, Hoffman, & Miller, 1980); skills, operations, and dispositions are easily extracted from original contexts through generalizations and a focus on the big ideas. Learning more readily targets relevant life skills as subject matter content becomes the vehicle for learning. For example, while studying about disease and the relationship to health and wellness, students learn the critical skills of cause and effect, comparing and contrasting, and drawing conclusions. The curiosity they experience drives continued and persistent inquiry, and they gain insight into the interdependence of all things. These are all processes they can take away with them. Knowledge, facts, and information are naturally the products of this learning, but perhaps more important, the students' tools of critical thinking are honed and their habits of mind begin to take shape.

Decontextualized learning chunks learning into discernible patterns that reveal universal attributes. These generalizable chunks are often mediated through analogies in which the generic pattern is uncovered and analogous ideas are slotted in, thereby chunking learning for future use (Perkins & Salomon, 1988). Decontextualized learning is fostered when process is the content because procedural learning is more neutral, or context free. For example, steps for problem solving are quite easily mediated toward generalizations that transfer to varied contexts: solving a "tower problem" is a typical strategic technique in which an analogous situation is recognized and the solution mitigated according to previously learned procedures.

Crystallized Learning: Diamonds Are Forever

When process instruction becomes the content of instruction, transfer is enhanced because learning is crystallized. As previously discussed, it is understood that skills, operations, and dispositions are taught through the vehicle of subject matter content. Students think well, with skill and grace and rigor, when they have something to think about; they work collaboratively and exemplify team skills when they are engaged in a project that requires cooperation; and they organize information when they have an abundance of data to manipulate. Thus, if students work with subject matter content in wholesome, project-oriented instruction, in which these very processes are the focus and transfer of learning, all learning is crystallized. Not only is content learning enhanced and deepened, but the processes, skills, operations, and dispositions are crystallized (Ben-Hur, 1994a).

In essence, understanding is deepened as students induce learning from specific situations and subsequently apply and use it in other situations. For example, as students are immersed in a problem-based learning scenario concerning Columbus's voyage and the near mutiny on board, they use analysis, conflict resolution, responsibility, and leadership skills and generate ideas. Also, they learn about historic moments, concept of exploration, and implications of the event. They gain insight into not only the knowledge base of the subject matter under scrutiny, but also the processes that undergird the learning of that knowledge base.

The crystallization of ideas elaborates, or fattens, the ideas and at the same time distills, or narrows, the learning until it is crystal clear. Process instruction provides an opportunity for this crystallization to occur both in the use of skills, operations, and dispositions and in the extrapolation of the knowledge base itself.

Recontextualized Learning: When Am I Ever Going to Use This?

Recontextualizing learning involves moving learning from one context to a new one. When process instruction becomes the content, transfer is enhanced as the skills, operations, and dispositions become portable as they are carried from one situation to the next and recontextualized into meaningful application and use.

Recontextualized learning often requires mediation toward future applications (Feuerstein et al., 1980). However, once realized, it prolongs episodic learning; it generates relevant connections and ensures the longevity of learning. Recontextualized learning is a necessary step in transfer. It is the moment of meaning that occurs as learners intentionally or unintentionally use skills, operations, and dispositions in similar or novel contexts.

One example of recontextualizing learning involves mindful abstraction, or bridging, of learning (Perkins & Salomon, 1988). A group of middle school students are expected to use argument and evidence to write a persuasive speech. The content of the argument, open to personal choice, encompasses issues of politics, economics, human rights, and the environment. Although the content of each speech is certainly one focus of importance, the process of arguing and providing evidence to support the argument is another critical focus of learning.

Although the content of the arguments may have transfer power, using argument and evidence as analysis techniques is a highly portable process. Argument and evidence move easily to proofs in math class, hypotheses and conclusions in science class, court cases in government class, and even artistic criticism in literature class. Argument and evidence are recontextualized in each, and although this may require some mediation to move from science to math to literature, the process appears to have universal qualities that expedite transfer. Recontextualized learning guarantees that the learning lives on—that it survives in other forms tailored to the new context.

Energized Learning: Beyond Pour and Store

Process instruction enhances transfer because it fights the inert knowledge syndrome; it shifts from the pour-and-store model of learning the facts, data, and information of subject matter content to the dynamics of process instruction itself. It shifts toward the fluid use of skills, the management of operations, and the fueling of dispositions as students use, apply, and transfer these behaviors to varied and relevant situations.

Energized learning moves learners from the "nobody taught me" refrain to the idea that they are the "generation of information and thereby can be engaged in the processes of discovery and creativity" (Ben-Hur, 1994a, p. 30). Energized learning is epitomized in process instruction because the *how* is highlighted, rather than (or along with) the *what*. Students are actively engaged in the steps and procedures of accomplishing something, rather than merely knowing of that something's existence. Inert knowledge, passive learners, and docile thinkers are instructional concerns that seem to disappear when process becomes content and is energized with action (Bransford, Sherwood, Vye, & Riser, 1986). For example, process instruction energizes learning even in the simplest of illustrations. Reading a chart of information and memorizing it for later recall form inert knowledge. Taking a survey, analyzing the results, and charting the data, on the other hand, constitute energized learning. The first scenario dictates passive learning, whereas the second creates active involved learning; one is content focused, the other is process focused.

When learning about coins in a process-oriented manner, youngsters are involved in using them to purchase items in their classroom store. Not only are the students cognizant of the value of the coins and why they are used, but they are also immersed in a simulation of appropriate use. Students are immersed in sets of skills and various operations—problem solving and decision making—as well as employment of the dispositions of efficacy and interdependence. The dynamics of interaction become as important as the content of the interaction. Learning is fluid, flexible, and changing. It is activated and energized with vigor. Process instruction lends power to learning because students use their capacities for action and involvement.

When process instruction energizes the learning into powerful, dynamic, and ever-changing ideas, transfer is enhanced. Once learning is in motion, it moves easily from one situation to the next. Process instruction, by its very nature, is mobile; it moves skills, operations, and dispositions into diverse circumstances. Process instruction is energized learning, and energized learning is portable, transferred learning.

Personalized Learning: Gotcha!

Process instruction enhances transfer because it personalizes learning. As the focus shifts toward skills, operations, and dispositions as content, students grasp universal aspects and adapt the processes to a personal style. For example, while students learn a generic methodology for problem solving, each develops a set of procedures particular to his or her own problem solving. One student may examine both sides by comparing and contrasting ideas, whereas another may prefer to gather multiple solutions before analyzing any of them.

Personalization is simply the way to fingerprint the technique or series of techniques that seem to work best for each individual. It is the unending tailoring necessary for students seeking the perfect fit for productivity and progress in their own endeavors. The personalization process is critical to the enhancement of transfer because it helps learners internalize learning in deeply significant and personally relevant ways.

The personalization process builds individuals' capacities not only for relevant, immediate transfer but also for long-term use. This allows learners to tap into their resource banks throughout their lives. Learners are better able to recall and initiate appropriate behaviors if and when they are tagged with a personal reference point or telling label.

The skill of prediction may be labeled by some people in their repertoire of strategies as guessing or intuiting outcomes on the basis of gut feelings. Others may refer to the same microskill of prediction as forecasting and rely in personal ways on the analysis of information to make predictions. Although differences between the two are subtle, they suggest the powerful role of personalization in the transfer process.

Process instruction, when more fully personalized, moves from tacit, implicit behaviors to aware, explicit actions. The tailoring process fosters metacognition (Brown, 1978). By understanding one's personal interpretation of craftsmanship as a feeling of pride in the completed task, the individual is more likely to explicitly transfer that disposition to multiple situations in life. For example, pride in craftsmanship may occur early in life. An individual may create a model airplane and have craftsmanship reappear later in a more abstract form of pride in a well-crafted argument (Fogarty, cited in Costa & Liebmann, 1997).

When teachers ask, "What will students need to know and be able to do 25 years from now?" they are asking what learning needs to transfer into students' adult lives. Students will need to know how to think, how to get along with others, how to solve problems, and how to make mindful decisions. At the same time, it seems that learning about learning, adopting a posture of inquiry, and acquiring a sense of efficacy are also desirable goals for learners. To achieve those goals, we must push learners to the edge.

Come to the edge, he said.

They said: We are afraid.

Come to the edge, he said.

They came.

He pushed them . . . and they flew.

(Apollinaire, quoted in Ferguson, 1980, p. 293)

Brainworks: Activities

Transfer Tales

In groups of three, use the jigsaw strategy. Assign each person in the group two levels of transfer (see Figures 8.9 and 8.10).

Person #1: Levels 1 and 2 (Ollie overlooks; Dan duplicates)

Person #2: Levels 3 and 4 (Laura replicates; Jonathan integrates)

Person #3: Levels 5 and 6 (Cathy maps; Samantha innovates)

Explain that we have all experienced the various levels of transfer. They are situational, and we have all been in situations as beginners and as experts. Tell each person in the group to decide on the important features of his or her metaphorical birds or levels of transfer and to think of personal stories of transfer (transfer tales) to illustrate each of the two birds. Then let each share in a teaching round so all members are informed about the six levels of transfer.

Brainstorms: Application

Create a list of possible reflection strategies and appropriate times to use those strategies.

Braindrain: REFLECTION

- Reflect on reflection with the Seesaw graphic (see Figure 7.7) balancing the "Yeah, buts" with "What ifs?"

BRAINWAVE #8: ASSESSMENT

There are those who believe that assessment drives instruction. While that may not be the whole story, there is a lot of truth to it. In this age of standards and accountability, teachers and students are feeling the pressure. In fact, schools are inundated with assessments and evaluations of all types.

This discussion covers the gamut of assessment strategies, from traditional measures such as tests, grades, report cards, and conferences to more dynamic assessments that utilize student portfolios and performance tasks with scoring rubrics. The reasoned voice advocates a balance in the assessment process, with traditional, portfolio, and performance assessments all playing a role in creating the complete picture of student growth and progress. In turn, the range of assessment tools and techniques are designated for both formative and summative assessments. The focus depends on how teachers choose to use the various assessments, yet all of these strategies must focus on self-assessing components. While dynamic assessments appear more metacognitive, traditional assessments can easily be adapted to include a self-reflective element.

BRAINWISE STATEMENTS

- There may be something going on in the brain that we don't have an inkling of at the moment.
- Your brain is smarter than you are.
- Instinct is what makes a genius a genius.

Braindrops: Strategies

Assessment issues abound in the educational arena. Yet a clear solution to the dilemma of how to assess student learning seems to be captured in the word *balance*. When assessment practices are balanced across the spectrum of strategies and across the dichotomy of formative and summative uses, a full and comprehensive picture emerges about the student. Therefore, this discussion fosters a balance between traditional measures and more dynamic methods of assessment (see Figure 8.11).

Traditional Assessments	Dynamic Assessments

Tests
   • Teacher made
   • Criterion referenced
   • Norm referenced
	Portfolio
	   • Working
	   • Showcase
	   • Electronic

Grades	Performance
Report cards	• Standards or goals • Performance tasks or evidence
Parent conferences	• Scoring rubrics or quality

Figure 8.11   Student Assessment

In the brain-compatible classroom, self-reflection and learning are expectations of all students. When students take charge of their own learning, they cannot help but be self-evaluative. By nature, learners want to know how they're doing. In the brain-compatible classroom, there are multiple ways for them to know how they're doing, including both traditional and dynamic assessments used in formative and summative ways.

Traditional Assessments

Traditional assessments are familiar tools that include many of the tried-and-true ways of evaluating student progress such as quizzes, tests, grades, report cards, and parent conferences.

Tests

Tests have weathered the test of time. They are embedded in everything we do in the school setting. There are the regular, run-of-the-mill quizzes and teacher-made tests that are used on a weekly and sometimes daily basis to motivate students to learn by keeping them accountable. Then there are the criterion-referenced tests published by textbook companies. Of course, states and provinces have gotten into the testing game and produce their own versions of criterion-referenced tests based on predetermined goals, aims, and objectives permeating the state standards. Again, these can serve a purpose in terms of indicators of district strengths and weaknesses in programs and curricula, but often they are not great indicators of individual student learning because of many uncontrollable variables.

And then there are the norm-referenced, or standardized, tests developed by national testing services and administered widely across the country. These give a comparison that is believed to be fair, constant, and reliable. The benefit of these tests and the information they provide comes in the form of demographic data for national and international comparisons. However, when these scores are used as gatekeepers to various opportunities for students, their value diminishes; they may not always be the best predictors of future successes.

Tests have a place in the overall assessment scheme; they do provide one form of feedback. However, their stature must not overshadow more dynamic forms of student evaluation.

Grades

In addition to the multitude of tests, traditional assessment includes assigning students grades. These are either letter grades (A, B, C, D, or F) or numerical grades (88 percent, 96 percent, etc.). Grades are given on daily work, homework, quizzes, tests, and in-class participation. While they are considered objective measures, often they are actually subjectively based on individual teacher standards.

Yet grades can be catalysts for learning—learners crave feedback from others. However, to make the grades meaningful motivators for learning, students must become integral partners in the process. They must understand the standards and requirements and accept responsibility for attaining and achieving them.

Report Cards

Report cards vary from checklists to letter grades to anecdotal comments, and they can have motivating and/or detrimental effects on learning. They are summative records, showing the results but not the process. While parents typically like the report card as a form for communicating how their children are doing in school, report cards tell only part of the assessment picture.

Parent Conferences

Parent conferences often complement the report card and are usually held once a year in the fall. More often than not, they are one-way communications by the teacher. However, teachers can, and sometimes do, include students in the conference and foster conversation and input from the parents. Often, they provide insight into the dynamics of the family.

Dynamic Assessments

Dynamic assessments employ the multiple intelligences approach and incorporate student portfolios and performances in the repertoire of assessment strategies. In the brain-compatible classroom, student portfolios provide viable tools for self-reflection, and performances put the responsibility on the learner to perform the task and demonstrate the learning. Assessment as instruction is brain friendly. Therefore, students whose brains function best visually or kinesthetically are able to use these means rather than the usual verbal or mathematical measures.

Portfolio

Student portfolios are selected collections of student work that demonstrate growth and progress toward certain predetermined goals. The portfolio process, in its most basic form, includes a series of stages often referred to as collection, selection, and reflection. In each of these phases, students take the lead in the process because the real essence of the portfolio process is in the self-evaluation it promotes.

The collection of artifacts usually occurs over time, and students gather items in a working portfolio. The portfolios are usually managed by the students, yet the teacher may require certain items to be included for the final selection process.

Periodically, the collected items are inventoried and sorted. Usually, this selection process is accompanied by the reflection process. As students decide to keep an item for their showcase, or final, portfolios, they take time to write reflections, justifying why they have selected particular items.

While traditional portfolios are real folders or folios used to hold student papers and other kinds of evidence of schoolwork, some classrooms and schools are using electronic portfolios—something like a student Web page. The power of this model is in the ease of storage and transport. The electronic version can be sent home via e-mail or the Web.

The ultimate stage in the portfolio process is including it in the parent conference. In this way, the conference becomes a three-way communication between teacher, student, and parent, with each having a vital role. The portfolio emphasizes the growth and development of the student, in contrast to the report card that only offers a look at grades and rankings.

Performance

Balancing the traditional measures and the portfolio process in the assessment repertoire is the strategy of performance assessments. Students demonstrate what they have learned through a performance of some sort. These range from doing a lab experiment to giving a speech to executing an intricate routine in gymnastics class.

To incorporate the performance assessment into a full repertoire of assessments, students must be informed of the standard expected for each performance. Once the standard is clear, criteria are delineated and indicators of meeting the criteria are explicitly described.

Performance tasks add the elements of relevance and transfer to the assessment picture and provide evidence of learning and the quality of that learning. Performance tasks are needed additions if the assessment strategies are to be balanced for the best and most holistic picture of the student.

The scoring guide for the performance task is a scoring rubric. It is, in essence, a chart or diagram that depicts the standards, criteria, indicators, and points assigned to each.

Brainworks: Activities

Folk Portfolio

Make the statement: "An owl pellet is a portfolio." Then elicit reactions from teachers about the idea that the collection of artifacts the owl has eaten is regurgitated as a "folk portfolio." In small groups, generate lists of suggestions for other folk portfolios. The ideas range from hope chests and jewelry boxes to the trunk of a car, a tool chest, and even the refrigerator door.

After the lists are completed and sampled, instruct the groups to list the characteristics or elements that these folk portfolios have in common. What is it that makes them portfolios?

After thinking about the attributes of a portfolio, have the groups synthesize their ideas into a definition of a portfolio. Read the definitions and discuss. Then, if time permits, show some student portfolios to illustrate how they have the same characteristics of the folk portfolios.

Brainstorms: Application

Create a riotous rubric activity as illustrated in Figure 8.12 around an entertaining topic to experience creating parallel structures. Then try a more serious rubric targeting an academic topic, as depicted in Figure 8.13.

Braindrain: REFLECTION

- Reflect on the assessment section using the Tri Pie graphic (see Figure 7.15). Compare three types of assessment: traditional, portfolio, performance. Finish with a discussion about formative and summative assessments—how they are alike and how they are different.

Standard:

Performance / Criteria				

- -

Romance

Standard: Adventurous, mysterious, encounter with ambience, and romantic setting.

	1	2	3	4
Secrecy Intrigue Mystery	All Know	Friends Know	Best Friend Knows	Only the Two of Us Know
Adventure	Comatose at Home	Theme Park	Weekend Getaway	Paris
Ambience	TV Dinner at Kitchen Table	Fast Food	Candlelight Dinner	Cruise
Setting	Later After the Game	Same Time Next Year	Lunch Date	Midnight Rendezvous

Figure 8.12 Riotous Rubric

Standard:

Performance \ Criteria				

- -

Integrated Curriculum

Standard: Rich, connected unit of study with rigor.

	1	2	3
RICHNESS (Multidimensional)	Contrived to fit across intelligences	Singular dimension	Breadth and depth across intelligences
RELATEDNESS (Connectedness)	No obvious connections across disciplines	Superficial connections across disciplines	Natural genuine connections across disciplines
RIGOR (Higher-Order Thinking)	Pour and store, recall and regurgitate	Challenge: follow rigorous procedure	Struggle: getting stuck and getting unstuck

Figure 8.13   Academic Rubric

Appendix A

Suggested Videos to Illustrate the Four-Corner Framework

Setting the Climate FOR Thinking	**Teaching the Skill OF Thinking**
Mr. Holland's Opus (High Expectations)	*Finding Forrester* (Skill Development)
Find the part in which the teacher sets the climate with the young athlete to "feel the rhythm" for marching to begin a discussion on creating a safe classroom climate and setting high expectations.	Find the part in which Forrester and the boy have the dialogue with conjunctions to demonstrate for skill development.
Structuring Interaction WITH Thinking	**Thinking ABOUT Thinking**
Pay It Forward (Experiential Learning)	*Dead Poets Society* (Reflection)
Find the part early in the film when Kevin Spacey places the assignment (or performance task) on the board for students.	Find the part in which the teacher has the boys rip the books and then recites "What will your verse be?" Use it as a lead-in about "big ideas" to reflect on.

Appendix B

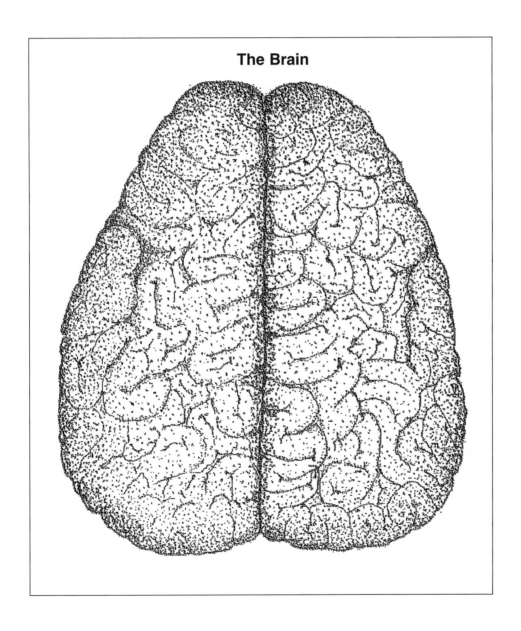

The Brain

Glossary

Amygdala*: the almond-shaped structure in the brain's limbic system that encodes emotional messages to long-term storage

Axon*: the neuron's long and unbranched fiber that carries impulses away from the cell to the next neuron

Bilateralization: two hemispheres of the brain working together

Binocular Vision: the ability to coordinate the images from both eyes

Brain-Compatible: teaching-learning processes that parallel or complement the way the brain/mind makes meaning and remembers

Brain Stem*: one of the three major parts of the brain; receives sensory input and monitors vital functions such as heartbeat, body temperature, and digestion

Cerebellum*: one of the three major parts of the brain; coordinates muscle movement

Cerebrum*: the largest of the three major parts of the brain; controls sensory interpretation, thinking, and memory

Chemical Signal: neurotransmitters that create connection between neurons (brain cells)

Chunking*: the brain's ability to perceive a coherent group of items as a single item, or a chunk

Closure: the time when the learner's mind can summarize for itself its perception of what has been learned; when the teacher gives specific directions for what the learner should mentally process and provides adequate time to accomplish it; usually the last opportunity the learner has to attach sense and meaning to the new learning, both of which are critical requirements for retention

Clustering: free-flowing technique to plot spontaneous verbal associations; used in writing to initiate, focus, or elaborate

Cooperative Group: small structured group in which members have designated roles and responsibilities

Cooperative Structures: interactive strategies used in small collaborative group work

Corpus Callosum*: the bridge of nerve fibers that connect the left and right cerebral hemispheres, allowing communication between them

Critical Thinking: using skills of analysis and evaluation to determine the worth of an idea; critiquing

Decision Making: judging choices and basing final selection on evaluation of criteria

Deductive Reasoning: reasoning from a general rule to a specific case (i.e., Does it fit the rule or generalization?)

Dendrite*: the branched extension from the cell body of a neuron that receives impulses from nearby neurons through synaptic contacts

Direct Instruction Model: Hunter's (1982) model of teaching that involves eight steps: an anticipatory set, a clear objective, instructor input, modeling, check for understanding, guided practice, independent application, and evaluation

DOVE Guidelines: guidelines to promote an open, nonjudgmental environment for group sharing: **d**efer judgment, **o**pt for original ideas, **v**ast number of ideas, **e**xpand by piggybacking on others' ideas

Electrical Impulse: activity inside the brain cell caused by a nerve impulse or sensory input of some sort

Embedded Application: use of a skill within a specific context (e.g., applying the skill of keyboarding during a word-processing activity)

Emotional Intelligence: ability to function effectively in the affective domain

Flow: state of immersed activity that creates a sense of harmony and effortlessness as defined by Csikszentmihalyi (2008)

Four-Corner Framework: teaching for, of, with, and about thinking

Glial Cells*: special "glue" cells in the brain that surround each neuron, providing support, protection, and nourishment

Graphic Organizer: visual format used to organize ideas, concepts, and information; also called visual organizer

Gray Matter: matter in brain where mental computation occurs and memories are stored; the topsoil of the brain; composed of densely packed neural cell bodies; the decision-making part of the nerve cell or neurons

Hemisphericity*: the notion that the two cerebral hemispheres are specialized and process information differently

Hippocampus*: a brain structure that compares new learning to past learning and encodes information from working memory to long-term storage

Journal: a student diary consisting of verbal and visual entries, usually including personal reflections, self-assessments, and spontaneous writing

Left Hemisphere: the logical hemisphere of the brain that monitors the areas for speech, reading, and writing; analyzes and evaluates factual material in a rational way; understands the literal interpretation of words; detects time and sequence; recognizes words, letters, and numbers

Limbic System*: the structures at the base of the cerebrum that control emotions

Log: a student record consisting of verbal and visual entries reflecting personal reactions to learning, usually in relation to a specific course or topic

Macroskill: critical and creative processes comprising several microskills (e.g., synthesis requires microskills of analyzing, brainstorming, evaluating, and prioritizing)

Metacognitive Processing: thinking about thinking; tracking how one thinks using structured discussion or written records

Microskill: skill taught in isolation (e.g., classifying, sequencing, comparing and contrasting)

Mirror Neurons: neuron systems that specialize in carrying out and understanding not just the actions of others but their intentions, the social meaning of their behavior, and their emotions

Moral Intelligence: ability to know one's way around; to act with wisdom and finesse

Mrs. Potter's Questions: four questions used to assess students' learning and performance: What was I expected to do? What did I do well? If I did the same task again, what would I do differently? What help do I need?

Multiple Intelligences: eight intelligences, as delineated by Gardner (1983, 1993, 1999b):

Verbal-Linguistic Intelligence: the ability to use with clarity the core operations of language

Musical-Rhythmic Intelligence: the ability to use the core set of musical elements

Logical-Mathematical Intelligence: the ability to use inductive and deductive reasoning, solve abstract problems, and understand complex relationships

Interpersonal-Social Intelligence: the ability to get along with, interact with, work with, and motivate others toward a common goal

Visual-Spatial Intelligence: the ability to perceive the visual world accurately and recreate one's visual experiences graphically

Intrapersonal-Introspective Intelligence: the ability to form an accurate model of oneself and to use that model to operate effectively in life

Bodily-Kinesthetic Intelligence: the ability to control and interpret body motions, manipulate physical objects, and establish harmony between the body and mind

Naturalist-Physical World Intelligence: the ability to see similarities and differences in one's environment and to understand the interrelationships of the ecosystem

Myelin*: a fatty substance that surrounds and insulates a neuron's axon

Neocortex: the outer layer of the brain; located just below the skull and pertaining to the cerebrum, or thinking brain

Neural Network or Pattern: a connection among neurons that forms a schema or pathway, which is strengthened through frequent use

Neural Plasticity: ability of the brain to wire and rewire itself by making and breaking connections between neurons

Neuron*: the basic cell making up the brain and nervous system; consists of a long fiber called an axon, which transmits impulses, and many shorter fibers called dendrites, which receive the impulses

Neurotransmitter*: one of over 50 chemicals stored in axon sacs; transmits impulses from neuron to neuron across the synaptic gap

Peak Performance: the expert performance or elegant solution

Portfolio: collection of student work, usually comprising a student's best work or work that shows development; also used to collect a group's or class's work

Problem Solving: specific strategies that use creative synthesis and critical analysis to generate viable alternatives to perplexing situations

Purpose: a statement defining why students should accomplish the learning objective (whenever possible, it should refer to how the new learning is related to prior and future learnings to facilitate positive transfer and meaning)

Reflection: the result of thoughts, ideas, or conclusions expressed in words (written or verbal); responses to thoughtful interludes

Right Hemisphere: the intuitive hemisphere of the brain; gathers information more from images than words; looks for patterns and can process many kinds of information simultaneously; interprets language through context, body language, and tone of voice, rather than through literal meanings; specializes in spatial perception and is capable of fantasy and creativity; recognizes places, faces, and objects

Rubric: assessment tool that specifies criteria for different levels of performance

Self-Assessment: any tool or strategy used by an individual to examine and evaluate his or her own work

Standard: criterion used to assess performance

Synapse*: the microscopic gap between the axon of one neuron and the dendrite of another

Three-Story Intellect Verbs or Questions: categorization of verbs to use in formulating questions that elicit responses based on different levels of thinking: one-story verbs prompt factual recall; two-story verbs ask for comparisons, reasoning, and generalizations; and three-story verbs stimulate imagination, hypotheses, and syntheses

Transfer*: a principle of learning described as a two-part process: (1) the effect that past learning has on the processing of new learning and (2) the degree to which the new learning will be useful to the learner in the future

Triune Brain: an early model of the brain defined by MacLean (1969) as the three different phases of the evolution of the human brain: reptilian, paleomammalian, neomammalian (this model is now suspect; see Chapter 1)

White Matter: matter that is the bedrock of the brain, underneath the gray matter; composed of millions of communication cables, each one containing an axon, coated with myelin; the axons connect neurons in one region of the brain to another

---

*SOURCE: Sousa, 1995.

References and Suggested Readings

Adler, M. J., & van Doren, C. (1972). *How to read a book.* New York: Simon & Schuster.

Ainsworth-Land, V., & Fletcher, N. (1979). *Making waves with creative problem solving.* Buffalo, NY: D.O.K.

American Educational Research Association. (1997a, March). *Expanding our concept of intelligence: What's missing and what could we gain?* Symposium at the American Educational Research Association Annual Meeting, Chicago.

American Educational Research Association. (1997b). *Neuroscience and education: What do we know about the brain that has implications for education?* (Audiotapes). Washington, DC: Author.

Armstrong, T. (1999). *Seven kinds of smart: Identifying and developing your many intelligences.* New York: Penguin.

Armstrong, T. (2000). *In their own way.* Los Angeles: J. P. Tarcher.

Aronson, E. (Ed.). (1978). *The jigsaw classroom.* Beverly Hills, CA: Sage.

Asp, K. (2006, July). A beautiful mind. *Southwest Airlines Spirit,* 86–92.

Association for Supervision and Curriculum Development. (1996). *The brain, the mind, and the classroom* (Audiotapes). Alexandria, VA: Author.

Ausubel, D. (1978). In defense of advance organizers: A reply to the critics. *Review of Educational Research, 48,* 251–257.

Baron, J. B., & Sternberg, R. J. (Eds.). (1987). *Teaching thinking skills: Theory and practice.* New York: W. H. Freeman.

Barrett, S. L. (1992). *It's all in your head: A guide to understanding your brain and boosting your brain power.* Minneapolis, MN: Free Spirit.

Beane, J. (Ed.). (1995). *Toward a coherent curriculum: 1995 yearbook of the ASCD.* Alexandria, VA: Association for Supervision and Curriculum Development.

Becoming a nation of readers: The report of the commission on reading. (1984). Washington, DC: National Academy of Education.

Begley, S. (2000a, May 8). Mind expansion: Inside the teenage brain. *Newsweek,* 68.

Begley, S. (2000b, Fall/Winter). Wired for thought. *Newsweek* [Special issue, Your Child: From Birth to Three], 25–30.

Begley, S. (2001a, July 9). The cellular divide. *Newsweek,* 22–26.

Begley, S. (2001b, May 7). Religion and the brain. *Newsweek,* 51–57.

Begley, S. (2007a, March 19). The evolution revolution: The new science of the brain and DNA is rewriting the story of human origins. *Newsweek,* 52–58.

Begley, S. (2007b, January 19). How the brain rewires itself. *Time,* 56–61.

Bellanca, J. (1984a). *Quality circles for educators.* Palatine, IL: IRI/SkyLight Training and Publishing.

Bellanca, J. (1984b). *Skills for critical thinking.* Palatine, IL: IRI/SkyLight Training and Publishing.

Bellanca, J., & Fogarty, R. (1986a). *Planning for thinking: A guidebook for instructional leaders.* Palatine, IL: IRI/SkyLight Training and Publishing.

Bellanca, J., & Fogarty, R. (1986b). *Teach them thinking.* Palatine, IL: IRI/SkyLight Training and Publishing.

Bellanca, J., & Fogarty, R. (1991). *Blueprints for thinking in the cooperative classroom.* Palatine, IL: IRI/SkyLight Training and Publishing.

Bellanca, J., & Fogarty, R. (1993). *Catch them thinking: A handbook of classroom strategies.* Palatine, IL: IRI/SkyLight Training and Publishing.

Bellanca, J., & Fogarty, R. (2002). *Blueprints for achievement in the cooperative classroom* (2nd ed.). Arlington Heights, IL: SkyLight Training and Publishing.

Ben-Hur, M. (Ed.). (1994a). *On Feuerstein's* Instrumental enrichment: A collection. Arlington Heights, IL: IRI/SkyLight Training and Publishing.

Ben-Hur, M. (1994b, December). *Thoughts on teaching and transfer.* Paper presented at the IRI/SkyLight Consultant Conference, Chicago.

Berman, S. (1997). *Project learning for the multiple intelligences classroom.* Arlington Heights, IL: SkyLight Training and Publishing.

Berman, S. (1999). *Service learning for the multiple intelligences classroom.* Arlington Heights, IL: SkyLight Training and Publishing.

Beyer, B. K. (1983). Common sense about teaching thinking skills. *Educational Leadership, 41*(3), 44–49.

Beyer, B. K. (1984). Improving thinking skills—Defining the problem. *Phi Delta Kappan, 65,* 486–490.

Beyer, B. K. (1985). Teaching thinking skills: How the principal can know they are being taught. *NASSP Bulletin, 69*(477), 70–83.

Beyer, B. K. (1987). *Practical strategies for the teaching of thinking.* Boston: Allyn & Bacon.

Biondi, A. (Ed.). (1972). *The creative process.* Buffalo, NY: D.O.K.

Black, H., & Black, S. (1981). *Figural analogies.* Pacific Grove, CA: Midwest.

Blakeslee, S. (2006, January 10). Cells that read minds. *New York Times,* p. F1.

Bloom, B. S. (1981). *All our children learning: A primer for parents, teachers, and other educators.* New York: McGraw-Hill.

Bloom, B. S., Engelhart, M. D., Furst, E. J., Hill, W. H., & Kratwohl, D. R. (1956). *Taxonomy of educational objectives: Book 1 Cognitive domain.* New York: Longman.

Bloom, F. E., & Lazerson, A. (1988). *Brain, mind, and behavior* (2nd ed.). New York: W. H. Freeman.

Brandt, R. (1988). On teaching thinking: A conversation with Arthur Costa. *Educational Leadership, 45*(7), 10–13.

Brandt, R. (1997, March). *How should educators use the new knowledge from the brain research?* Moderated session at the 52nd Annual Conference of the Association for Supervision and Curriculum Development, Baltimore.

Bransford, J., Sherwood, R., Vye, N., & Riser, J. (1986). Teaching thinking and problem solving: Research foundations. *American Psychologist, 41,* 1078–1089.

Brink, S. (2001, May 7). Your brain on alcohol. *U.S. News & World Report,* 50–57.

Brooks, J. G., & Brooks, M. G. (1993). *In search of understanding: The case for the constructivist classroom.* Alexandria, VA: Association for Supervision and Curriculum Development.

Brown, A. L. (1978). Knowing when, where, and how to remember: A problem of metacognition. In R. Glaser (Ed.), *Advances in instructional psychology* (Vol. 1, pp. 77–165). Hillsdale, NJ: Lawrence Erlbaum.

Bruer, J. (2002). *Myth of the first three years: A new understanding of early brain development and lifelong learning.* New York: Free Press.

Bruner, J. S. (1973). Readiness for learning. In J. Anglin (Ed.), *Beyond the information given: Studies in the psychology of knowing* (pp. 413–425). New York: Norton.

Bruner, J. S., Goodnow, J., & Austin, G. A. (1986). *A study of thinking.* New York: Wiley.

Burns, M. (1975). *I hate mathematics.* Boston: Little, Brown.

Burns, M. (1976). *The book of think: Or how to solve a problem twice your size.* Boston: Little, Brown.

Buscaglia, L. F. (1996). *Love: What life is all about.* Thoroughfare, NJ: Slack.

Buzan, T. (1984). *Make the most of your mind.* New York: Simon & Schuster.

Cahill, L. (2005, May). His brain, her brain. *Scientific American,* 22–29.

Caine, G., Caine, R. N., & Crowell, S. (1994). *Mindshifts: A brain-based process for restructuring schools and renewing education.* Tucson, AZ: Zephyr Press.

Caine, R. N., & Caine, G. (1991). *Making connections: Teaching and the human brain.* New York: Innovative Learning/Addison-Wesley.

Caine, R. N., & Caine, G. (1993). *Making connections: Teaching and the human brain* (2nd ed.). New York: Innovative Learning/Addison-Wesley.

Caine, R. N., & Caine, G. (1997). *Education on the edge of possibility.* Alexandria, VA: Association for Supervision and Curriculum Development.

Caine, R. N., & Caine, G. (2008). *Making connections: Teaching and the human brain.* Thousand Oaks, CA: Corwin.

Caine, R. N., Caine, G., McClintic, C. L., & Klimek, K. J. (2007). *12 brain/mind learning principles in action: The fieldbook for making connections, teaching, and the human brain.* Thousands Oaks, CA: Corwin.

Calvin, W. H. (1997). *How brains think: Evolving intelligence, then and now.* New York: Basic Books.

Carmichael, M. (2007, March 26). Stronger, faster, smarter. *Newsweek,* 38–46.

Chapman, C. (1993). *If the shoe fits . . . : How to develop multiple intelligences in the classroom.* Palatine, IL: IRI/SkyLight Training and Publishing.

Chudler, E. H. (2001). *Neuroscience for kids.* University of Washington. Retrieved December 11, 2008, from http://faculty.washington.edu/chudler/neurok.html

Coles, R. (1998). *The moral intelligence of children: How to raise a moral child.* New York: Random House.

College Board. (1983). *Academic preparation for college: What students need to know and be able to do.* New York: Author.

Cooney, W. C., Cross, B., & Trunk, B. (1993). *From Plato to Piaget: The greatest theorists from across the centuries and around the world.* New York: University Press of America.

Costa, A. (1981). Teaching for intelligent behavior. *Educational Leadership, 39*(1), 29–32.

Costa, A. (1991). *The school as a home for the mind.* Palatine, IL: IRI/SkyLight Training and Publishing.

Costa, A. (2007). *The school as a home for the mind.* Palatine, IL: IRI/SkyLight Training and Publishing.

Costa, A., & Kallick, B. (2000). *Discovering and exploring: Habits of mind.* Alexandria, VA: Association for Supervision and Curriculum Development.

Costa, A., & Liebmann, R. (Eds.). (1997). *Envisioning process as content: Towards renaissance curriculum.* Thousand Oaks, CA: Corwin.

Csikszentmihalyi, M. (2008). *Flow: The psychology of optimal experience.* New York: HarperPerennial.

Damasio, A. R. (2000). *The feeling of what happens: Body and emotion in the making of consciousness.* New York: Harcourt.

Damasio, A. R. (2005). *Descartes' error: Emotion, reason, and the human brain.* New York: Penguin.

Danielson, C. (2007). *Enhancing professional practice: A framework for teaching.* Alexandria, VA: Association for Supervision and Curriculum Development.

D'Arcangelo, M. (2000). The scientist in the crib: A conversation with A. Meltzoff. *Educational Leadership, 58*(3), 8–13.

Davis, J. (1997). *Mapping the mind.* New York: Carol.

Davis, J. (2000). *Mapping the mind.* New York: Replica Books.

deBono, E. (1999). *Six thinking hats for schools: K–2 resource book.* Des Moines, IA: Back Bay Books.

Dewey, J. (1938). *Experience and education.* New York: Free Press.

Diamond, M. (1988). *Enriching heredity: The impact of the environment on the anatomy of the brain.* New York: Free Press.

Diamond, M., & Hobson, J. (1998). *Magic trees of the mind: How to nurture your child's intelligence, creativity, and healthy emotions from birth to adolescence.* New York: Dutton.

Eisner, E. (1997). Cognition and representation: A way to pursue the American dream? *Phi Delta Kappan, 78,* 348–353.

Epstein, H. (Ed.). (1978). *Education and the brain: The 77th yearbook of the National Society for the Study of Education.* Chicago: University of Chicago Press.

ESS Science Series. (1966). *Problem cards: Attribute games and problems.* New York: Webster Division of McGraw-Hill.

Ferguson, M. (1980). *The Aquarian conspiracy: Personal and social transformation in our time.* New York: Putnam.

Ferguson, M. (1987). *The Aquarian conspiracy: Personal and social transformation in the 1980s.* Los Angeles: J. P. Tarcher.

Feuerstein, R. (1978). *Learning potential assessment device.* Baltimore: University Park Press.

Feuerstein, R. (1980). *Instrumental enrichment: An intervention program for cognitive modifiability.* Glenview, IL: Scott-Foresman.

Feuerstein, R. (1990). *Instrumental enrichment.* Baltimore: University Park Press.

Feuerstein, R., Rand, Y., Hoffman, M. B., & Miller, R. (1980). *Instrumental enrichment: A collection.* Baltimore: University Park Press.

Fields, D. (2008, March). White matter matters. *Scientific American, 42–49.*

Flavell, J. H. (1979). Metacognition and cognitive monitoring: A new area of cognitive-developmental inquiry. *American Psychologist, 34,* 906–911.

Foer, J. (2007). Remember this. *National Geographic, 212*(5), 32–57.

Fogarty, R. (1989). From training to transfer: The role of creativity in the adult learner. Unpublished doctoral dissertation, Loyola University of Chicago.

Fogarty, R. (1991). *The mindful school: How to integrate the curricula.* Palatine, IL: IRI/SkyLight Training and Publishing.

Fogarty, R. (1994). *The mindful school: How to teach for metacognitive reflection.* Palatine, IL: IRI/SkyLight Training and Publishing.

Fogarty, R. (1997). *Problem-based learning and other curriculum models for the multiple intelligences classroom.* Arlington Heights, IL: IRI/SkyLight Training and Publishing.

Fogarty, R. (2001a). *Differentiated learning: Different strokes for different folks.* Chicago: Fogarty & Associates.

Fogarty, R. (2001b). *Making sense of the research on the brain and learning.* Chicago: Fogarty & Associates.

Fogarty, R. (2001c). *A model for mentoring our teachers: Centers of pedagogy.* Chicago: Fogarty & Associates.

Fogarty, R. (2001d). *Student learning standards: A blessing in disguise.* Chicago: Fogarty & Associates.

Fogarty, R. (2001e). *Teachers make the difference: A framework for quality.* Chicago: Fogarty & Associates.

Fogarty, R., & Bellanca, J. (1993). *Patterns for thinking, patterns for transfer.* Palatine, IL: IRI/SkyLight Training and Publishing.

Fogarty, R., & Berman, S. (1997). *Project learning for the multiple intelligences classroom.* Arlington Heights, IL: SkyLight Training and Publishing.

Fogarty, R., Perkins, D., & Barell, J. (1992). *The mindful school: How to teach for transfer.* Palatine, IL: IRI/SkyLight Training and Publishing.

Fogarty, R., & Pete, B. (2007). *How to differentiate curriculum, instruction, and assessment.* Thousands Oaks, CA: Corwin.

Fogarty, R., & Stoehr, J. (2008). *Integrating curricula with multiple intelligences: Teams, themes, and threads.* Thousands Oaks, CA: Corwin.

Fox, M. (2001). *Reading magic: Why reading aloud to our children will change their lives forever.* San Diego, CA: Harcourt.

Franklin, J. (2005). Mental mileage: How teachers are putting brain research to work. *Education Update, 47*(6), 2–7.

Gagne, R. M. (1968). Learning hierarchies. *Educational Psychologist, 6,* 1–9.

Gardner, H. (1983). *Frames of mind: The theory of multiple intelligences.* New York: Basic Books.

Gardner, H. (1993). *Multiple intelligences: The theory in practice.* New York: HarperCollins.

Gardner, H. (1999a). *The disciplined mind: What all students should understand.* New York: Simon & Schuster.

Gardner, H. (1999b). *Intelligence reframed: Multiple intelligences for the 21st century.* New York: Basic Books.

Gelber, A. (1997, Spring/Summer). Your child: From birth to three [Special issue]. *Newsweek, 129.*

Gibbs, N. (1995, October 2). The EQ factor. *Time,* 60–68.

Gick, M. L., & Holyoak, K. J. (1987). The cognitive basis of knowledge transfer. In S. M. Cormier & J. D. Hagman (Eds.), *Transfer of training* (pp. 9–46). San Diego, CA: Academic Press.

Gilbert, D., & Buckner, R. (2007, January 19). Time travel in the brain. *Time,* 55.

Goldberg, E. (2001). *The executive brain: Frontal lobes and the civilized mind.* New York: Oxford.

Goleman, D. (1995a). *Emotional intelligence: Why it can matter more than IQ.* New York: Bantam Books.

Goleman, D. (Speaker). (1995b). *Emotional intelligence: Why it can matter more than IQ* (Audiotape). Los Angeles: Macmillan Audio.

Goleman, D. (Speaker). (1997). *Emotional intelligence: A new model for curriculum development* (Audiotape). Alexandria, VA: Association for Supervision and Curriculum Development.

Goodlad, J. I. (1980). How laboratory schools go awry. *UCLA Educator, 21*(2), 46–53.

Goodlad, J. I. (1984). *A place called school: Prospects for the future.* New York: McGraw-Hill.

Gopnik, A., Meltzoff, A., & Kuhl, P. (1999). *The scientist in the crib: Minds, brains, and how children learn.* New York: William Morrow.

Gould, S. J. (1981). *The mismeasure of man.* New York: Norton.

Hannaford, C. (2005). *Smart moves: Why learning is not all in your head.* Arlington, VA: Great River Books.

Harmin, M. (1994). *Inspiring active learning: A handbook for teachers.* Alexandria, VA: Association for Supervision and Curriculum Development.

Hart, L. (2002). *Human brain, human learning.* Kent, WA: Books for Educators.

Healy, J. M. (1987). *Your child's growing mind: A guide to learning and brain development from birth to adolescence.* New York: Doubleday.

Healy, J. M. (1990). *Endangered minds.* New York: Touchstone/Simon & Schuster.

Hemingway, E. (1952). *The old man and the sea.* New York: Scribner.

Herrmann, N. (1995). *The whole brain business book.* New York: McGraw-Hill.

Howard, P. J. (2006). *The owner's manual for the brain: Everyday applications from the mind-brain research.* Austin, TX: Bard Press.

Hunter, M. (1971). *Transfer.* El Segundo, CA: TIP.

Hunter, M. (1982). *Teaching for transfer.* El Segundo, CA: TIP.

Isaacson, R. L. (1982). *Limbic system* (2nd ed.). New York: Plenum Press.

Jensen, E. (1988). *SuperTeaching: Master strategies for building student success.* Del Mar, CA: Turning Point.

Jensen, E. (1995). *The learning brain.* Del Mar, CA: Turning Point.

Jensen, E. (1996a). *Brain-based learning.* Del Mar, CA: Turning Point.

Jensen, E. (1996b). *Brain research/learning.* National Educational Conference of Texas, Austin.

Jensen, E. (1996c). *Completing the puzzle: A brain-based approach to learning.* Del Mar, CA: Turning Point.

Jensen, E. (1997a). *Brain-compatible strategies: Hundreds of easy-to-use brain-compatible activities that boost attention, motivation, learning and achievement.* Del Mar, CA: Turning Point.

Jensen, E. (Speaker). (1997b). *Links between diversity training and brain research* (Audiotape). Alexandria, VA: Association for Supervision and Curriculum Development.

Jensen, E. (1997c, March). *A new vision for assessment: Matching assessment reforms with current brain research.* Presentation at the 52nd Annual Conference of the Association for Supervision and Curriculum Development, Baltimore.

Jensen, E. (1999). *Teaching with the brain in mind.* Alexandria, VA: Association for Supervision and Curriculum Development.

Jensen, E. (2000). Moving with the brain in mind. *Educational Leadership, 58*(3), 34–37.

Jensen, E. (2008a). Exciting times call for collaboration. *Phi Delta Kappan, 89,* 428–431.

Jensen, E. (2008b). A fresh look at brain-based education. *Phi Delta Kappan, 89,* 408–417.

Johnson, D., Johnson, R., & Holubec, E. J. (1986). *Circles of learning: Cooperation in the classroom.* Alexandria, VA: Association for Supervision and Curriculum Development.

Johnson, D., Johnson, R., & Holubec, E. J. (1994). *The new circles of learning: Cooperation in the classroom.* Alexandria, VA: Association for Supervision and Curriculum Development.

Johnson, R., & Johnson, D. (1982). Cooperation in learning: Ignored but powerful. *Lyceum, 5,* 22–26.

Joyce, B. (1983). *Power in staff development through research and training.* Alexandria, VA: Association for Supervision and Curriculum Development.

Joyce, B. R. (1986). *Improving America's schools.* New York: Longman.

Joyce, B. R., & Showers, B. (1980). Improving inservice training: The messages of research. *Educational Leadership, 37,* 379–385.

Joyce, B., & Weil, M. (1983). Models of teaching. Englewood Cliffs, NJ: Prentice Hall.

Kagan, S. (1992). *Cooperative learning.* San Juan Capistrano, CA: Resources for Teachers.

Karplus, R. (1974). *Science curriculum improvement study: Teachers handbook.* Berkeley: University of California.

Kerman, S. (1979). Teacher expectations and student achievement. *Phi Delta Kappan, 60,* 716–718.

King, K., & Gurian, M. (2006). With boys in mind: Teaching to the minds of boys. *Educational Leadership, 64*(1), 56–61.

Klein, J. (1997, March 17). Clintons on the brain: Will this be their legacy? Letter from Washington. *New Yorker*, 59–63.

Kotulak, R. (1996). *Inside the brain: Revolutionary discoveries of how the mind works.* Kansas City, MO: Andrews and McMeel.

Kovalik, S. (1993). *Integrated thematic instruction (ITI).* Kent, WA: Discovery Press.

Krupp, J.-A. (1981). *Adult development: Implications for staff development.* Manchester, CT: Adult Development and Learning.

Krupp, J.-A. (1982). *Adult learner: A unique entity.* Manchester, CT: Adult Development and Learning.

Lach, J. (1997, Spring/Summer). Your child's first steps: Turning on the motor. *Newsweek* [Special Issue, Your Child: From Birth to Three], 26–27.

Larkin, J. H., McDermott, J., Simon, D. P., & Simon, H. A. (1980, June 20). Expert and novice performance in solving physics problems. *Science*, 1335–1342.

Larson, C. (2008, February 11). Keeping your brain fit. *U.S. News & World Report*, 41–49.

Lazear, D. (1991). *Seven ways of teaching.* Palatine, IL: IRI/SkyLight Training and Publishing.

LeDoux, J. E. (1998). *The emotional brain: The mysterious underpinnings of emotional life.* New York: Simon & Schuster.

Lewkowicz, A. (2006). *Teaching emotional intelligence: Making effective choices.* Thousand Oaks, CA: Corwin.

Lipman, M., Sharp, A. M., & Oscanyan, F. (1980). *Philosophy in the classroom.* Philadelphia: Temple University Press.

Lozanov, G. (1978). *Suggestology and outlines of suggestology.* New York: Gordon and Breach.

Luria, A. (1976). *Working brain: An introduction to neuropsychology.* New York: Basic Books.

Lyman, F., & McTighe, J. (1988). Cueing thinking in the classroom: The promise of theory-embedded tools. *Educational Leadership*, 45(7), 18–24.

Machado, L. A. (1980). *The right to be intelligent.* New York: Pergamon Press.

MacLean, P. D. (1969). New trends in man's evolution. In *A triune concept of the brain and behavior* (pp. 68–84). Ann Arbor, MI: Books on Demand, University Microfilms International.

MacLean, P. D. (1978). A mind of three minds: Educating the triune brain. In J. Chall & A. Mirsky (Eds.), *Education and the brain* (pp. 308–342). Chicago: University of Chicago Press.

Mangan, M. (2006). *Brain-compatible science.* Thousand Oaks, CA: Corwin.

Maraviglia, C. (1978). *Creative problem-solving think book.* Buffalo, NY: D.O.K.

Marcus, S. (2007). *The hungry brain: The nutrition/cognition connection.* Thousand Oaks, CA: Corwin.

Margulies, N. (1997). *Inside Brian's brain: Interactive comics* (Vol. 3). Tucson, AZ: Zephyr Press.

Marzano, R. J., & Arredondo, D. E. (1986). Restructuring schools through the teaching of thinking skills. *Educational Leadership*, 43(8), 20–26.

Marzano, R., Pickering, D., & Pollock, J. (2001). *Classroom instruction that works: Research-based strategies for increasing student achievement.* Alexandria, VA: Association for Supervision and Curriculum Development.

Mayer, J. D., & Salovey, P. (1993). The intelligence of emotional intelligence. *Intelligence*, 17, 422–433.

Mayer, J. D., & Salovey, P. (1995). Emotional intelligence and the construction and regulation of feelings. *Applied and Preventive Psychology*, 4, 197–208.

Mayer, J. D., & Salovey, P. (1997). What is emotional intelligence? In P. Salovey & D. Sluyter (Eds.), *Emotional development and emotional intelligence: Implications for educators* (pp. 3–31). New York: Basic Books.

McCloskey, M., Carmazza, A., & Green, B. (1980, December 5). Curvilinear motion in the absence of external forces: Naive beliefs about the motion of objects. *Science*, 1139–1141.

Nash, J. M. (1997a, May 5). Addicted. *Time*, 68–74.

Nash, J. M. (1997b, February 3). Fertile minds. *Time*, 47–54.

Nickerson, R. S. (1982). *Understanding understanding.* BBN Report No. 5087.

Nickerson, R. S. (1983). Computer programming as a vehicle for teaching thinking skills. *Thinking: The Journal of Philosophy for Children, 4*(3 & 4), 42–48.

Nickerson, R. S., Perkins, D. N., & Smith, E. E. (1985). *Teaching thinking.* BBN Report No. 5575.

Nickerson, R. S., Shepard, W. S., & Hermstein, J. (1984). *The teaching of learning strategies.* BBN Report No. 5578.

Nisbett, R., & Ross, L. (1980). *Human inference: Strategies and shortcomings of social judgment.* Englewood Cliffs, NJ: Prentice Hall.

Noller, R. (1977). *Scratching the surface of creative problem solving: A bird's eye view of CPS.* Buffalo, NY: D.O.K.

Noller, R., Parnes, S., & Biondi, A. (1983). *Creative action book.* New York: MacMillan.

Noller, R., Treffinger, D., & Houseman, E. (1979). *It's a gas to be gifted: Scratching the surface: Creative problem solving in math.* Buffalo, NY: D.O.K.

Oakes, J., & Lipton, M. (1992). Detracking schools: Early lessons from the field. *Phi Delta Kappan, 73,* 448–454.

Ogle, D. (1986). KWL: A teaching model that develops active reading of expository text. *Reading Teacher, 39,* 564–570.

Ogle, D. (1989). Implementing strategic teaching. *Educational Leadership, 46*(4), 47–48, 57–60.

O'Keefe, J., & Nadel, L. (1973). *The hippocampal syndrome: Persistence or something more?* Paper presented at the Conference on Partial Reinforcement and Persistence Phenomena, Sussex, United Kingdom.

O'Keefe, J., & Nadel, L. (1974, June 27). Maps in the brain. *New Scientist,* 749–751.

O'Keefe, J., & Nadel, L. (1975). *The psychology of space.* Invited address to the Canadian Psychological Association, Quebec City, Canada.

O'Keefe, J., & Nadel, L. (1978). *The hippocampus as a cognitive map.* Oxford, England: Clarendon Press.

O'Keefe, J., & Nadel, L. (1979). Precís of O'Keefe and Nadel's *The hippocampus as a cognitive map* and author's response to commentaries. *Behavioral and Brain Sciences, 2,* 487–534.

Ornstein, R., & Sobel, D. (1987). *The healing brain: Breakthrough discoveries about how the brain keeps us healthy.* New York: Malor Books.

Osborn, A. F. (1963). *Applied imagination.* New York: Charles Scribner & Sons.

Palincsar, A. S., & Brown, A. (1984). Reciprocal teaching of comprehension-fostering and comprehension-monitoring activities. *Cognition and Instruction, 1,* 117–175.

Park, A. (2007, January 29). What the mouse brain tells us. *Time,* 61.

Parker, S. (1995). *Brain surgery for beginners and other major operations for minors.* Brookfield, CT: Millbrook Press.

Parker, S., & West, D. (1995). *Brain surgery for beginners and other major operations for minors.* Brookfield, CT: Millbrook Press.

Parnes, S. (1972). *Creativity: Unlocking human potential.* Buffalo, NY: D.O.K.

Parnes, S. (1975). *Aha! Insights into creative behavior.* Buffalo, NY: D.O.K.

Parry, T., & Gregory, G. (2006). *Designing brain-compatible learning.* Thousand Oaks, CA: Corwin.

Pearson, C. (1980). Can you keep quiet for three minutes? *Learning, 8*(6), 40–43.

Perkins, D. N. (Ed.). (1986). *Knowledge as design.* Hillsdale, NJ: Lawrence Erlbaum.

Perkins, D. N. (1988, August). *Thinking frames.* Paper presented at Association for Supervision and Curriculum Development Conference on Approaches to Thinking, Alexandria, VA.

Perkins, D. N. (1992). *Smart schools: From training memories to educating minds.* New York: The Free Press.

Perkins, D. N. (1995). *Outsmarting IQ: The emerging science of learnable intelligence.* New York: Free Press.

Perkins, D. N., & Salomon, G. (1988). Teaching for transfer. *Educational Leadership, 46*(1), 22–32.

Perkins, D. N., & Salomon, G. (1989). Are cognitive skills context bound? *Educational Researcher, 18,* 16–25.

Pert, C. (1999). *Molecules of emotions: Why you feel the way you feel.* New York: Simon & Schuster.

Pete, B. (In press). *Active brains, engaged minds: Experience the difference.* Chicago: Fogarty & Associates.

Peters, T., & Austin, N. (1985). *Passion for excellence: The leadership difference.* New York: Random House.

Peters, T., & Waterman, R., Jr. (2004). *In search of excellence.* New York: Collins.

Piaget, J. (1954). *The construction of reality in the child.* New York: Basic Books.

Piaget, J. (1970). Piaget's theory. In P. Mussen (Ed.), *Carmichael's manual of child psychology* (pp. 703–732). New York: Wiley.

Pinker, S. (1997). *How the mind works.* New York: W. W. Norton.

Pinker, S. (2007, January 19). The mystery of consciousness. *Time,* 45–54.

Polette, N. (1981). *Exploring books for gifted programs.* Metuchen, NJ: Scarecrow Press.

Polya, G. (2004). *How to solve it: A new aspect of mathematical method.* Princeton, NJ: Princeton University Press.

Posner, M. I., & Keele, S. W. (1973). Skill learning. In R. M. W. Travers (Ed.), *Second handbook of research on teaching* (pp. 805–821). Chicago: Rand McNally.

Potter, B., & Orfali, S. (1993). *Brain boosters: Foods and drugs that make you smarter.* Berkeley, CA: Ronin.

Ratey, J. (2003). *A user's guide to the brain.* New York: Abacus Books.

Raths, L. (1967). *Teaching for thinking.* Columbus, OH: Merrill.

Raymond, J. (2000, Fall/Winter). The world of senses. *Newsweek* [Special Issue, Your Child: From Birth to Three], 16–18.

Rico, G. (1983). *Writing the natural way: Using right brain techniques to release your expressive powers.* Los Angeles: J. P. Tarcher.

Rico, G. (1991). *Pain and possibility: Writing your way through personal crisis.* New York: G. P. Putnam's Sons.

Ronis, D. (2006). *Brain-compatible mathematics.* Thousand Oaks, CA: Corwin.

Ronis, D. (2007). *Brain-compatible assessments.* Thousand Oaks, CA: Corwin.

Rowe, M. B. (1972). *Wait-time and rewards as instructional variables: Their influence in language, logic, and fate control.* Paper presented at the National Association for Research in Science Teaching, Chicago. (ERIC Document Reproduction Service No. ED061103)

Rowe, M. B. (1987). Wait-time: Slowing down may be a way of speeding up. *American Educator, 11,* 38–43, 47. (ERIC Document Reproduction Service No. EJ351827)

Rowe, M. B. (1996). Science, silence, and sanctions. *Science and Children, 34*(1), 35–37.

Salomon, G., & Perkins, D. (1988). Rocky roads to transfer: Rethinking mechanisms of a neglected phenomenon. *Educational Psychologist, 24,* 113–142.

Salovey, P., & Mayer, J. D. (1990). Emotional intelligence. *Imagination, Cognition, and Personality, 9,* 185–211.

Scardamalia, M., Bereiter, C., & Fillion, B. (1979). *The little red writing book: A source book of consequential writing activities.* Toronto, Ontario, Canada: OISE Pedagogy of Writing Project.

Schoenfeld, H. A. (1980). Teaching problem-solving skills. *American Mathematical Monthly, 87,* 794–805.

Sergiovanni, T. (1987). Will we ever have a true profession? Supervision in context. *Educational Leadership, 44*(8), 44–49.

Shapiro, L. (1997, March 1). Your child's health: Beyond an apple a day. *Newsweek,* 52–53.

Sharan, S., & Sharan, Y. (1976). *Small-group teaching.* Englewood Cliffs, NJ: Educational Technology.

Shaywitz, S., & Shaywitz, B. (2007). What neuroscience really tells us about reading instruction. *Educational Leadership, 64*(5), 74–76.

Siegel, D. (2000, January). *The developing mind.* Speech given at the Learning Brain Expo, San Diego, CA.

Sizer, T. (2004). *Horace's compromise: The dilemma of the American high school.* Boston: Mariner Books.

Slavin, R. E. (1983). *Cooperative learning.* New York: Longman.

Smith, F. (1986). *Insult to intelligence: The bureaucratic invasion of our classrooms.* New York: Arbor House.

Solso, R. (Ed.). (1997). *Mind and brain sciences in the 21st century.* Cambridge, MA: MIT Press.

Sousa, D. (1995). *How the brain learns: A classroom teacher's guide.* Reston, VA: National Association of Secondary Schools.

Sousa, D. (2000). *How the brain learns: A classroom teacher's guide* (2nd ed.). Thousand Oaks, CA: Corwin Press.

Specter, M. (2001, July 23). Rethinking the brain. *New Yorker,* 42–53.

Sperry, R. W. (1968). Hemisphere disconnection and unity conscious awareness. *American Psychologist, 23,* 723–733.

Sprenger, M. (1999). *Learning and memory: The brain in action.* Alexandria, VA: Association for Supervision and Curriculum Development.

Sprenger, M. (2005). Inside Amy's brain. *Educational Leadership, 62*(7), 28–32.

Sternberg, R. J. (1981). Intelligence as thinking and learning skills. *Educational Leadership, 39*(1), 18–21.

Sternberg, R. J. (1984). How can we teach intelligence? *Educational Leadership, 42*(1), 38–48.

Sternberg, R. J. (1986). *Intelligence applied: Understanding and increasing your intellectual skills.* New York: Harcourt Brace Jovanovich.

Sternberg, R. J. (1997). What does it mean to be smart? *Educational Leadership, 54*(6), 20–24.

Sternberg, R. (2008). The answer depends on the question: A reply to Eric Jensen. *Phi Delta Kappan, 89,* 418–420.

Sternberg, R. J., & Berg, C. A. (Eds.). (1992). *Intellectual development.* New York: Cambridge University Press.

Stevens, J., & Goldberg, D. (2001). *For the learner's sake: A practical guide to transform your classroom and school.* Tucson, AZ: Zephyr Press.

Strong, M. (1996). *The habit of thought: From Socratic seminars to Socratic practice.* Chapel Hill, NC: New View.

Swartz, R. J., & Perkins, D. N. (1989). *Teaching thinking: Issues and approaches.* Pacific Grove, CA: Midwest.

Swartz, R. J., & Perkins, D. N. (1995). *Teaching thinking: Issues and approaches.* Pacific Grove, CA: Midwest.

Sylwester, R. (1995). *A celebration of neurons: An educator's guide to the human brain.* Alexandria, VA: Association for Supervision and Curriculum Development.

Sylwester, R. (1996). *A celebration of neurons: A conversation about the educational applications of recent cognitive science developments.* Alexandria, VA: Association for Supervision and Curriculum Development.

Sylwester, R. (1997, March). *How should educators use new knowledge from brain research?* Presentation at the 52nd Annual Conference of the Association for Supervision and Curriculum Development, Baltimore.

Sylwester, R. (Ed.). (1999). *Student brains, school issues: A collection of articles.* Thousand Oaks, CA: Corwin.

Sylwester, R. (2000a). *A biological brain in a cultural classroom.* Thousand Oaks, CA: Corwin.

Sylwester, R. (2000b). Unconscious emotions, conscious feelings. *Educational Leadership, 58*(3), 20–24.

Thorndike, E. (1903). *Educational psychology.* New York: Lemke & Buechner.

Thorndike, E. (1906). *Psychological review.* New York: Appleton-Century-Crofts.

Tierno, S. F. (1996). *Brain B.I.T.S.: Brain connections to bilingual integrated thinking and thematic strategies.* Danbury, CT: Creative Thinkers.

Tolkien, J. R. R. (1937). *The hobbit.* New York: Ballantine Books.

Torrance, E. P. (1979). *The search for satari and creativity.* Buffalo, NY: Creative Educational Foundation.

Trowbridge, D. E., & McDermott, L. C. (1980). Investigation of student understanding of the concept of velocity in one dimension. *American Journal of Physics, 48,* 1010–1028.

Tversky, A., & Kahneman, D. (1974, September 27). Judgment under uncertainty: Heuristics and biases. *Science,* 1124–1131.

Tyler, R. W. (1987). The five most significant curriculum events in the twentieth century. *Educational Leadership, 44*(4), 36–38.

Underwood, V. L. (1982). *Self-management skills for college students: A program in how to learn.* Unpublished doctoral dissertation, University of Texas.

U.S. Department of Education. (1986). *What works: Research about teaching and learning.* Washington, DC: Author.

Von Oech, R. (1986). *A kick in the seat of the pants: Using your explorer, artist, judge, and warrior to be more creative.* New York: HarperCollins.

Von Oech, R. (2008). *A whack on the side of the head: How you can be more creative.* New York: Business Plus.

Vygotsky, L. S. (1978). *Mind in society: The development of higher psychological process.* Cambridge, MA: Harvard University Press.

Wallace, R. (1966). *The world of Leonardo 1452–1519.* New York: Time.

Wallis, C. (2006a, May 15). Inside the autistic mind. *Time,* 42–48.

Wallis, C. (2006b, May 15). A tale of two schools. *Time,* 48–51.

Warner, S. A. (1986). *Teacher.* New York: Touchstone Books.

Wason, P. C. (1974). The psychology of deceptive problems. *New Scientist, 63,* 382–385.

Wayman, J. (1981). *The other side of reading.* Carthage, IL: Good Apple.

Weaver, R., & Cotrell, H. (1986). Using interactive images in the lecture hall. *Educational Horizons, 64,* 180–185.

Weber, P. (1978a). *Promote . . . Discovering ways to learn and research.* New York: D.O.K.

Weber, P. (1978b). *Question quest: Discovering ways to ask worthwhile questions.* New York: D.O.K.

Weinstein, C. E., & Underwood, V. L. (1983). Learning strategies: The how of learning. In J. Segal, S. Chipman, & R. Glaser (Eds.), *Relating instruction to basic research* (pp. 241–259). Hillsdale, NJ: Lawrence Erlbaum.

Westwater, A., & Wolfe, P. (2000). The brain-compatible curriculum. *Educational Leadership, 58*(3), 49–52.

Whimbey, A. (1975). *Intelligence can be taught.* New York: Lawrence Erlbaum.

Williams, F. E. (1970). *Classroom ideas for encouraging thinking and feeling.* Buffalo, NY: D.O.K.

Willington, D. (2008). When and how neuroscience applies to education. *Phi Delta Kappan, 89,* 421–423.

Willis, J. (2007a). The gully in the brain glitch theory. *Educational Leadership, 64*(5), 68–73.

Willis, J. (2007b). Toward neurological reading instruction. *Educational Leadership, 64*(5), 80–82.

Willis, J. (2008). Building a bridge from neuroscience to the classroom. *Phi Delta Kappan, 89,* 424–427.

Wingert, P., & Brant, M. (2005, August 15). Reading your baby's mind. *Newsweek,* 32–40.

Wittrock, M. C. (1967). Replacement and nonreplacement strategies in children's problem solving. *Journal of Educational Psychology, 58*(2), 69–74.

Wolfe, P. (Speaker). (1994). *A staff developer's guide to the brain* (Audiotape). Front Royal, VA: National Cassette Services.

Wolfe, P. (Speaker). (1996). *Live seminars on tape: Translating brain research into classroom practice* (Audiotape). Alexandria, VA: Association for Supervision and Curriculum Development.

Wolfe, P. (2001). *Brain matters: Translating brain research into classroom practice.* Alexandria, VA: Association for Supervision and Curriculum Development.

Index

CORWIN

A SAGE Company

The Corwin logo—a raven striding across an open book—represents the union of courage and learning. Corwin is committed to improving education for all learners by publishing books and other professional development resources for those serving the field of PreK–12 education. By providing practical, hands-on materials, Corwin continues to carry out the promise of its motto: **"Helping Educators Do Their Work Better."**